THE CAMBRIDGE COMPAN

Hailed as the father of black literature in the twentieth century, Richard Wright was an iconoclast, an intellectual of towering stature whose multidisciplinary erudition rivals only that of W. E. B. Du Bois. This collection captures Wright's immense power, which has made him a beacon for writers across decades, from the civil rights era to today. Individual essays examine Wright's art as central to his intellectual life and shed new light on his classic texts *Native Son* and *Black Boy*. Other essays turn to his short fiction and nonfiction, as well as his lesser-known work in journalism and poetry, paying particular attention to manuscripts in Wright's archive – unpublished letters and novels, plans for multivolume works – that allow us to see the depth and expansiveness of his aesthetic and political vision. Exploring how Wright's expatriation to France facilitated a broadening of this vision, contributors challenge the idea that expatriation led to Wright's artistic decline.

Glenda R. Carpio is Professor of African and African American Studies and English at Harvard University. She is the author of *Laughing Fit to Kill: Black Humor in the Fictions of Slavery* (2008). She coedited *African American Literary Studies: New Texts, New Approaches, New Challenges* (2011) with Professor Werner Sollors and is currently at work on a book tentatively titled *Migrant Aesthetics*, a study of contemporary immigrant fiction.

A complete list of books in the series is at the back of this book

THE CAMBRIDGE
COMPANION TO
RICHARD WRIGHT

THE CAMBRIDGE
COMPANION TO

RICHARD WRIGHT

EDITED BY

GLENDA R. CARPIO

Harvard University

CAMBRIDGE
UNIVERSITY PRESS

CAMBRIDGE
UNIVERSITY PRESS

University Printing House, Cambridge CB2 8BS, United Kingdom

One Liberty Plaza, 20th Floor, New York, NY 10006, USA

477 Williamstown Road, Port Melbourne, VIC 3207, Australia

314–321, 3rd Floor, Plot 3, Splendor Forum, Jasola District Centre,
New Delhi – 110025, India

79 Anson Road, #06–04/06, Singapore 079906

Cambridge University Press is part of the University of Cambridge.

It furthers the University's mission by disseminating knowledge in the pursuit of
education, learning, and research at the highest international levels of excellence.

www.cambridge.org
Information on this title: www.cambridge.org/9781108475174
DOI: 10.1017/9781108567510

First published 2019

Printed and bound in Great Britain by Clays Ltd, Elcograf S.p.A.

A catalogue record for this publication is available from the British Library.

Library of Congress Cataloging-in-Publication Data
NAMES: Carpio, Glenda, editor.
TITLE: The Cambridge companion to Richard Wright / edited by Glenda R. Carpio.
DESCRIPTION: Cambridge ; New York, NY : Cambridge University Press,
2019. | Includes bibliographical references and index.
IDENTIFIERS: LCCN 2018061286 | ISBN 9781108475174 (alk. paper) |
ISBN 9781108469234 (pbk.)
SUBJECTS: LCSH: Wright, Richard, 1908–1960 – Criticism and interpretation.
CLASSIFICATION: LCC PS3545.R815 Z6127 2019 | DDC 813/.52–dc23
LC record available at https://lccn.loc.gov/2018061286

ISBN 978-1-108-47517-4 Hardback
ISBN 978-1-108-46923-4 Paperback

For Werner Sollors, with love

CONTENTS

CONTENTS

CONTRIBUTORS

GLENDA R. CARPIO is Professor of African and African American Studies and English at Harvard University. She is the author of *Laughing Fit to Kill: Black Humor in the Fictions of Slavery* (2008) and coedited *African American Literary Studies: New Texts, New Approaches, New Challenges* (2011) with Professor Werner Sollors. Currently at work on a book tentatively titled *Migrant Aesthetics*, a study of contemporary immigrant fiction, she has published in American Literature, Critical Inquiry, ASAP: The Association for the Study of the Arts of the Present, Transition, and Public Books, among other venues.

LAURENCE COSSU-BEAUMONT is Associate Professor at the University Sorbonne Nouvelle Paris 3 in Paris. Her work focuses on the intersection between African American studies and book history, and on intercultural exchanges between France and the United States. She has edited the forgotten text of *Gustave de Beaumont, Tocqueville's fellow traveller, in French: Marie or Slavery in the United States* (2014).

ALICE MIKAL CRAVEN is Professor of English and Comparative Literature as well as affiliated faculty in the Department of Film Studies at the American University of Paris. She is author of *Visible and Invisible Whiteness: American White Supremacy Through the Cinematic Lens* (2018). She is also coeditor of *Richard Wright: New Readings in the 21st Century (2011) and Richard Wright in a Post-Racial Imaginary* (2015), winner of Choice Magazine's Outstanding Academic Title for 2016.

JAY GARCIA is Associate Professor of Comparative Literature at New York University. He is the author of *Psychology Comes to Harlem: Rethinking the Race Question in Mid-Twentieth Century America* (2012), which examines the work of Richard Wright, Lillian Smith, James Baldwin, and other mid-twentieth-century literary artists and critics. He teaches courses on transnationalism in African American letters, comparative approaches to the study of American literature, and modern critical practices, including the emergence of American studies and cultural studies.

GEORGE HUTCHINSON is the Newton C. Farr Professor of American Culture at Cornell University. He is the author of *In Search of Nella Larsen: A Biography of* the *Color Line* (2006), *The Harlem Renaissance in Black and White* (1996), and *The Ecstatic Whitman: Literary Shamanism and the Crisis of the Union* (1986). He also edited *The Cambridge Companion to the Harlem Renaissance* (2007) and coedited *Publishing Blackness: Textual Constructions of Race since 1850* (2013). His latest books are *Facing the Abyss: American Literature and Culture in the 1940s* (2018) and the *Penguin Classics edition of Jean Toomer's Cane* (2019).

GENE ANDREW JARRETT is Seryl Kushner Dean of the College of Arts and Science and Professor of English at New York University. He specializes in African American literary history from the eighteenth century to the present; US literary history between the Civil War and World War II; race, ethnic, and cultural studies; and theories of literature, aesthetics, and intellectual historiography. He is the author of *Representing the Race: A New Political History of African American Literature* (2011) and *Deans and Truants: Race and Realism in African American Literature* (2007). He is the editor of eight books that examine the long-standing negotiations of African American writers with racial representation.

STEPHAN KUHL is Assistant Professor at the Institute for English and American Studies of Goethe University Frankfurt, Germany. He has published several essays on Richard Wright, most recently "Intellectual Disposition and Bodily Knowledge: Richard Wright's Literary Practice" (2018), and he is the author of *Crude Psychology: Richard Wright's Literary Practice* (forthcoming). Besides African American literature and culture, his research interests include comparative literature, psychoanalysis, and relational sociology.

ERNEST JULIUS MITCHELL is a Lecturer in History and Literature at Harvard University. He is the author of "Zora Neale Hurston's Politics" (2013) and "Black Renaissance: A Brief History of the Concept" (2010). His Ph.D. dissertation, "Zora's Moses," (Harvard 2018) argues that Hurston's fifth novel, "Moses, Man of the Mountain" (1939), should be more widely read: for its literary quality as the work of a modernist author working at the height of her powers; for the historical insight it affords into the politics and culture of the interwar era; and for the bold theological implications it carries for several religions.

NATHANIEL F. MILLS is Assistant Professor of English at the University of Minnesota. His research focuses on the political commitments of twentieth-century American and African American literature, specifically literary engagements with the 1930s–1950s Communist left and with political movements of the Cold War and Civil Rights eras. He is the author of *Ragged Revolutionaries: The Lumpenproletariat and African American Marxism in Depression-Era Literature* (2017).

NICHOLAS T RINEHART is a PhD candidate in English at Harvard University. His dissertation, "Narrative Events: Slavery, Testimony, and Temporality in the Afro-Atlantic World," provides an account of New World slave testimony challenging scholarly preoccupation with the American slave narrative tradition and its attendant critical conventions. His publications include "Vernacular Soliloquy, Theatrical Gesture, and Embodied Consciousness in *The Marrow of Tradition*" (2018), "Native Sons; or, How 'Bigger' Was Born Again," (2018), "The Man That Was a Thing: Reconsidering Human Commodification in Slavery" (2016), and "'I Talk More of the French': Creole Folklore and the Federal Writers' Project." (2016).

KATHRYN S. ROBERTS is Assistant Professor in the Program in American Studies at the University of Groningen. She is the author of "Writing 'Other Spaces': Katherine Anne Porter's Yaddo," (2015) and is completing *The New Monastics*, a book about how participation in creative communities such as Yaddo and the MacDowell Colony shaped twentieth-century literature. Her research focuses on twentieth- and twenty-first-century American literature and culture; African-American Literature; media studies; critical theory; feminist and queer theory; and the sociology of literature. She is currently developing a new project on podcasts as a form of civic media.

TOMMIE SHELBY is the Caldwell Titcomb Professor in the Department of African and African American Studies and the Department of Philosophy at Harvard University. He is the author of *We Who Are Dark: The Philosophical Foundations of Black Solidarity* (2005) and *Dark Ghettoes: Injustice, Dissent, and Reform* (2016). His research and teaching interests include social and political philosophy, Africana philosophy, philosophy of law, critical philosophy of race, history of black political thought, and philosophy of social science. He is also the coeditor of *Hip Hop and Philosophy: Rhyme 2 Reason* (2005) and *To Shape a New World: Essays on the Political Philosophy of Martin Luther King, Jr.* (2018).

ROBERT B. STEPTO is Professor of English and African American Studies at Yale University. His research focuses on American and African American autobiography, fiction, poetry, and visual arts since 1840. His publications include A *Home Elsewhere: Reading African American Classics in the Age of Obama* (2010), *Blue As the Lake: A Personal Geography* (1998), and *From Behind the Veil: A Study of Afro-American Narrative* (1979). His editing projects include (with Jennifer Greeson) *the Norton Critical Edition of Charles Chesnutt's Conjure Stories (2011)*, (with Michael Harper) *Chant of Saints: Afro-American Literature, Art, and Scholarship* (1979), and (with Dexter Fisher) *Afro-American Literature: The Reconstruction of Instruction* (1990).

ACKNOWLEDGMENTS

This edited volume would not have been possible without the steady commitment of all of its contributors and the aid of two fine young minds, Donald "Field" Brown, a PhD candidate in English at Harvard University, and Julian Lucas, associate editor at *Cabinet* and web editor at *The Point*. Field helped with every stage of production, including editing and proofreading essays, and preparing the Chronology and Guide for Further Reading. I am forever grateful to him for his sound and good-natured approach to our work together. Julian's precise and insightful editing brought the introduction and several essays to full fruition. Ray Ryan, senior editor of English and American Literature at Cambridge University Press, was an indefatigable supporter of this project who made sure to keep it going, especially when time was of essence. My gratitude goes to him and to the members of his office. The dedication to Werner Sollors is one way to express deep respect and gratitude for the model of scholarship that he has provided me and many contributors in this volume, and for his own excellent work on Richard Wright's brilliant career. Finally, I would like to thank all of the students who have participated in courses I have has taught on Richard Wright at Harvard University, both with Professors Sollors and with Professor Tommie Shelby, whose contribution to this volume is indispensable. As my students have made clear, reading Richard Wright is a revelation, both of the power of fiction and of the political conditions of people of color in the United States and the world. This volume hopes to reach their peers and readers in general, especially in these troubled times.

CHRONOLOGY

1908   Richard Nathaniel Wright is born on September 4 on a plantation in Roxie, Mississippi, located twenty miles east of Natchez, Mississippi. It was one of the most impoverished and segregated areas in the Deep South. His father, Nathan, was a sharecropper, and his mother, Ella, was a schoolteacher who started to work on a farm shortly after Richard was born.

1910   Richard Wright's brother, Leon Alan Wright, is born on September 24. He was the second and last child of Nathan and Ella Wright.

1911–1912   Ella Wright leaves the farm with her children to live with her parents in Natchez, and Nathan joins them later. Wright's maternal grandmother was a strict Seventh-Day Adventist and strong disciplinarian.

1913–1915   Wright sets his maternal grandparents' house on fire by accident, and the Wrights move up the river to Memphis to find better employment. Nathan works as a night porter in a hotel and Ella cooks for a white family. Nathan then leaves his family for another woman, and Ella acquires an illness that eventually disables her for the remainder of her life. Richard Wright enrolls at Howe Institute in Memphis.

1916   As their mother becomes more ill, Wright and his brother Leon are placed in an orphanage for a month. This experience surely influenced his posthumously published novel *Rite of Passage*. Ella eventually moves with her children to Jackson, Mississippi, for the summer to stay with Wright's grandmother. After that, they move to Elaine, Arkansas, to live with Ella's sister and brother-in-law, Maggie and Silas Hopkins.

1917–1918   Wright's Uncle Silas is murdered by whites due to his thriving business as a saloonkeeper. The Wrights escape to West Helena, Arkansas, and ultimately move back to Jackson to live with Ella's mother again. For the next two years, they oscillate between West Helena and Jackson, and Wright's schooling is irregular. During this time, Wright becomes conscious of the depth of American racism and violence in the Deep South.

1919   Wright begins school in West Helena as his mother's health continues to deteriorate. As her health worsens, he must leave school to make money for his family. After Ella has a paralyzing stroke, the Wrights move back to Jackson to live with Ella's mother. Wright attends a Seventh-Day Adventist school yet rebels against the strict guidelines laid out there.

1921–1923   Wright attends Jim Hill School and Smith Robertson Junior High, and does well academically and socially. He works an array of jobs after school during the summer and reads pulp fiction in his spare time.

1924   He publishes his first short story, "The Voodoo of Hell's Half-Acre," in Jackson's *Southern Register*.

1925   Wright graduates from Smith Robertson as valedictorian but refuses to give the speech prepared for him by the principal. Upon graduation, he moves to Memphis and begins to take reading and writing more seriously.

1926   Richard is drawn to H. L. Mencken's writing due to his courage to criticize American society and modern life. He is also attracted to American naturalists (e.g. Theodore Dreiser, Sherwood Anderson, and Sinclair Lewis) and European realists (Henrik Ibsen, Emile Zola, and Fyodor Dostoevsky). This period intensely awakens him and confirms his desire to write.

1927–1928   Wright moves to Chicago and begins to work in a post office.

1928–1930   During these early years in Chicago, he develops a strong interest in modernist literature, such as the works of T. S. Eliot and Gustave Flaubert. After the 1928 stock market crash, he loses his job as a postal clerk and is forced to support himself and his family with low-paying jobs while living in the Chicago slums. Such an experience influenced both *Lawd Today!* and *Native*

	Son. In 1930, he becomes an aide to the South Side Boys Club and works with young men in Chicago's street gangs.
1931	He publishes another short story, "Superstition," in a black magazine. He also starts working with the Federal Negro Theatre and becomes a writer for the Illinois Writers' Project.
1932–1934	Wright joins the John Reed Club, a Communist Party–sponsored literary organization. There he writes poems about revolution and is published in *Left Front*, the magazine for Midwestern John Reed Clubs. In 1933, he officially joins the Communist Party. He is eventually elected secretary of the Chicago John Reed Club and becomes coeditor of *Left Front*. He continues to read nineteenth- and twentieth-century fiction, and is greatly influenced by Fyodor Dostoevsky, with whom he is often compared.
1935–1936	He continues publishing poetry, ventures into journalism, and expands his connections in Marxist and leftist circles. He also joins the Federal Writers' Project, where he does research on the history of blacks in Chicago, which influences *Twelve Million Black Voices*. He also tries to sell his first novel, *Lawd Today!*, but without success. Nevertheless, he publishes "Big Boy Leaves Home" in *Negro Caravan* in 1936 and begins working on *Native Son* and other short stories that will be included in *Uncle Tom's Children*.
1936	Wright organizes the South Side Writers' Group, which consisted of black writers and intellectuals such as Frank Marshall Davis, Horace Cayton, and Margaret Walker.
1937	Due to ideological differences over artistic freedom, Wright leaves Chicago's John Reed Club and moves to New York City in June. In New York, he assists in founding *New Challenge*. He also becomes a writer and editor for the Harlem Bureau of the *Daily Worker*. Moreover, he is on a rigorous schedule as he works on *Native Son*.
1937	He publishes his literary manifesto, "Blueprint for Negro Writing," in the *Daily Worker* and publishes "The Ethics of Living Jim Crow" in *American Stuff: WPA Writers' Anthology*. He also wins a $500 first prize in *Story Magazine*'s contest for his short story "Fire and Cloud."

1937   This is also the year Langston Hughes connects Wright with Ralph Ellison. They become friends as they discuss modernist literature and even attend the Second American Writers' Congress together in Carnegie Hall, where Ernest Hemingway gave the plenary address. Wright gives Ellison his first opportunity to write, requesting that he write a review for *New Challenge*'s first issue.

1938   *Uncle Tom's Children* is published and receives positive reviews. Wright continues to work on *Native Son*. He does research on the Robert Nixon case, in which an 18-year-old black man was accused of murdering a white woman, to help flesh out the novel more.

1939   Wright wins the Guggenheim Fellowship in June, and this helps him complete *Native Son*. He marries his first wife, Dhimah Meadman, in August. Ralph Ellison is the best man.

1940   *Native Son* is published on March 1 by *Harpers* as a Book of the Month Club selection. It sells 215,000 copies by early April and becomes a bestseller. Wright and Dhimah Meadman get divorced. Later in the year, he collaborates with Paul Green on a stage version of the novel. He also starts working on *Twelve Million Black Voices*.

1941   Wright marries Ellen Poplar, a Communist Party organizer, on March 12. On March 25 *Native Son* opens on Broadway. *Twelve Million Black Voices* is published by Viking Press. For his many literary accomplishments, the NAACP awards him with the Spingarn Medal. Wright begins to doubt his relationship with the Communist Party due to their de-emphasis on American racial issues.

1942   He officially leaves the Communist Party. His daughter Julia is born, and he publishes the short story "The Man Who Lived Underground" in *Accent*. The existentialist story details the life of a man who dwells in the city sewers after being falsely accused of a murder. This short story deeply influenced *Invisible Man*, and obvious connections can be made between the two.

1943–1944   Wright visits the Deep South and gives a lecture at Fisk University. Traveling back to the South inspires him to write his own autobiography. In August of 1944, he publishes

"I Tried to Be a Communist" in *The Atlantic Monthly*. A young James Baldwin meets Richard Wright. Baldwin visits Wright's apartment in Brooklyn, and they discuss his novel over a bottle of bourbon. Wright agrees to read his draft, eventually supports the novel, and recommends him for the Eugene Saxton Fellowship (which Baldwin wins in 1946).

1945   *Black Boy* is published in March as a Book of the Month Club selection. It is an autobiography that covers his childhood and teenage years in the South. Like *Native Son*, it becomes an instant bestseller. He does not keep the success all to himself. On top of supporting Baldwin, he helps Gwendolyn Brooks publish her first book of poetry, *A Street in Bronzeville*, by giving a glowing review of her work when asked by Harper & Brothers. Wright and Brooks knew each other from their shared literary circle in Chicago.

1946–1947   The Wrights sail to France on invitation from the French government. While there, they make friends with Gertrude Stein. Upon returning to the United States, he experiences racism again and they decided to move to France permanently. He quickly adapts to the French scene and makes friends with the likes of Andre Gide, Jean-Paul Sartre, and Simone de Beauvoir. He also connects with members of the African diaspora living in Paris, such as Aimé Césaire, George Padmore, and Léopold Senghor. Wright helps Senghor, Césaire, and Alioune Diop launch *Présence Africaine*.

1948   Baldwin writes to him, curious to learn more as he decides whether he should follow Wright's footsteps. Wright responds and encourages him to do so, and Baldwin moves to France in 1948. Wright continues to explore his intellectual curiosities by reading the works of Heidegger and Husserl, and forms friendships with European writers Carlo Levi, Arthur Koestler, and Ignazio Silone.

1949   His second daughter, Rachel, is born in January. Baldwin begins to criticize Wright's literary aesthetic with the first of two scathing critiques of Wright's fiction (see "Everybody's Protest Novel" [1949] and "Many Thousands Gone" [1951]), and their relationship never recovers. Nevertheless, Wright continues to produce and begins to write the script for the film version of *Native Son*.

1949   While in Chicago filming for *Native Son*, Wright was encouraged by Ben Burns to write three articles for *Ebony*, which became "Richard Wright Explains Ideas about Movie Making" (published in January 1951); "The Shame of Chicago" (published in December 1951); and "I Choose Exile," which was never published by *Ebony*. Burns and *Ebony* had problems with Wright's bleak outlook on the Negro problem after World War II. They preferred he give a more optimistic story about African American success. Therefore "I Choose Exile" was never published. *Ebony* had problems with "The Shame of Chicago," but "I Choose Exile," an essay about why he decided to leave racist American society and flee to Paris, crossed a line. The essay still has not been published. It is held by Kent State University, with use restricted by Wright's inheritors.

1950   Wright begins to work on *The Outsider* as he continues to work on the film version of *Native Son*. He also forms the Franco-American Fellowship with a group of African-American expatriates. The goal of the fellowship was to encourage better relations with France and America during the Cold War. They fought against racism back in America, and internationally.

1951   On June 14, 1951, up-and-coming Negro writer William Gardner Smith writes Richard Wright with questions about moving to Paris. After Wright responds graciously, encouraging him to move and offering to help him make the transition, Smith gets on the *Liberté* to join Wright and Baldwin in Paris in October of 1951. *Native Son* the film is released on June 16, 1951, with Wright starring as Bigger Thomas.

1953   Wright helps Chester Himes find a place to stay when he moves to Paris. He also introduces him to his friends and other important contacts in the publishing world. Maybe most importantly, to help Himes's reputation in France, Wright writes a laudatory preface to the French translation of *Lonely Crusade*. Wright's *The Outsider* is published in March, but the reviews are not as praiseworthy as his earlier works. In July of 1953, William Gardner Smith publishes a major profile on Richard Wright in *Ebony* entitled "Black Boy in France," which gives the people back home a picture of a day in the life of the famed writer. Wright spends the summer in the Gold Coast, now Ghana, and records his experiences in a travel diary.

1954   Wright travels in Spain and publishes two books: *Black Power: A Report of Reaction in a Land of Pathos*, about his experiences in the Gold Coast; and the novel *Savage Holiday*.

1955   He travels to Indonesia to report on the Bandung Conference, the first large-scale meeting of newly independent African and Asian states.

1956   *The Color Curtain: A Report on the Bandung Conference* is published in March. He helps to organize the first Congress of Negro Writers and Artists in Paris, an important meeting of writers from across the African diaspora in which they discuss the role of literature and culture in the freedom of black people worldwide. The meeting is held in September.

1957   *Pagan Spain* and *White Man, Listen!* are published.

1958   *The Long Dream* is published. Wright works on a few other novels as well, which are not published in his lifetime.

1959   Wright adapts a play from Louis Sapin's *Papa Bon Dieu* and produces *Daddy Goodness* in Paris. After visiting Africa, Wright is diagnosed with amoebic dysentery and is hospitalized. In the hospital, he experiments with haiku.

1960   *The Long Dream* appears on Broadway, but only for one week. Wright continues to battle illnesses. On November 28, he dies of a heart attack at the Clinique Eugene Gibez. He is cremated at Père Lachaise Cemetery on December 3, along with a copy of *Black Boy*.

1960–1961   Richard Wright's career is universally praised in France, especially by French-speaking Africans. Many elegiac articles are written about his contribution to freedom for the world at large. And the three black novelists Wright helped move to Paris all praise him in their work following his death: Baldwin in "Alas Poor Richard" (1961); Himes in an *Ebony* article, "The Last Days of Richard Wright" (February 1961) and later in *My Life of Absurdity* (1972); and William Gardner Smith in a *Two Cities* article, "The Compensation for the Wound"

(Summer 1961). *Eight Men*, a collection of short stories, is posthumously published.

1963   *Lawd Today!*, which was originally declined by several publishers in the 1930s, is published.

1968   *Negro Digest* polls the most prominent African American writers of the time, asking who the most important writer in African American literary history is. In their January issue, "A Survey: Black Writers' Views on Literary Lions and Values," they publish their results. Richard Wright is voted number one. The cover of that issue is subtitled "Richard Wright: 'The Leading Lion,'" with a big picture of Wright on the cover.

1977   *American Hunger*, a continuation of the autobiography *Black Boy*, is published by Harper & Row.

1986   *Callaloo* publishes a special issue on Richard Wright, "Richard Wright and the Chicago Renaissance School," dedicated to his work and aesthetics.

1991   The Library of America publishes a two-volume edition of Richard Wright's work in which they restore cuts and changes made by publishers and others.

1994   Wright's young adult fiction novel, *Rite of Passage*, is published by HarperCollins.

1995   *Rite of Passage* wins Notable 1995 Children's Trade Books in Social Studies (National Council for Social Studies/Children's Book Council).

1998   A selection of Richard Wright's haiku is published by Arcade Publishers under the title *Haiku: This Other World*.

2001   On November 9, *The New York Times* publishes an article that outlines a "literary tour" of "Richard Wright's Left Bank" experience in Paris. The tour was created by Monique Wells, who released a book, *Paris Reflections: Walks Through African-American Paris*, in 2002.

2005   Julia Wright, his daughter, publishes *Daughter of a Native Son* with Random House. It is a memoir about her father.

2008   Two major conferences are held to celebrate Richard Wright's centennial. On March 29, acclaimed writers Sonia Sanchez and John Wideman, along with Richard Wright biographer Hazel Rowley and his daughter Julia Wright form a panel in which they discuss the importance of his body of work. This is moderated by Professor Maryemma Graham at the Schomburg Center ("Richard Wright at 100"). On June 21, the American University of Paris hosts the International Richard Wright Centennial Conference in Paris. In the same year, Harper Perennial publishes a draft of a novel by Wright, *A Father's Law*.

2015   University of Missouri Press publishes some of Wright's early leftist journalism under the title *Byline, Richard Wright: Articles from the Daily Worker and New Masses*.

GLENDA R. CARPIO

Introduction

Richard Wright's Art and Politics

Richard Wright is best known as a hard-edged writer of political protest. Often contrasted with other major African American figures – specifically James Baldwin, Zora Neale Hurston, and Ralph Ellison – as more dedicated to politics than art, Wright's unflinching focus on the racial violence and class warfare that compromise American democracy has solidified his legacy as a preeminent social critic. But Wright was also a daring artist whose dazzling formal innovation was central to his politics, grounding a precocious exploration of the intersections between race, gender, class, and global imperialism. This made him at once an inviting sparring partner for contemporaries and a model for younger writers to live up to or transcend. While occasionally categorized as a "naturalist," he used a variety of styles – from a robust modernism to a razor-sharp realism to mixed-media collaborations in photography and film; from elegiac poetry to noir-influenced experiments with pulp fiction – to call attention to the existential, ontological, and material marginalization of African Americans. As scholar Werner Sollors puts it, "the point was to use any technique that was likely to shake up readers and direct them towards serious questions ... of class inequality and racial segregation."[1] Wright consistently emphasized that, what used to be called "the Negro Problem" – a phrase he and Baldwin derided – was both unique to the United States and connected in a myriad of ways to power struggles worldwide, refracting the plight of people of color across nations. Wright's aesthetic experimentation and globalist point of view were intrinsically connected, making him one of the most radical writers and controversial social critics of the twentieth century.

Richard Nathaniel Wright was born in 1908 to a family of sharecroppers on a plantation located between Roxie and Natchez, Mississippi, and died fifty-two years later in Paris after almost fifteen years of what he once described as "voluntary exile."[2] Named after his formerly enslaved grandfathers, Wright grew up poor in the Jim Crow South (first in Elaine, Arkansas, and Jackson, Mississippi, then in Memphis, Tennessee) and had limited formal schooling. But he was also an autodidact who, according to his younger brother, "seemed to live almost exclusively in a world of books and ideas."[3] He devoured "everything he could lay his hands on, textbooks belonging to his young neighbors, old almanacs, and local weekly papers."[4] His "first reader was the Sunday paper," which he learned to decipher with the help of his mother, Ella Wilson. Before giving up her trade for farming, Wilson had been a schoolteacher, and she instructed Wright at home until he was approximately eight years old.[5] Wright attended school sporadically – only at the age of thirteen was he able to complete a full year – largely because of the poverty his immediate family suffered after his father abandoned them and, later, when his mother suffered an incapacitating stroke. Sent to live with his intensely devout maternal grandmother, a Seventh Day Adventist, Wright made the best of the religious schooling she forced upon him. He "learned to decipher the system of representation set forth" in church sermons and parables, and "later borrowed some of his most beautiful images" from preachers and the "biblical mythology with which he became so familiar."[6] At the same time, Wright rejected the grim austerity of his grandmother's faith, asserting, even at an early age, his individual right to create his own system of thought and belief.

At sixteen he published his first short story. At nineteen he moved to Chicago, where he worked as postal clerk and insurance salesman but continued writing in his spare time. He wrote poetry and short stories while reading widely and deeply across disciplines, especially sociology, philosophy, and psychology. He joined the Chicago John Reed Club – a local chapter of the national organization for Marxist intellectuals and artists – then the Communist Party. Although he publicly broke from the latter in his 1944 *Atlantic Monthly* essay "I Tried to Be a Communist," the Federal Bureau of Investigation file on his activities would grow thick over time. He moved to New York in 1937 to pursue a literary career but left the United States ten years later, weary of racial discrimination and anti-Communist persecution. By the time he, his second wife, and their daughter had moved to Paris, Wright was *the* most prominent black American writer, his reputation resting on the short-story collection *Uncle Tom's Children* (1938); his nonfiction project *Twelve Million Black Voices: A Folk History of the United States* (1941), which combines a poetic, incisive account of anti-black oppression in America with photographs of contemporary black life; and above all his novel *Native Son* (1940) and his autobiography *Black Boy* (1945), which both achieved great critical and financial success. Less well-known but equally important works from this early period include Wright's numerous journal articles for the *Daily Worker, The New Masses,* and other left-leaning periodicals; several important essays, including "Blueprint for Negro Writing" (1937); and two adaptations of *Native Son*, one a stage play directed by Orson Welles (1941) and the other a film with French director Pierre Chenal (1951). In exile, Wright's prolific career continued with three major novels, *The Outsider* (1953), *Savage Holiday* (1954), and *The Long Dream* (1958), as well as four collections of travel writing and reportage.

Best known for *Native Son* and *Black Boy*, both still fixtures on high school and university syllabi, Wright produced ten works of fiction (including his unpublished and posthumously published works), one collection of haiku, three plays, several books of essays, and nonfiction works on topics including the black urban migration of the early twentieth century, African decolonization, and global communism. Interdisciplinary in practice, international in range, and interracial in thematic concern, Wright's oeuvre is without a question a towering achievement. His fearless ability to provoke, his enormous capacity for personal, political, and artistic growth, and the sheer richness of his writing made him a favorite literary ancestor for radical black thinkers of the 1960s and the subject of intense scholarly interest for decades.[7] But Wright is also freshly relevant for new generations of scholars, students, and cultural critics. His work speaks not only to anxieties about the meaning of racial progress in a world where – despite premature declarations of "post-blackness" – stunning racial violence erupts with deadly consistency, but also to questions of globalization and national belonging, as well as debates about the role of fiction and writing in general as methods of political intervention. Witness the publication of Ta-Nehisi Coates's widely discussed *Between the World and Me* (2015), a book that not only takes its title from one of Wright's poems but that also carries forward Wright's radical critique of racial violence; or Isabel Wilkerson's celebrated *The Warmth of Other Suns* (2010), another book with a title borrowed from Wright's verse and infused with his lyricism in its epic account of the Great Migration. More broadly, the success and reception of Claudia Rankine's *Citizen: An American Lyric* (2014), Colson Whitehead's *The Underground Railroad* (2016), and Jesmyn Ward's *Sing, Unburied, Sing* (2017), among others, reflect a resurgence of demand for black politics through literature for which Wright's career set the pattern.

The centennial of Wright's birth (2008) and the fifty-year anniversary of his death (2011) occasioned conference papers and lectures in the United States, Western Europe, and across the world.[8] The scholarship resulting from these occasions offers insight on Wright's late and unpublished writings, on his exile from the United States, and on his work as a global intellectual and transnational humanist. It also considers his experimentation in genres not normally associated with him: drama and film.[9] Our *Companion* joins this renaissance in Wright studies, while disputing persistent myths about Wright's political vision and artistry. It is divided in two sections, both of which highlight the genres and modes of Wright's craft as integral to his political project. The first focuses on Wright's development as a writer in the United States and the second turns to the works he produced as an expatriate in France and during his travels through Africa and Asia. But this two-part structure does not entail a dichotomy. Challenging a well-known argument that Wright's expatriation contributed to his supposed literary decline, each section of the *Companion* traces overlooked connections between Wright's life in America and abroad. Far from dimming, Wright's vision developed as he left the United States, exile both sharpening his political perspective and allowing him to experiment with form relatively unconstrained by the expectations placed upon writers of color in America. Yet critics insisted that his work's worth rested in its engagement with racial strife in America, largely ignoring Wright's evolving aesthetics and his often-prescient views of globalization. Since his death, this critical tendency has continued, as scholars emphasize Wright's political views, specifically his insights into the sociology and psychology of race, at the expense of exploring the full reach of his artistic achievements. By contrast, *The Cambridge Companion to Richard Wright* focuses on the inseparable connection between Wright's art and politics while offering fresh insights on his oeuvre.

Chapters in Part I, "Native Son in Jim Crow America," consider the influence of publishers on the shape of Wright's major works – for instance, the splitting of his autobiography into *Black Boy* and *American Hunger*, the latter unpublished until 1977; and the editorial abridgement of *Native Son*, published in its entirety only in 1991 – shedding new light on texts that, while classics, have not always been available in their fullest expression. Other essays explore his engagement with non-literary disciplines (psychology, sociology) and other arts (music, photography), as these dovetailed with his political development. The chapters in this section also offer new ways of seeing Wright's representation of masculinity and challenge how his involvement with the Communist Party has been understood. Chapters in Part II, "'I Choose Exile': Wright Abroad," focus on Wright's leading role among black expatriate artists in Paris, as well as the development of his political worldview in the works of nonfiction that he published in the 1950s. This section pays particular attention to manuscripts in Wright's archive – unpublished letters and novels, plans for multivolume works – that illuminate the depth and expansiveness of his aesthetic and political vision.

Categorizing Wright

As an expatriate in Paris, Wright "removed himself from purely American preoccupations," broadening a global view of race and the human condition that, as Nicholas T. Rinehart's chapter in this volume argues, he had begun to cultivate long before his expatriation.[10] He also deepened his engagement with existential philosophy, producing a novel, *The Outsider*, which Tommie Shelby's contribution to the *Companion* reads as a "searching dialogue with canonical works and figures in the tradition,"[11] including Kierkegaard, Nietzsche, Dostoevsky, and Heidegger, as well as Wright's contemporaries in Paris: Camus, Beauvoir, and Sartre. During this time, Wright also kept his keen eye on the political and economic challenges of postwar Europe, particularly the persistence of totalitarianism. His only book about a European country, *Pagan Spain* (1956), details life under Francisco Franco's fascist government. But Wright's principal orientation in this phase of his career was toward liberation movements in the so-called third world. His travel books and essays, *Black Power* (1954), on the Gold Coast before its independence as Ghana; *The Color Curtain* (1956), on the Bandung Conference, the first large-scale meeting of newly independent African and Asian states; and *White Man, Listen!* (1957), a collection of essays on topics ranging from African American literature to African nationalism to the psychology of racial oppression, constitute foundational texts in what became known, after the publication of Edward Said's *Orientalism* (1978), as postcolonial studies.[12]

In Paris, Wright became a leading figure not only among the other black American expatriates who, following his lead, moved to France, but also the African and Caribbean writers and intellectuals who converged on the cosmopolitan capital. Writers James Baldwin, Chester Himes, William Gardner Smith, and Richard Gibson; the cartoonist Oliver Harrington; the painters Larry Potter, Beauford Delaney, Herb Gentry, and Walter Coleman; and numerous black musicians "made up a veritable black colony" in Paris during the 1950s.[13] Key places for their "encounters, discussions, [and] confrontations" included the "Montmartre and Tournon cafes in the Latin Quarter," the ex-GI Leroy Haynes' soul food restaurant on the Rue Clauzel,[14] and Wright's apartment, which as Himes recalled, "occupied the entire fourth floor of the building" and was "the inner sanctum to which only selected visitors were ever invited."[15] If Wright was selective about invitations to his home, he was often generous in other ways, procuring financial support, jobs, and contacts (as he had in the United States) for younger writers such as Gwendolyn Brooks, Langston Hughes, and Ralph Ellison. He was instrumental in getting James Baldwin financial support to write his first novel, similarly helping Himes, Gardener Smith, and others.[16] Wright also collaborated with leading African and Caribbean literary figures, including Aimé Césaire, George Padmore, Alioune Diop, and Léopold Sédar Senghor. He assisted Césaire and Diop in launching *Présence Africaine*, a political and literary magazine that evolved into a publishing house, a bookstore, and key institution of the Pan-African movement for decolonization.

Wright differed ideologically with many of the writers he supported but did not see disagreement as an impediment to collaboration; rather, he valued debate as a cornerstone of artistic and intellectual progress. His position in the Pan-African movement was complicated by his rejection of Négritude, "the politically charged assertion by some Francophone African nationalists of a transhistorical, transnational black cultural unity."[17] Wright rejected such "black essentialism in favor of 'modern' (non-primordial) political coalitions, and, in the same vein, formed at times close relationships to the (white) intelligentsia of France," which made some of his black peers uneasy.[18] Baldwin distrusted his associations with French intellectuals, arguing that, for instance, "Sartre, de Beauvoir, and company" did not see Wright's full humanity. "I always sensed in Richard Wright a Mississippi pickaninny, mischievous, cunning, and tough," Baldwin wrote, "like some fantastic jewel buried in tall grass." The French, Baldwin concluded, offered "very little" that Wright could use; it "was painful to feel that the people from his adopted country were no more capable of seeing this jewel than were the people of his native land, and were in their own way as intimidated by it."[19] Writing to Albert Murray in 1953, Ralph Ellison expressed a similar view.[20] Fellow artists in the black expatriate community in Paris wondered if Wright had been away from home "for too long," if he made a mistake by cutting "himself from his roots."[21] His self-imposed exile, they argued, had not only alienated him personally but also corrupted, if not destroyed, "the authenticity" of his artistic vision.[22]

As Ellison's letter to Murray attests, this view of Wright's expatriate years took shape even before his death. Though Wright's pre-exile work was overwhelmingly well received, the books he wrote abroad received tepid if not outright negative reviews. The influential critic Irving Howe characterized Wright's later work as "clumsy" and "uneven" and others echoed his view.[23] In the decades after his death, this account of Wright hardened, not only obfuscating his prescient critique of essentialism and diminishing his artistic accomplishments but also revealing the stubborn tendency to tether Wright's artistic vision to his racial identity. Harold McCarthy's 1972 essay for *American Literature* summarizes this distorted critical consensus:

6

Such American novelists as Henry James, Hemingway, and Henry Miller did not discover how to cope as artists with their experience until their sense of American life had been placed in a European perspective. With Richard Wright the opposite was true. When he left for Paris ... his best fiction had been written and exile was only to dilute his capacity for dealing with American life ... Critics of Wright's work seem fully agreed that as a result of leaving America he lost touch with *the source of his strength as a writer, namely, his being a Negro*, a man immersed in the American Negro experience, and a spokesman for black causes (emphasis added)[24]

In *The Black Atlantic: Modernity and Double Consciousness* (1993) Paul Gilroy trenchantly critiqued this view, rightly arguing that American critics "overshadow" the "range and diversity of Wright's work" by separating his pre- and post-exile output.[25] It is worth pausing over the assumptions that sustain this split, for they continue to crop up in one guise or another. According to the critical consensus that McCarthy highlights, Wright's inspiration and talent lay in his racial identity, which, like his writing, could only remain "pure" in the United States. In his review of Wright's posthumously published short story collection *Eight Men* (1961), Howe goes even further, identifying Wright's expatriation with his supposedly misguided desire to experiment with form. For Howe, Wright was not "a writer of the first rank," because, by abandoning the United States and, by extension, the "naturalist" literary style associated with his early work, Wright had abdicated his true calling as a writer of protest fiction.[26] Or was that "true calling" to stay black and angry? By locating the source of Wright's talent in an "authentic" racial essence, and by tethering that talent to the protest tradition, critics have implied as much. But Wright always operated in many registers and used a variety of aesthetic forms. This was both evidence of his artistic deftness and key to his political vision. For it was *through* form – and not only through theme – that he challenged racial and class oppression, and it was by *varying* the aesthetic means through which he represented social reality that he offered new ways of imagining our world. As his talent expanded, in *both* his pre- and post-exile years, Wright amassed a richer arsenal for exposing injustice and for imagining freedom. To see Wright only as an American protest writer is to limit the scope of his formidable achievement.

Native Son in Jim Crow America

As a young man still living in Memphis, Wright was transformed by what he called the "naturalism of the modern novel,"[27] which he discovered through H. L. Mencken's cultural and literary criticism. He was drawn to the style, especially in the novels of Theodore Dreiser, for its illustration of how "social systems drive the individual," and determine "consciousness and psychology."[28] *Uncle Tom's Children, Native Son,* the novella "The Man Who Lived Underground" (a key precursor to Ellison's *Invisible Man*), and *Black Boy* all bear marks of Wright's encounter with naturalism. When Wright moved to Chicago, his engagement with urban sociology deepened his understanding of how social structures shape individual consciousness, an influence especially evident in *Native Son* and *Black Hope*, an unfinished novel focused on African American women workers.[29]

As Gene Andrew Jarrett argues in his contribution to this collection, "Sincere Art and Honest Science: Richard Wright and the Chicago School of Sociology," Wright, like Ralph Ellison and Albert Murray, saw how racial bias distorted sociological interpretations of African American life. But he nevertheless believed that literature and sociology together could provide a "multidimensional image of African American life." He was particularly interested in the work of Horace Cayton and John St. Claire Drake, two sociologists whose years researching black life in Chicago through the Works Progress Administration program culminated in the seminal *Black Metropolis: A Study of Negro Life in a Northern City* (1945). Wright admired it so much that he wrote the introduction. In his literary work, Wright combined the formal qualities of literary naturalism with the environmental and characterological insights exemplified by scholarship by Cayton and St. Clair Drake, striving to expose race- and class-based exploitation and social domination as vividly as possible. Jarrett argues that Wright "sought to balance an artistic sensibility, which could capture the nuances of human experience, with empirical acumen, which could attend to potential thematic patterns discernible within raw data." [30]

Wright's combined use of sociological insight with the aesthetics of literary naturalism rhymed with his commitment to Marxist theory and Communist politics. He not only laid bare the intrinsic connection between race- and class-based oppression with gripping precision and realism, he also explicitly figured Communist characters struggling, often in solidarity across race, gender, and class barriers, to bring forth change. This brought on anti-Communist critique but also gave his prose a force that stunned readers. Irving Howe declared that the day "*Native Son* appeared, American culture was changed forever," for "Wright's novel brought out into the open, as no one ever had before, the hatred, fear, and violence that have crippled and may yet destroy our culture."[31] Wright wanted to "assault his readers' sensibilities, not curry their favor or indulge their sentimentality."[32] Judging from the responses garnered by the novel in the two years after its publication, he succeeded for readers "regardless of race or region" found it a "searing emotional force that gripped [them] with or against their will."[33] But others, especially Baldwin, saw Wright as sacrificing his literary talents in the name of politics. In his famous critique of *Native Son*, "Everybody's Protest Novel," Baldwin argued that the novel dispenses with the "niceties of style or characterization" in favor of abstractions like "the good of society"; that it reduces human complexity to political and sociological formulas.[34] Ellison and Hurston recognized Wright's artistic talent, praising him at the level of craft, but nevertheless echoed Baldwin's view, adding that Wright's blind embrace of Marxism not only kept him from "discovering the forms of American Negro humanity" but also led him to depict black life in overly dire ways.[35]

The tension between art and politics implicit in this criticism was informed by arguments particular to African American letters, as the debate between W. E. B. Du Bois and Alain Locke during the 1920s attests.[36] Yet, as Nathaniel Mills argues in his contribution "Marxism, Communism, and Richard Wright's Depression-Era Work," the binary was also "hegemonic in the Cold War era."[37] Revelations of Stalin's crimes resulted in vast disillusionment with Communism and led to vehement rejection of viewpoints and practices associated with it. Critics aligned literary naturalism "with totalitarian tendencies and instead valued ethical ambiguity, aesthetic experimentation, and the internal complexities of individual human experience."[38] It was in this critical climate that Wright's so-called protest fiction came to be seen as wanting. But, as several chapters in this volume show, it has always been misguided to see Wright's engagement with Marxism as separate from his aesthetic experimentation and commitment to exploring human complexity. It is also not true that Marxism left him disconnected from African American culture.[39] As Mills shows, Wright *adapted*, rather than merely implemented Marxist theory, providing a corrective to the racial blinders of historical materialism. Wright drew from "Marxism to depict blackness not in simple terms of deprivation or victimhood, as Ellison, Baldwin, and Hurston variously suggested, but as culturally sustained and capable of effecting revolutionary historical progress" through specifically African American "vernacular communal knowledge and traditional religious sensibilities."[40]

Mills's chapter, like others in this volume, helps us resolve a curious contradiction in Wright scholarship. Wright has been derided both as a formulaic Marxist (early phase) *and* as an experimentalist (later years); in each case he is cast as a writer disconnected from authentic black experience. But the contradiction falls apart when we see that his Depression-era work did not doggedly adhere to Marxist philosophy, and that, instead, in the early part of his career, Wright experimented with form to challenge stereotyped notions of "authentic" black experience. In the latter part of his career he continued to do so, deepening his engagement with philosophy and global politics while reimagining himself as a writer; this speaks to a consistency in his work that critics have undermined. Because Wright challenged not only black essentialism but also parochial representations of race; because he insisted on what we now call the intersectionality of race, class, and gender, he has been a puzzle and a worry for critics. Rather than meet Wright's challenge – and perhaps intimidated by it – scholars have tended to force him into preconceived frameworks, missing, as Baldwin put it, the "fantastic jewel buried in tall grass." The writers in this *Companion* welcome the opportunity to examine that jewel from multiple perspectives.

Chapters in this volume explore a wide range of intellectual and aesthetic developments in Wright's work that the label "protest writer" has obscured. George Hutchinson's opening chapter, "The Literary Ecology of *Native Son* and *Black Boy*," attends to the centrality of ecology in Wright's "general theory of literary expression" and "social processes."[41] As Hutchinson shows, Wright was drawn to the Communist party for its vision of human unity through revolution, but he also came to see the limitations that such a vision placed on both artistic and human development. After breaking with the party, Wright put his faith in the power of literary experimentation to create a "humanist and ecological" model of self-fashioning that promoted not only human unity but also greater interconnection among life forms.

In "Richard Wright's Planned Incongruity: *Black Boy* as 'Modern Living'," Jay Garcia argues that Wright's familiarity with literary and cultural criticism, especially his knowledge of the writings of Kenneth Burke, allowed him to produce a different kind of storytelling about the Jim Crow South, one that rendered it emblematic of, rather than peripheral to, modernity. Garcia offers a new reading of *Black Boy*, which has long been interpreted through the limited strictures of autobiography, or else contested on the grounds of its deviation from the biographical record. As Garcia shows, Wright adopted what Burke called a "perspective by incongruity" or "planned incongruity" by positing his younger self as the source of a detached critical perspective that could devise fresh, often psychological, insights into the workings of the Jim Crow social order. This was especially provocative because, at the time of the book's publication, "black youth remained segregated and marginalized not only in fact, but also in mainstream thought, which placed them in liminal relation to conceptions of the human." Giving his younger self "a critical function and psychological perspicacity incongruous with this role," Wright "produced a personality ... unlike but not altogether different from those of his readers," thereby affirming his "sense of segregated sociality and racial hierarchy as modes of 'modern living,' not marginal or aberrant patterns." As Garcia notes, many critics failed to recognize Wright's efforts, but there were those, notably Lionel Trilling and Mary McCarthy, who rightly saw that the book investigates "racism as a feature of modernity."[42]

Robert B. Stepto's "Rhythms of Race in Richard Wright's 'Big Boy Leaves Home'" explores the centrality of music, particularly the blues, to one of Wright's earliest short stories. As Stepto argues, Wright not only uses the blues to give lyrical expression to the personal catastrophe of the main character, Big Boy, but also creates his own linguistic rhythms by alternating prose forms between the vernaculars spoken by black and white Americans. Wright uses these rhythms to represent, *in language*, the racial warfare enacted in the story, and demonstrates his authorial control by intertwining these rhythms with Standard English. At the same time, Wright deploys contemporary popular music, such as the Broadway hit "Is It True What They Say About Dixie?" to contrast the song's "mythic fantasy about the South" with the reality of Big Boy's experience, especially as represented through the blues. The essay provides a corrective to critical assessments of Wright which, until recently, have failed to account for his use of African American musical forms in his fiction.[43]

In "Outside Joke: Humorlessness and Masculinity in Richard Wright," Kathryn S. Roberts provides another corrective. Critics who have framed Wright as a grimly serious writer[44] have not been attentive to how he combined "elements of humor – whether representations of men laughing, comically exaggerated symbolism, or more complex formal irony" – with a studied refusal to afford readers the "escape valve of laughter." This is what Roberts calls Wright's humorlessness, his strategy of distancing his readers from the laughter in his work. In *Lawd Today!* (1963), Wright's first, yet posthumously published novel, this use of humor becomes a calculated method of representing black male laughter while protecting it from the distortions of black gaiety produced by racial stereotyping. In "Big Boy Leaves Home," as well as in his late novel *The Outsider*, Wright uses humorlessness to represent modes of homosocial intimacy within and across racial borders, encounters that should provoke "laughter or embarrassment" within the contexts of "white supremacy, patriarchy, and heteronormativity," but in Wright open up possibilities for human connection.[45] As Roberts demonstrates, Wright's deployment of humorlessness has found literary heirs today in Ta-Nehisi Coates's 2015 epistolary memoir *Between the World and Me* and Barry Jenkins's 2016 film *Moonlight*.

"I Choose Exile": Wright Abroad

The chapters in the second part of the *Companion* explore the broadening of Wright's artistic and political vision catalyzed by his expatriation as well as the intertwined nature of the work Wright produced abroad and in the United States. In the first chapter, "Freedom in a Godless and Unhappy World: Wright as Outsider," Tommie Shelby traces Wright's adaptation of elements from European existential philosophy in *The Outsider* "to pursue in depth" two "common themes in his writings – family life and religion." Though it was decried as the novel most alienated from Wright's American "roots," *The Outsider* reprises Wright's earlier work, principally *Native Son*, and "The Man Who Lived Underground," two fictions that also address family life and religion from an existentialist perspective. But *The Outsider* shifts focus away from racial identity. Instead, Wright reflects "upon the human condition *through* black characters, representing black individuals, even those facing oppressive and violent treatment, as all-too-human embodiments of universal motifs." In so doing, Shelby argues, Wright also opens "a window" into his "own emotional life and strivings."[46]

If Shelby's chapter allows us to see connections between Wright's pre- and post-expatriation fiction, Laurence Cossu-Beaumont's "Richard Wright, Paris Noir, and Transatlantic Networks: A Book History Perspective," shows us Wright at "the center of an ongoing publication network between the United States and France" that also reached "African and West Indian intellectuals."[47] Challenging the myth of Wright as an isolated native son in exile, Cossu-Beaumont highlights the intellectual exchanges in which Wright was a key figure, arguing that understanding these exchanges requires considering not only the publication, circulation, and reception history of pertinent texts but also the work of translators, publishers, agents, critics, and journalists.

Turning to Wright's last published novel, *The Long Dream* (1958), and his unpublished manuscript "Island of Hallucination," Alice Mikal Craven explores how Wright fictionalized the aspirations and internal tensions of the black American expatriate community in Paris. As Craven notes in "Expatriation in Wright's Late Fiction," black American artists went to France "seeking ways to exercise their individual creativity" but their expectations were frustrated by intergroup pressure to address racial conflict at home.[48] This pressure was exacerbated by the atmosphere of suspicion and paranoia prompted by the US government's surveillance of black artists through the Central Intelligence Agency and the Federal Bureau of Investigation. Offering close analyses of Wright's late fiction in conversation with John A. Williams's novel *The Man Who Cried I Am* (1967), an expatriate *roman à clef* that includes a character based on Wright, Craven shows that despite the pressures assailing them, black American artists "managed to create lasting documents" attesting to the value of their comradeship and artistic freedom.[49]

In "Richard Wright's Globalism," Nicholas Rinehart takes a long view of Wright's work, arguing that his racial consciousness was forged from a "globalist" perspective that extended beyond national boundaries even before Wright lived abroad. This outlook was not, as some critics have maintained, a "late-stage development" in Wright's career, but "rather the predominant theme that unites his oeuvre." Wright's ongoing elaboration of this perspective is evident not only in his fiction, but also in "essays, journalism, poetry, letters, and unpublished pieces spanning from the beginning of his career in the mid-1930s to his deathbed writings of 1960." As Rinehart argues, Wright's globalist racial consciousness crystallizes and shifts registers across time, from his "anti-fascist political solidarity framed by Marxist internationalism, to an affective kinship among formerly colonized peoples expressed through existentialist proto-postcolonialism, and finally to a transcendent poetics in search of a universal humanism."[50]

Stephan Kuhl's chapter, "Richard Wright's Transnationalism and His Unwritten *Magnus Opus*" complements Rinehart's. Focusing on the wealth of material he left unpublished as well as his late fiction, Kuhl demonstrates that Wright planned to produce three multivolume fictions of expansive global vision and historical depth. The first series of novels, "Voyage," would have followed one "ageless individual from tribal life in Africa" through the "Middle Passage into American slavery and urban life." The second, "Celebration," would have extended "from the early stages of European colonialism to the mid-twentieth century," bridging five continents. The third series would have focused on Fishbelly, a character featured in his last published novel *The Long Dream* as well as the unpublished manuscript "Island of Hallucination." Kuhl shows that Wright conceived the latter two texts and the novel *Savage Holiday* (1954) as parts of a multivolume whole, giving us hard evidence for how it would have taken shape. He also reads Wright's travelogues, *Black Power*, *Pagan Spain*, and *The Color Curtain*, in tandem with *Savage Holiday*, reconstructing an interconnected critique of Western modernity – particularly Wright's nascent skepticism that Western secularism and industrialism "should serve as the ideal for emerging nations in Asia and Africa" – that unfolds across these texts much as it might have in his never-realized masterwork. Kuhl's intertextual approach enacts a central stylistic conceit in Wright's planned *magnus opus*: he imagined the individual novels of his series as standalone texts that would receive their highest significance and meaning only when read as part of the larger map.[51]

Ernest Julius Mitchell's concluding chapter, "Tenderness in Early Richard Wright," returns our attention to the issues raised in this introduction and throughout the collection regarding the publication and reception history of Wright's oeuvre. Since most of Wright's works were first published in their final form only after his death, and some of his texts were only published posthumously, a broad assessment of Wright's work has been possible only relatively recently. There are two waves of posthumous publications: the first occurred shortly after Wright's death (1961–1977), covering works from the beginning of his career, such as the collection of short stories, *Eight Men* (1961) and *Lawd Today!* (1963); while the second (1991–2008) covers works Wright wrote at the end of his life such as the novella *Rite of Passage* (1994), concerning a tragic afternoon in the life of a black adolescent and *A Father's Law* (2008), a novel about a black Chicago police officer and his son. When one takes into account these posthumous publications, Mitchell argues, one discovers a version of Wright that differs radically from the image that formed about him based only on his most well-known texts. Offering an incisive reading of *Lawd Today!* as a case in point, Mitchell shows how it reframes well-known texts such as *Native Son* and *Black Boy*, especially when these are read in their unexpurgated editions. Such reframing allows us to see that Wright, far from being an author who gratuitously and compulsively represented violence, as Baldwin and others have claimed, was involved in a lifelong attempt "to dissect and diagnose the roots of misogyny, homophobia, and masculine violence."[52] Perhaps most surprisingly, Mitchell argues, a review of Wright's posthumously published work allows us to reconsider the key role that *tenderness* plays in his fiction. Our *Companion* thus ends with a call, present in various forms throughout its chapters, to rediscover a writer who has been for too long shrouded in myth.

Reevaluating Wright

I began this Introduction by noting the current renaissance in Wright studies and I end by highlighting this boon once more. Especially in today's dark political climate, we need Wright's penetrating vision to guide us, to help us understand the resurgence of white supremacy, and the broad economic, political, and structural context which has caused it to surge now and will likely cause it to surge again. The new scholarship reevaluating Wright's contributions unearths sources from his archive, and in this way makes his prescient views more available in this time of need.

Barbara Foley's work on Wright's unpublished novel *Black Hope* is a case in point. *Black Hope* focuses on black women domestic workers and furthers Wright's "investigation into the nature of fascism" (he had explored the topic in *Lawd Today!* and in *Native Son*) underscoring the interconnections between sexism, racism, capitalism, and right-wing mass movements.[53] As Foley shows, the novel highlights the "potential psychological appeal" of such movements "to all sectors of the population – even those whose material interest should lead them to reject [them] most passionately" because they play on the experience of alienation.[54] Fascism and similar movements are "ruling-class-instigated" but deceptively appear as the antidote for the economic and psychological maladies produced by systems of inequality. Foley argues that the novel radically positions women, particularly black women, in the "vanguard of antifascism." With a title that uncannily echoes recent political rhetoric, *Black Hope* imagines an egalitarian future in which "black people are the principal articulators of hope" with women at the center of that "liberatory project."[55] Foley's scholarship broaches new territory, encouraging a reassessment of Wright's politics and ethics.[56] Wright, who has often been "viewed as oblivious to gender issues, if not outrightly misogynist, was in fact deeply interested in the condition of women as an issue in its own right as well as its broader social and political connections."[57] Arguably the most radical of Wright's novels, *Black Hope* has yet to be published.

Wright ultimately envisioned an egalitarian world where racial and class categories would be null, "a social order free of exploitation of all kinds."[58] He works to represent this vision in his oeuvre, but it is in his haiku, the Japanese poetic form he turned to after learning that he was terminally ill, that gave this vision its most robust shape. Producing over 4,000 poems and preparing 817 for publication in the posthumous collection *This Other World* (1998), Wright used haiku to imagine a world in which "fearless African American writers such as himself" could divest themselves of their "socio-historical and racial circumstances" and produce a global literature buttressed by a "universal humanism and ecological holism."[59] Scholarly work on Wright's haiku has been scant until recently. As it has burgeoned, it has highlighted the *aspirational* aspects of Wright's late poetry, his consciously quixotic mode. In combination with Wright's unwavering critique of our world – with its brutal structures of inequality and rapacious systems of greed – this ideal vision deserves our attention.[60] His turn to haiku reminds us of Wright's versatility, of his ingenuity. It takes us back to the young boy from rural Mississippi who devised ingenious ways to educate himself and who, as an artist, used any means necessary to shake his readers awake, and keep them socially and politically engaged. For as much as Wright's intellectual prowess accomplished, it was his play with form that made up his extraordinary insight, the lyricism with which he fearlessly drew and daringly dreamed alternatives to our woefully imperfect world.

Notes

1. Werner Sollors, "The Clock, the Salesman, and the Breast," in *The Cambridge History of American Literature*, ed. Sacvan Bercovitch (Cambridge, UK: Cambridge University Press, 1994), 495.
2. Richard Wright, "I Choose Exile," Richard Wright Papers, Box 6, Folder 110, James Weldon Johnson Collection, Yale Collection of American Literature, Beinecke Rare Book and Manuscript Library, Yale University, 1.
3. Leon Wright, as quoted in Hazel Rowley, *Richard Wright: The Life and Times* (New York: Henry Holt and Company, 2001), 325.
4. Michel Fabre, *The Unfinished Quest of Richard Wright*, trans. Isabel Barzum (Chicago: University of Illinois Press, 1993), 38.
5. Ibid., 15.
6. Ibid., 35.
7. See for instance, Keneth Kinnamon, *The Emergence of Richard Wright* (Urbana: University of Illinois Press, 1972); John M. Reilly, ed., *Richard Wright: The Critical Reception* (New York: Burt Franklin, 1978); Yoshinobu Hakutani, ed. *Critical Essays on Richard Wright* (Boston: G. K. Hall, 1982); Michel Fabre, *The World of Richard Wright* (Jackson: University Press of Mississippi, 1985); Henry Louis Gates Jr. and K. A. Appiah, eds., *Richard Wright: Critical Perspectives Past and Present* (New York: Amistad Press, 1993); Arnold Rampersad, ed., *Richard Wright: A Collection of Critical Essays* (Englewood Cliffs: Prentice Hall, 1995); and Keneth Kinnamon, ed., *New Essays on Native Son* (Cambridge; New York: Cambridge University Press, 1990) and *Critical Essays on Richard Wright* (Woodbridge: Twayne Publishers, 1997).
8. Two new collections, *Richard Wright: New Readings in the 21st Century* (New York: Palgrave Macmillan, 2011) and *Richard Wright in a Post-Racial Imaginary* (New York: Bloomsbury, 2014), both edited by William Dow and Alice Mikal Craven, a contributor to this volume, emerged from a 2008 centenary conference in Paris. They focus on Wright's late and unpublished writings, on questions of national alienation as well as international belonging.
9. See for instance Bruce Allen Dick, "Forgotten Chapter: Richard Wright, Playwrights, and the Modern Theater," in *Richard Wright in a Post-Racial Imaginary*, ed. William Dow and Alice Mikal Craven (New York: Bloomsbury Academic, 2014), 179 –195; and Emily Lordi, *Black Resonance: Iconic Women Singers and African American Literature* (New Brunswick: Rutgers University Press, 2013). Connecting Wright's reflections on the blues, specifically Bessie Smith, to his theatrical and film adaptations of *Native Son* with Orson Welles and Pierre Chenal, Lordi reveals how Wright, whose work is "generally thought to devalue both black women *and* black music, creates nonfictional and cinematic works in which song becomes the medium of expressive alliance between black men and women." (27)

10. Fabre, *The Unfinished Quest*, 316.

11. See Tommie Shelby in this volume, p.121.

12. See Sudhi Rajiv, "Expanding Metaphors of Marginalization: Richard Wright, Sharankumar Limbale, and a Post-Caste Imaginary," in *Richard Wright in a Post-Racial Imaginary*, 234. Rajiv highlights the similarities between Wright's desire "to eliminate racial categorization as a vector of national (un) belonging" and Limbale's tireless quest for a "post-caste" Indian society." (7)

13. Michel Fabre, *From Harlem to Paris: African Americans: Black American Writers in France, 1840–1980* (Chicago: University of Illinois Press, 1991), 5–6.

14. Fabre, *From Harlem to Paris*, 5–6.

15. Chester Himes, *My Life of Absurdity* (New York: Doubleday, 1976), 197–198.

16. Ibid., 197–198. After Wright's death, Himes, Gardener Smith, and Harrington all wrote tributes to their mentor, highlighting his generosity. See Gardener Smith, "The Compensation for the Wound," *Two Cities* 6 (Summer 1961): 67–69; Chester Himes, "The Last Days of Richard Wright," *Ebony* 16 (February 1961), later reprinted in *My Life of Absurdity*; and Oliver Harrington, "The Last Days of Richard Wright," *Ebony* 16 (February 1961) reprinted in *Why I Left American and Other Essays* (Jackson: University Press of Mississippi, 1993), 20–25. Baldwin's "Alas, Poor Richard" [1961] is a tortured account of his indebtedness to Wright mixed with a critique of the older writer's worldview and artistry. See Baldwin, *Collected Essays*, ed. Toni Morrison (New York: Library of America, 1998), 247–268.

17. Kevin Gaines, as quoted in Alexa Welk, "'The Uses and Hazards of Expatriation': Richard Wright's Cosmopolitanism in Process," *African American Review* 41, no. 3 (Fall 2007): 462. See Kevin Gaines, "Revisiting Richard Wright in Ghana: Black Radicalism and the Dialectics of Diaspora," *Social Text* 19, no. 2 (2001): 76.

18. Welk, "'The Uses and Hazards of Expatriation'," 462.

19. James Baldwin, "Alas, Poor Richard," in *Collected Essays*, 249. See also "Many Thousands Gone" [1951] in the same volume, 19–34.

20. Ellison frames Wright as an artist in decline and argues that he is an example of what happens "when you go elsewhere looking for what you already had at home. Wright goes to France for existentialism," he writes, but any "blues Negro could tell him things that would make that cock-eyed Sartre's head swim." See Ralph Ellison and Albert Murray, *Trading Twelves: The Selected Letters of Ralph Ellison and Albert Murray*, ed. John Callahan (New York: Vintage Books, 2001), 43.

21. Baldwin, "Alas, Poor Richard," 260.

22. Welk, "'The Uses and Hazards of Expatriation'," 462.

23. Irving Howe, "Richard Wright: A World of Farewell," review of *Eight Men* by Richard Wright, *New Republic*, February 13, 1961. In her review of *The Outsider*, Lorraine Hansberry plainly states that, because "Wright has been away from home a long time," he is unable to create a believable character in protagonists Cross Damon, calling him "someone you will never meet on the Southside of Chicago or Harlem." She argues that Damon is a violent monster who functions as a "propaganda piece for the enemies of the Negro people." See Lorraine Hansberry, review of *The Outsider*, by Richard Wright, *Freedom* (April 1953), 7. Wright's literary agent, Paul Reynolds, also worried that he

had been away from America for too long. "I haven't any question about your ability to write very fine novels," he wrote Wright after the publication of *The Outsider* and *Savage Holiday*, "I have lots of doubts as to whether a man who has been nine years away from this country can successfully write them laid in this country." As quoted in Hazel Rowley, *Richard Wright: The Life and Times*, 471. For an account of *The Outsider* as an "abysmal flop" and the demise of Wright's career in Paris, "dragged down by the wreckage of *The Outsider*," see James Campbell, *Paris Interzone: Richard Wright, Lolita, Boris Van, and Others of the Left Bank 1946–1960* (London: Secker and Warbug, 1994), 105–106.

24. See Harold McCarthy, "Richard Wright: The Expatriate as Native Son," *American Literature* 44, no. 1 (March 1972): 97. McCarthy partially challenges this consensus but still maintains that Wright's source of inspiration was his racial identity.

25. Paul Gilroy, *The Black Atlantic: Modernity and Double Consciousness* (Cambridge: Harvard University Press, 1993): 155–61.

26. Howe, "Richard Wright: A World of Farewell," 17–18.

27. Wright quoted in Fabre, *The Unfinished Quest*, 68.

28. James Smethurst, "After Modernism: Richard Wright Interprets the Black Belt," in *Richard Wright in a Post-Racial Imaginary*, ed. William Dow and Alice Mikal Craven (New York: Bloomsbury, 2014), 18–19.

29. For an excellent discussion of this unpublished manuscript, see Barbara Foley, "'A Dramatic Picture ... of Woman from Feudalism to Fascism': Richard Wright's *Black Hope*," in *Richard Wright in a Post-Racial Imaginary*, 113–126.

30. See Jarrett in this volume, p. 89.

31. Irving Howe, "Black Boys and Native Sons," *Dissent* 10, no. 4 (Fall 1963): 353–368.

32. Keneth Kinnamon, "Introduction," in *New Essays on Native Son*, ed. Keneth Kinnamon (Cambridge, UK: Cambridge University Press, 1990), 18. See also Fabre, *The Unfinished Quest*. Malcolm Cowley, along with other critics, praised the novel, "comparing Wright with Dreiser, Dostoevsky, Steinbeck, and Dickens." (178)

33. Kinnamon, "Introduction," 19.

34. James Baldwin, *Notes of a Native Son* (Boston: Beacon Press, 2012), 18–19.

35. See Ralph Ellison, "The World and the Jug," in *The Collected Essays of Ralph Ellison*, ed. John Callahan (New York: Modern Library, 2003), 167. See Hurston, review of *Uncle Tom's Children* by Richard Wright, *Saturday Review of Literature* (April 2, 1938), 32–33; and James Baldwin's essay "Many Thousands Gone," *Collected Essays*, 19–35, which argues that *Native Son* represents Negro life as "debased and impoverished." (31)

36. In his 1926 essay "Criteria of New Art" W. E. B. Du Bois argued for the necessity of black art to explicitly challenge racial inequality, while Alain Locke, in his 1928 essay "Art or Propaganda?" called for black artists to be free to choose between group and individual expression, arguing that black political art is a form of propaganda that "perpetuates the position of group inferiority."

37. Mills, this volume, p. 58.

38. See Nathaniel F. Mills in this volume, p. 71, note 3.

39. Harold Cruse's reflections on Richard Wright best summarize this consensus: "Poor Richard Wright! He sincerely tried, but he never got much beyond that starting point that Marxism represented for him ... Uncharted paths existed for the Negro creative intellectuals to explore, if only they could avoid being blinded by Communist Party propaganda." See *The Crisis of the Negro Intellectual* [1967] (New York: New York Review Books, 2005), 188.
40. Mills in this volume, p. 61.
41. Hutchinson in this volume, p. 23.
42. Garcia in this volume, pp. 42, 52.
43. For an excellent exception to this trend, see Emily Lordi's "Vivid Lyricism: Richard Wright and Bessie Smith's Blues," in *Black Resonance*, 27–65.
44. For instance, Hurston wrote that the stories in *Uncle Tom's Children* are "so grim that the Dismal Swap of race hatred must be where they live." Hurston, review of *Uncle Tom's Children*, 32–33.
45. Roberts in this volume, pp. 105, 114, 109.
46. Shelby in this volume, p. 122
47. Cossu-Beaumont in this volume, p. 140.
48. Craven in this volume, p. 152. For another view of the tensions compromising the aspirations of black American expatriates in Paris, see Laila Amine, "The Paris Paradox: Colorblindness and Colonialism in African American Expatriate Fiction," *American Literature* 87, no. 4 (2015): 739–768. As Amine shows, black artists had to contend with France's colonial legacy, especially as their expatriation coincided with the Algerian war for independence from France (1954–1962).
49. Craven in this volume, p. 153
50. Rinehart in this volume, p. 166.
51. Kuhl in this volume, pp. 187, 188, 190.
52. Mitchell in this volume, p. 199.
53. Wright was working on *Black Hope* in 1940, as *Native Son* neared publication. See Foley, "A Dramatic Picture," pp. 113, 119. Wright also articulated his views of fascism's nature in "How Bigger Was Born," his account of the *Native Son* protagonist's genesis. Originally delivered as a talk at Columbia University, Wright published it as an essay for the *Saturday Review of Literature* in 1940 and included it in subsequent printings of *Native Son*.
54. Foley, "A Dramatic Picture," 121.
55. Ibid., 122.
56. Ibid.
57. Ibid., 113. For critical discussions of Wright's purported misogyny, see Trudier Harris, "Native Sons and Foreign Daughters," in Keneth Kinnamon, ed., *New Essays on Native Son*; Sherley Anne Williams, "Papa Dick and Sister-Woman: Reflections on Women in the Fiction of Richard Wright" in Arnold Rampersad, ed., *Richard Wright: A Collection of Critical Essays*; and Sondra Guttman, "What Bigger Killed For: Rereading Violence against Women in Native Son," *Texas Studies in Literature and Language* 43:2 (Summer, 2001): 169–193.
58. Foley, "A Dramatic Picture," 119.

59. Sandy Alexandre, "Culmination in Miniature: Late Style and the Essence of Richard Wright's Haiku," in *Richard Wright in a Post-Racial Imaginary*, 246–247.

60. For further scholarship on Wright's haiku see Yoshinobu Hakutani, *Richard Wright and Haiku* (Columbia: University of Missouri Press, 2014); Jianqing Zheng, ed., *The Other World of Richard Wright: Perspectives on His Haiku* (Jackson: University of Mississippi Press, 2011); Eugene E. Miller, *Voice of a Native Son: The Poetics of Richard Wright* (Jackson: University of Mississippi Press, 1990); and Michel Fabre, *The World of Richard Wright* (Jackson: University of Mississippi Press, 1985).

PART I

Native Son in Jim Crow America

I

GEORGE HUTCHINSON

The Literary Ecology of *Native Son* and *Black Boy*

We have long known that Richard Wright was deeply impressed by the work of the Chicago sociologists as he wrote *Native Son*. Lawrence Buell has usefully interpreted *Native Son* in the context of environmental determinism, in line with literary naturalists and "urban fiction" going back to Dickens.[1] However, the specifically ecological discourse Wright employs in *Native Son* and *Black Boy* commands attention, shedding light on his general theory of literary expression as well as social processes.

The very sociologists who influenced Wright were in close collaboration with leading-edge ecologists, particularly in botany. Sociological terms and concepts of community shaped botanists' work, for example, while botanists' studies of biological "succession" and the like informed social theory, ideas of social "metabolism," and what Robert Park called "human ecology."[2] Ernest W. Burgess, for example, spoke of urban transformation in biological terms of "metabolism," adopting then-current tendencies of plant and animal ecologists to think of biotic zones as organisms. (Later "organism" was rethought as "community" and eventually "ecosystem" beginning in the 1940s.) According to ecological theories of succession, the organisms in any space prepared the ground for other species that would in turn alter the local biota, such that the place would be taken over by new life forms, the soil would be altered by these, and so on. Sociologists imported this concept to their studies of urban "zones."

In *Native Son*, Boris Max echoes such theories: "injustice blots out one form of life, but another grows up in its place with its own rights, needs, and aspirations."[3] White men have attempted to prevent this form of life from spreading into their own habitat, have "marked up the earth and said, 'Stay there!' But life is not stationary."[4] Max emphasizes the interconnection of life forms and the consequences of attempting to segregate one form of life from others. Such attempts had helped create, he says, "our whole sick social organism"[5]: "I plead with you to see a mode of *life* in our midst, a mode of life stunted and distorted, but possessing its own laws and claims, an existence of men growing out of the soil prepared by the collective but blind will of a hundred million people."[6] This new life form, Max asserts, expresses itself in terms of its own fulfillment, not in terms of white society's "good" and "bad."

Max uses biological terms metaphorically at times, but his argument is explicitly ecological throughout. To refer to Bigger Thomas as a new form of life is not merely a metaphor. And a city is not what "nature" is not, but rather one of the kinds of habitats that human animals build. These habitats become death traps for some – like Bigger's apartment for the rat he kills at the opening of the novel – for all life within them is interconnected. Only by understanding how strongly Bigger's life and fate are linked to everyone else's in the society can "we" find, asserts Max, "the key to our future, that rare vantage point upon which every man and woman in this nation can stand and view how inextricably our hopes and fears of today create the exultation and doom of tomorrow."[7]

As Wright presents it, the Marxist explanation of history, which also pervades Max's speech, has much to recommend it but fails to address Bigger's most fundamental need. Bigger's cry for understanding to Max in their final conversation, "what I killed for I *am*!" – which repels even Max – makes complete sense from an ecological point of view.[8] Wright affirms the import of Bigger's search for *meaning*, a value the author considered essential to human life. As the philosopher Thomas Alexander has recently put it in his book subtitled *Eco-Ontology and the Aesthetics of Existence*:

> Human beings seek to live with a concrete, embodied experience of meaning and value in the world. We *need* to feel that our own lives are meaningful and have value. This is a biological claim insofar as if this need is denied we either die or become filled with destructive rage.[9]

To Wright, writing came from a visceral need to wring meaning out of deadlocking tensions and was thus a key to survival.

Ralph Ellison later took Wright to task for environmental determinism, for not giving enough attention to individual agency, to which Wright replied, "I don't mean to say that I think that environment *makes* consciousness ... but I do say that I felt and still feel that the environment supplies the instrumentalities through which the organism expresses itself, and if that environment is warped ... the mode and manner of behavior will be affected toward deadlocking tensions."[10] In *Black Boy*, Wright emphasizes that his childhood *environment* gave no encouragement to writing; he had to leave to find the instrumentalities to express and thus save himself.

For Wright, imaginative writing was a sort of naturally occurring weapon that, while battling injustice, could liberate those hidden springs of action – feelings, the affects – lying between bodily experience and consciousness. He joined a growing contingent of left-oriented writers and artists of the late 1930s and 1940s discontented with Marxist orientations that subordinated aesthetics and creative expression to political and economic theory. These artists were rethinking the genesis and goals of creative expression as an inherent aspect of human nature. Its relationship to the environment was potentially ontological, the processes of its utterance understood as forces in the ecosystem.[11] Muriel Rukeyser, for example, called poetry a "transfer of human energy."[12] The dynamics and "meanings" of a poem do not inhere in the words or images but emerge in the relations among its elements:

> The science of ecology, is only one example of an elaboration of the idea, so that the life of land may be seen in terms of its tides of growth, the feeding of one group on another, the equilibrium reached, broken, and the drive toward another balance and renewal.
>
> But in areas dealing with emotion and belief, there is hesitation. Their terms have not been invented . . . a poem, a novel, or a play *act emotions out* in terms of words, they do not describe.[13]

Initiated at the meeting point of individual consciousness and the world, Rukeyser stresses, poems are about the "*in*vironment, where live the inner relationships."

Rukeyser emphasized "the moving relation between the individual consciousness and the world . . . I think human energy may be defined as consciousness, the capacity to make change in existing conditions."[14] Sociopolitical conditions are part of a more encompassing environment that inspires, even forces, creative expression. A similar attitude toward novel writing serves as the dynamic core of Wright's autobiography.

I should say "autobiographies," for the original *American Hunger* was shortened for Book of the Month Club adoption, ultimately with the new title *Black Boy: A Record of Childhood and Youth*. In the 1970s, the second part of the original, dealing with Wright's experiences after leaving the South for Chicago, was separately published as *American Hunger*; and finally the Library of America published the "original" version in 1991, annotated by Arnold Rampersad, with both parts – "Southern Night" and "The Horror and the Glory" – under the title *Black Boy (American Hunger)*.

Although Wright had already written and published portions of what eventually went into Part One of his autobiography, he claimed that he gained inspiration for the book when delivering a talk in 1942 to an interracial audience at Fisk University. Without a formal plan in advance, he began talking about his early life and the role of racism and racial self-hatred in his experience. As he warmed to his theme, he felt a rising tension in the room.

> There was but little applause. Indeed, the audience was terribly still, and it was not until I was half-way through my speech that it crashed upon me that I was saying things that Negroes were not supposed to say publically, things that whites had forbidden. What made me realize this was a hysterical, half-repressed, tense kind of laughter that went up now and then from the white and black faces.[15]

His characterization of the laughter coming up from "white and black faces" suggests an involuntary, physical, and collective response – signaling the ethical impasse of the occasion. His tale of his own experience forced his audience to face the truth of their bad faith in their relationships with each other – a truth they routinely repressed. Inspired by the charged energy in the room ignited by his story, Wright abandoned a novel on which he was working to write an autobiography.[16] The effect of his outspokenness at Fisk would be mirrored in the effect he sought to achieve in his autobiography. During a radio interview, he added that his main desire "was to render a judgment on my environment. That judgment was this: the environment the South creates is too small to nourish human beings, especially Negro human beings."[17]

Wright was writing about not only the barbarity of southern racism but also white liberals' inability to face their implication in white dominance, their responsibility for helping sustain the silence around black experience. However, in *Black Boy*, as in *Native Son*, the protagonist's own shortcomings due to fear and shame are also central. To acknowledge one's fear and shame is a special duty of the writer who aims to bring to consciousness the buried truth of human "feeling." For human beings, to Wright, are those earthbound organisms whose complex feelings have a particularly strong bearing on their destiny.

Black Boy begins with young Richard at age four, being chastised for talking and then, trying to manage his boredom, accidentally setting fire to his house. He is overcome by fear and then is beaten nearly to death by his mother. The chapter ends with the grown Richard Wright re-meeting his father and contemplating how far he has come in consciousness. The rest of the book details how he got from here to there and escaped his father's fate. One of Wright's main emphases, as in *Native Son*, is how fear and shame prevent human communion by interrupting honest self-examination and communication – hence the importance of writing.

Chapter Two shows Richard's dawning grasp of the line between "white" and "black," which is all the more confusing because his grandmother is "white" in appearance. Hearing stories about white atrocities awakened "confused defensive feelings"; as these feelings became conscious, he fantasized about defying white power, which enabled him to keep his "emotional integrity":

> These fantasies were no longer a reflection of my reaction to the white people, they were a part of my living, of my emotional life; they were a culture, a creed, a religion. The hostility of the whites had become so deeply implanted in my mind and feelings that it had lost direct connection with the daily environment in which I lived ... Tension would set in at the mere mention of whites and a vast complex of emotions, involving the whole of my personality, would be aroused. It was as though I was continuously reacting to the threat of some natural force whose hostile behavior could not be predicted. I had never in my life been abused by whites, but I had already become as conditioned to their existence as though I had been the victim of a thousand lynchings.[18]

His reference to the "tension" aroused by the mention of whites suggests a response centered in the body, and "the threat of some natural force whose hostile behavior could not be predicted" binds his physiological response to Wright's larger ecological cast of thought.

In fact, Wright presents the responses of blacks and whites to each other as almost pre-linguistic, physiological, even though they are ultimately productions of a particular social history and its ideologies. These affects, in Wright's case, had been transmitted not (at first) through contact with whites but by way of his family and black acquaintances. They have both deeply personal and collective aspects.[19] No creature is autonomous, no individual or species disconnected from the whole. Growing older, Wright learned to make friends with older boys "by subscribing to certain racial sentiments. The touchstone of fraternity was my feeling toward white people, how much hostility I held toward them ... None of this was premeditated, but sprang spontaneously out of the talk of black boys who met at the crossroads."[20]

When his mother had a stroke and nearly died, Richard was sent to live with an uncle. The suffering of his mother profoundly affected him as he came to the conviction that "the meaning of living came only when one was struggling to wring a meaning out of meaningless suffering."[21] From his mother's anguish, he gained insight into the suffering of others. This dawning awareness drew him to writing, especially to fiction. At the end of Chapter Four, he tells about the first story he wrote and shared with a girl who asked what it was for and why he wrote it. He tells her he "just wanted to." The point here is how alien written fiction was to his world: "My environment contained nothing more alien than writing or the desire to express one's self in writing."[22] Yet the episode also emphasizes the instinctive nature of his drive toward creative self-expression.

Up to the point when he discovers the public library in Memphis, the book details Richard's conditioning by and resistance to his environment, demonstrating a kind of inborn sense of integrity that makes him "dangerous" (to his own survival as well as others') and that makes the South dangerous to him. He becomes conscious of how his feelings are stunted and shaped to the fear and terror around him. He sees it in others, too. In this state, however, he comes upon the power of the written word to express unspoken feelings.

A newspaper article denouncing H. L. Mencken inspires him to acquire Mencken's *A Book of Prefaces* from the library. The writing stuns him: "what amazed me was not what he said, but how on earth anybody had the courage to say it."[23] Before this, Wright has constantly gotten himself in trouble for what he *says* – first to his grandmother in an early scene, then his uncle, his mother, and ultimately white coworkers and others. The danger of speech is a constant refrain. He has had to learn to guard his words and his feelings. So this bare use of words as weapons is a revelation. "Who were these men about whom Mencken was talking so passionately?"[24]

His impulse to dream, to imagine, was reawakened. Again, the impulse is almost precognitive, physiological: "Now it surged up again and I hungered for books, new ways of looking and seeing. It was not a matter of believing or disbelieving what I read, but of feeling something new, of being affected by something that made the look of the world different."[25] This was, in other words, an aesthetic/affective awakening primarily, but with ethical consequences. The meaning of "Hunger" in the text now attaches to the hunger to read and to write.

The effect of reading continues to change the atmosphere: "I went to work, but the mood of the book would not die; it lingered, coloring everything I saw, heard, did."[26] It's all about the *feelings* the books are able to express and evoke in the reader. Reading fiction that Mencken praised, Richard found that "[t]he novels created moods in which I lived for days."[27] Coming to greater understanding of the people around him, he writes that now he "could feel the very limits" of his boss's "narrow life" after reading Sinclair Lewis's account of George F. Babbitt.[28] Dreiser's novels "revived in me a vivid sense of my mother's suffering."[29]

He could not at this time express what he derived from the novels, "for it was nothing less than a sense of life itself. All my life had shaped me for the realism, the naturalism, of the modern novel."[30] The ecological point of view in *Black Boy* grows insistent. "I now knew what being a Negro meant. I could endure the hunger. I had learned to live with hate. But to feel that there were feelings denied me, that the very breath of life itself was beyond my reach, that more than anything else hurt, wounded me. I had a new hunger"[31] – a hunger to *feel* and to *write*. His survival depended on it. "I no longer *felt* that the world about me was hostile, killing; I *knew* it. A million times I asked myself what I could do to save myself, and there were no answers."[32] He has a hunger for "books that opened up new avenues of feeling and seeing."[33]

He came to realize that he could not survive in the South. If he organized with other blacks and fought, they would lose. If he fought openly he would die. Submitting to the "genial slave" life was "impossible."[34] It becomes a matter of survival that he move North and pursue his dream of reading and writing.

The second part of the "original" *American Hunger* is set in Chicago, but more than being about the North as such (as critics usually emphasize) it is chiefly about Wright's experience with the Communist Party in relationship to the hunger driving him. The title itself, "The Horror and the Glory," pertains not to "the North" but to Communism. The "glory" is the vision of human unity, of all hearts beating as one, of collective *feeling*, that Communism offered him. The "horror" is the blindness and ignorance that the party bred in its members.

When Richard first tried to master narrative, partly inspired by Stein's *Three Lives*, he would pound out "disconnected sentences for the sheer love of words."[35]

> My purpose was to capture a physical state or movement that carried a strong subjective impression, an accomplishment which seemed supremely worth struggling for. If I could fasten the mind of the reader upon words so firmly that he would forget words and be conscious only of his response, I felt that I would be in sight of knowing how to write narrative. I strove to master words, to make them disappear, to make them important by making them new, to make them melt into a rising spiral of emotional stimuli, each greater than the other, each feeding and reinforcing the other, and all ending in an emotional climax that would drench the reader with a sense of a new world. That was the single aim of my living.[36]

This kind of writing might be called a transfer of energy. But Wright lacked a framework, a reference to social reality, and "theories to light up the shadows of conduct."[37] It's at this juncture, while working at the post office in Chicago, that he becomes connected with the John Reed Club, an arm of the Communist Party that nurtures young writers and artists.

Through the John Reed Club, magazines published by the Communist Party, and the Federal Writers Project (where party members helped him), Wright was able to find work as an author, and comradeship, for the first time. In effect, he became dependent on the party for sustaining himself as a writer. But gradually he came up against the party's hostility to "intellectuals" and its attempts to limit what he read and wrote.

Much as Bigger Thomas's search escapes the understanding of Boris Max, Wright's struggle for expression of African American experience escaped his comrades' comprehension. Taking notes on the lives and vigorous speech of the "black boys" of the South Side, Wright observed that "Wrestling with words gave me my moments of deepest meaning."[38] Such wrestling, for Wright, meant allowing images to take shape "out of the depths of me ... feeling my way, trying to find the answer to my question," as opposed to beginning with an answer.[39] For this he was suspected of Trotskyism. His very ability to continue writing honestly was imperiled, and we have seen how central writing was to his sense of survival. His response was visceral: "Must I discard my plot-ideas and seek new ones? No. I could not. My writing was my way of seeing, my way of living, my way of feeling; and who could change his sight, his sense of direction, his senses?"[40] He had to quit the party to preserve his sense of integrity.

If Part One, "Southern Night," had ended with a new hunger, for feelings denied him – the feelings of other people and a feeling of oneness with them – Part Two concludes after Wright witnesses such oneness in the Communists' trial of a friend. The condemned man, after being "sundered" from the group through alleged wrongdoing, confessed his guilt and begged for forgiveness. To Wright, this was "a spectacle of glory; and yet, because it had condemned me, because it was blind and ignorant, I felt that it was a spectacle of horror."[41] As a result, Wright knows he "would never be able to feel with that simple sharpness about life, would never again express such passionate hope, would never again make so total a commitment of faith."[42]

After his break with the Communist Party, Wright believed humanity must discover a new unity; this hunger for unity was inborn in the human heart. Wright's vision remains both humanist and ecological: "If this country can't find its way to a human path, if it can't inform conduct with a deep sense of life, then all of us, black as well as white, are going down the same drain ... "[43] This realization sets Wright's task before him. He must use words to bring human beings together; and yet he must do so knowing that in some sense words and feelings stand opposed; this tension defines the aesthetic challenge that drives literary creation.

> I picked up a pencil and held it over a sheet of white paper, but my feelings stood in the way of my words. Well I would wait, day and night, until I knew what to say. Humbly now, with no vaulting dream of achieving a vast unity, I wanted to try to build a bridge of words between me and that world outside.[44]

Rather than trying to represent the path toward a human unity already envisioned, he would have to write experimentally. That is, without a teleology, a faith that provided answers in advance, he would have to "hurl words into the darkness and wait for an echo, and if an echo sounded, no matter how faintly, I would send other words to tell, to march, to fight, to create a sense of the hunger for life that gnaws in us all, to keep alive in our hearts a sense of the inexpressibly human."[45]

As Wright's literary reputation grew, his dependence on the Communist Party waned. His biggest break came when the Book-of-the-Month Club (BOMC) offered to adopt *Native Son* as a main selection, which would very likely help it become a best-seller. The club asked for changes to particular scenes of a primarily sexual content, and Wright rewrote those scenes. These changes, which have been exhaustively studied, indicate the compromises that Wright had to make in order to reach the wider readership the Book Club would open up, while Harper & Brothers had already accepted the book without those changes and had it in galleys.[46]

This episode indicates the publishing environment black writers (and not only black writers) of the time had to negotiate. Yet Wright did not feel the changes he made compromised his integrity; nor did they prevent the book from setting off a shock wave in the literary field and selling 200,000 copies in just three weeks.[47] *Native Son* was immediately recognized as epochal in importance by exposing Americans' bad faith on issues of race, freedom, and democracy. Probably no book by a black author has had a more profound impact on American writers' treatments of race. And, together with Wright's next major book, his autobiography, it made Wright artistically self-sufficient.

As with *Native Son*, in 1944 BOMC approached Wright's editor and agent about offering *American Hunger* as a main selection. But they wanted only "Southern Night," the first part of the book (about two-thirds of the whole). Clifton Fadiman, one of the judges, suggested changing the title to "First Chapter," which would suggest another chapter to come.[48] According to Arnold Rampersad, Wright attributed their demand to Communist influence, since most of Part Two concerned his involvement with and then alienation from the Communist Party.

Ignoring this possibility and that suggested by Fadiman's title, recent scholars have speculated that BOMC judges objected to Wright's attacks on racism in the North and the suggestion that no place in America was safe for a black man. Both hypotheses are plausible, but the attack on Southern culture in the first part of the book was far more likely to limit national distribution than the second part. It seems just as likely that the club considered the first part of the book more interesting as a story for a general middle-class audience and functional as a unit in its own right. They may also have been worried about paper allotments in the midst of wartime rationing, when print runs had to be cut back and books came out with slim margins on cheap paper, in small type.

Regardless of the reasoning behind the BOMC request that "The Horror and the Glory," be dropped, Wright had to rewrite the ending of what had been "Southern Night." It was too abrupt to end the book. As Fadiman requested, he should "summarize briefly, and make explicit, the meaning that is now implicit in the preceding pages."[49]

Wright could have declined the BOMC offer since Harper & Brothers already had *American Hunger* in page proofs, with a dust jacket designed and ready for publication. Critics have lamented the fact that the book club opportunity convinced him to change the book, ending it on a note that seems more conventionally optimistic than he had originally intended. Michel Fabre expressed this attitude most succinctly in his "Afterword" to the 1977 edition of *American Hunger*: "*Black Boy* is commonly construed as a typical success story, and thus it has been used by the American liberal to justify his own optimism regarding his country."[50] But Wright did nothing to compromise his integrity while turning the editorial challenge to his advantage.

In the revised ending, Wright muses on what had made him feel as he did:

> From where in this southern darkness had I caught a sense of freedom? Why was it that I was able to act upon vaguely felt notions? What was it that made me feel things deeply enough for me to try to order my life by my feelings? ... How dare I consider my feelings superior to the gross environment that sought to claim me?[51]

In the expanded conclusion to what had been "Southern Night," the ecological Wright comes once again to the fore:

> Whenever my environment had failed to support or nourish me, I had clutched at books. ... In the main, my hope was merely a kind of self-defense, a conviction that if I did not leave I would perish ... The substance of my hope was formless and devoid of any real sense of direction ... The shocks of southern living had rendered my personality tender and swollen, tense and volatile, and my fight was more a shunning of external and internal dangers than an attempt to embrace what I felt I wanted ... It had been my accidental reading of fiction and literary criticism that had evoked in me vague glimpses of life's possibilities ... And it was out of these novels and stories and articles, out of the emotional impact of imaginative constructions of heroic or tragic deeds, that I felt touching my face a tinge of warmth from an unseen light; and in my leaving I was groping toward that invisible light, always trying to keep my face

so set and turned that I would not lose the hope of its faint promise, using it as my justification for action.[52]

Wright had used the metaphor of "a tinge of warmth from an unseen light" in the original version of the book, near the end of Chapter Fifteen in "The Horror and the Glory," and shifted it to this more expansive conclusion to what had been "Southern Night." He was responding to Fadiman's suggestion that he summarize and make explicit the themes of the narrative, and to Dorothy Canfield Fisher's desire that he indicate more clearly how American writers had given him hope.[53]

All of this suggests pressure to accommodate the BOMC's need to be assured of wide sales to justify its low prices, and to respond to a white supporter who had previously vouched for *Native Son*. (Fisher, a judge for the BOMC, had a long history of supporting African American civil rights and black writers, going back to the early years of the century.) Wright remained opposed to ending the book on an optimistic or patriotic note, which he did not believe the narrative could support. However, Fisher never offered her recommendations as conditions for acceptance of the manuscript, and the original *American Hunger* had already prominently featured the importance of H. L. Mencken, Sinclair Lewis, and Theodore Dreiser to Wright's literary awakening, as we have seen. In a letter to Fisher, he also argued that Mencken, Dreiser, and Lewis had been influenced by European thinkers.

Fisher insisted he should do nothing contrary to his own artistic sensibilities. She wanted him to mention the dissenting voices of American literature but concluded, "of course, (this goes without saying) if you don't honestly believe this is true, if I am mistaken even a single word would be a dreadful travesty."[54] Fisher remained worried and highly self-conscious about her recommendations: "Anything I say is just a personal notion of mine, and you must not take it too seriously. ... *You certainly are the best judge*. Whatever you decide to do, I'll accept without question."[55]

About a week later, after learning from Wright's editor that he was finishing revisions in response to her suggestions, she wrote Wright to say that this news made her

> very uneasy for fear you are going beyond what you really feel is honest. I'd never forgive myself if (in my own attempt to be honest) I had stepped beyond the line of permissible influence on a younger writer! Don't you put in a single word which is not from your heart, like all the rest of your fine book! You have a grand ending as it is. I feel I shouldn't have written as I did, that second time![56]

She was showing the kind of honesty Wright asked of his readers, without insisting that he accommodate her feelings. He made revisions to recap and emphasize, in his new concluding chapter, the inspiration he had received from American writers. Critics have suggested that these additions hardly provided the kind of patriotic endorsement Fisher might have been hoping for as World War II approached its close. But in fact it was precisely the dissenting voices in American writing that she, recently descended from radical abolitionists and an admirer of Thoreau, was moved by.[57] Fisher wrote a review of *Black Boy* for the BOMC newsletter, sharing it with Wright for his approval, and the book club added a portion of this review to the front matter (again with Wright's approval) as an "Introductory Note."

As far as we know, Wright never regretted his revisions, and he was overjoyed when the book appeared. "It is a beautiful book, slender, modern-looking, and with a good binding. It is strange that when reality comes true you cannot think of what to say; the moment fails; the look of things remains the same ... you strain to feel what it is that you dreamed."[58] Two days later he wrote, "I fell asleep thinking that *Black Boy* was out over the land, that people were reading about my life, about how I grew up, about how I felt and feel."[59]

Most of "The Horror and the Glory" had been or would be published in the mainstream liberal *Atlantic* (where "I Tried to Be a Communist" ran in two long installments in August and September 1944), *Harper's* ("What You Don't Know Won't Hurt You" in December 1942), *Cross Section* 1945, and *Mademoiselle*.[60] The book itself topped the best-seller list from April to June of 1945 and by July had sold 425,000 copies (30 percent more than *Native Son* had sold in five years), inspiring a reissue of his first book, *Uncle Tom's Children*.[61] Between the wider sales of a shorter book and the money received from the magazines, Wright undoubtedly made more money than if the BOMC had published his original manuscript as accepted by Harper & Brothers, let alone if he had passed up the BOMC offer entirely. It made his career sustainable for the foreseeable future.

As for the contemporary reception of *Black Boy*, Theodore Bilbo of Mississippi had this to say on the floor of the US Senate:

> There is another book which should be taken off the book racks of the nation; it should be removed from the book stores; its sales should be stopped. It is the recent book of the month, which has had such great sale. . . . It is entitled "Black Boy," by Richard Wright. . . . The purpose of the book is to plant the seeds of hate in every Negro in America against the white men of the South or against the white race anywhere, for that matter. That is the purpose. Its purpose is to

plant the seeds of devilment and trouble-breeding in the days to come in the mind and heart of every American Negro. Read the book if you do not believe what I am telling you. It is the dirtiest, filthiest, lousiest, most obscene piece of writing that I have ever seen in print.[62]

It did indeed plant seeds that one finds sprouting in such subsequent books as the Filipino-American Carlos Bulosan's *America Is in the Heart* (1946). That it had been selected by the Book-of-the-Month Club made the book all the more dangerous to the American public, in Bilbo's view. Black critics including W. E. B. Du Bois worried that the book was "unrepresentative," giving a bleak view of black culture. By contrast, a reviewer for Boston's *Morning Globe* managed to find in its publication and wide distribution proof of American exceptionalism, for only in America would such an eloquent rebel against his own country get so wide a hearing.[63]

With the financial success of *Black Boy*, Wright was able to move with his family to Paris, secure in his profession as no black author preceding him had ever been. Today we are fortunate to have the "original" autobiography as Harper's would have published it, something made possible by modern textual scholarship and Wright's place on college syllabi since the 1970s. Yet the transfer of energy the book delivered in its first published version could be most shocking only in the environment and climate that brought it into being. Today, read mainly as an assignment in college courses and in relation to African-American literary tradition, the book does different work.

Notes

1. Lawrence Buell, *Writing for an Endangered World: Literature, Culture, and Environment in the U.S. and the World* (Cambridge: Belknap/Harvard University Press, 2001), 131–142.
2. Emanuel Graziano, "Ecological Metaphors as Scientific Boundary Work: Innovation and Authority in Interwar Sociology and Biology," *American Journal of Sociology* 101 (1996): 874–907; and Gregg Mitman, *The State of Nature: Ecology, Community, and American Social Thought, 1900–1950* (Chicago: University of Chicago Press, 1992).
3. Richard Wright, Native Son, in *Early Works: Lawd Today!, Uncle Tom's Children, Native Son* (New York: Library of America, 1991), p. 812. All subsequent citations of *Native Son* refer to this text.
4. Ibid., 815.
5. Ibid., 809.
6. Ibid., 809.
7. Ibid., 803–804.
8. Ibid., 849.

9. Thomas Alexander, *The Human Eros: Eco-Ontology and the Aesthetics of Existence* (New York: Fordham University Press, 2013), 6.
10. Richard Wright, "How Bigger Was Born," in *Early Works*, 862.
11. One excellent example is John Steinbeck, whose friend and collaborator Edward F. Ricketts was a marine biologist who earned his PhD at the University of Chicago under the influential ecologist W. C. Allee. See especially John Steinbeck and Edward F. Ricketts, *Sea of Cortez: A Leisurely Journal of Travel and Research* (1941; New York: Penguin, 2009).
12. Muriel Rukeyser, prefatory statement to *The Life of Poetry* (New York: A. A. Wyn, 1949), n.p.
13. Ibid., 9–10.
14. Ibid., n.p.
15. "Richard Wright Describes the Birth of *Black Boy*," *New York Post*, November 30, 1944, B6.
16. Trudi McCullough, "Author Richard Wright Champion of Negro Rights," New Haven Sunday Register, April 8, 1945, sec. III, 10; Rpt. in Keneth Kinnamon and Michel Fabre, eds., *Conversations with Richard Wright* (Jackson: University Press of Mississippi, 1993), 61–62.
17. Anonymous, "How Richard Wright Looks at *Black Boy*," *PM*, April 15, 1945, 3–4. Rpt. in *Conversations*, 64–65.
18. Richard Wright, *Black Boy (American Hunger)*, in *Later Works: Black Boy (American Hunger) and The Outsider* (New York: Library of America, 1991), 72. All subsequent citations of *Black Boy (American Hunger)* refer to this text.
19. For an impressive treatment of this phenomenon, see Teresa Brennan, *The Transmission of Affect* (Ithaca: Cornell University Press, 2004).
20. Wright, *Black Boy (American Hunger)*, 75
21. Ibid., 96.
22. Ibid., 116
23. Ibid., 237.
24. Ibid.
25. Ibid., 238.
26. Ibid.
27. Ibid.
28. Ibid.
29. Ibid., 239.
30. Ibid.
31. Ibid.
32. Ibid.
33. Ibid., 240.
34. Ibid., 241.
35. Ibid., 267.
36. Ibid., 268.
37. Ibid., 271.
38. Ibid., 324.
39. Ibid.
40. Ibid., 329.
41. Ibid., 356.
42. Ibid., 363.

43. Ibid., 356, ellipsis in original.

44. Ibid., 365.

45. Ibid.

46. For discussions of the changes Wright made to *Native Son* to gain BOMC adoption, see especially John K. Young, "'Quite as Human as It Is Negro': Subpersons and Textual Property in *Native Son* and *Black Boy*," in George Hutchinson and John K. Young, eds., *Publishing Blackness: Textual Constructions of Race since 1850* (Ann Arbor: University of Michigan Press, 2013), 67–81; Yoshinobu Hakutani, *Richard Wright and Racial Discourse* (Columbia: University of Missouri Press, 1996), 63–64, 82–83; Claudine Raynaud, "Changing Texts: Censorship, 'Reality,' and Fiction in *Native Son*," in Alice Mikal Craven and William E. Dow, eds., *Richard Wright: New Readings in the 21st Century* (New York: Palgrave Macmillan, 2011); Arnold Rampsersad, "Too Honest for His Own Time," in Robert J. Butler, ed., *The Critical Response to Richard Wright* (Westport: Greenwood Press, 1995), 164–166 (rpt. from New York Times Book Review, December 29, 1991, 3); and Hazel Rowley, *Richard Wright: The Life and Times* (New York: Henry Holt, 2001), 180–184.

47. Young, "'Quite as Human as It Is Negro'," 78.

48. Rowley, Richard Wright: The Life and Times, 286–287.

49. Clifton Fadiman quoted in Young, "'Quite as Human as It Is Negro'," 84, from Selected Records of Harper & Brothers, Rare Books and Special Collections, Princeton University Library.

50. Michel Fabre, "Afterword," in Richard Wright, *American Hunger* (New York: Harper & Row, 1977), 140

51. Richard Wright, *Later Works*, 878, n. 246.5.

52. Ibid., 878–879, n. 246.5

53. See Dorothy Canfield Fisher to Richard Wright, July 12, 1944, in Mark Madigan, *Keeping Fires Night and Day: Selected Letters of Dorothy Canfield Fisher* (Columbia: University of Missouri Press, 1993), 234, 235.

54. Dorothy Canfield Fisher to Richard Wright, July 1, 1944, in *Keeping*, 233.

55. Fisher to Wright, July 12, 1944, in *Keeping*, 234, 235.

56. Fisher to Wright, July 21, 1944, *Keeping*, 236.

57. See especially Fisher to Wright, July 23, 1944, *Keeping*, 236–237. For other discussions of the changes to *American Hunger* Wright made to satisfy the Book-of-the-Month Club and Fisher, see especially Rowley, *Richard Wright: The Life and Times*, 286–290; Janice Thaddeus, "The Metamorphosis of *Black Boy*," in Henry Louis Gates Jr., and K. A. Appiah, eds., *Richard Wright: Critical Perspectives Past and Present* (New York: Amistad, 1993), rpt. from *American Literature* 57.2 (May 1985): 199–214; Jeff Karem, "'I Could Never Really Leave the South': Regionalism and the Transformation of Richard Wright's *American Hunger*," *American Literary History* 13.4 (Winter 2001): 694–715; and Young, "'Quite as Human as It Is Negro'," 81–88.

58. Richard Wright to Leon Wright, February 14, 1945, quoted in Rowley, *Richard Wright: The Life and Times*, 309.

59. Ibid.

60. Wright, "Early Days in Chicago," in Edwin Seaver, ed., *Cross-Section 1945: A Collection of New American Writing* (New York: L. B. Fischer, 1945),

306–342; "American Hunger," *Mademoiselle* 21 (September 1945): 164–165, 299–301.

61. Karem, "'I Could Never Really Leave the South'," 710.

62. June 27, 1945, 79th Congress, 1st Session, Congressional Record Volume 91, 6808.

63. Karem, "'I Could Never Really Leave the South'," 711.

2

JAY GARCIA

Richard Wright's Planned Incongruity

Black Boy as "Modern Living"

Not long after the publication of his autobiographical narrative *Black Boy*, Richard Wright expressed frustration over the public response. Readers seemed to say, "how bad this life was; how did he learn to write; we must do something."[1] Such consternation puzzled him. "Frankly I don't know why people read my work; it upsets them terribly," he wrote to Gertrude Stein.[2] "It may be that they like to be upset," he speculated, "not knowing what to do in life about feeling and living, they can live and feel with a book."[3] Many had failed to connect his story of the Jim Crow South to the "theme of modern living," confining its relevance to the proverbial "Negro problem."[4] As if this was not discouraging enough, *Black Boy* as an instance of modern letters and criticism went unexplored: "In no review does anyone link me with what is being done in writing in the world."[5]

In *Black Boy*, Wright identifies the anxieties and neurotic patterns of the Jim Crow South as belonging to a continuum with those of the nation and the modern world at large, positing the very ordinariness of the Jim Crow South not as the "Negro problem" but instead as nothing more or less than "modern living." What Wright wanted to describe in *Black Boy* was all too often rendered as the world of a marginal strata, peripheral to American life. Yet he believed that if writers contended forthrightly with the situations and experiences dissembled by the "Negro problem" euphemism, the effects could be dramatic: "Honest grappling" and a "therapeutic and loosening process could enter our culture, our feelings, and allow us to react freely."[6] That larger aspiration led Wright to veer away from rebuke and invective even as he relentlessly and indelibly depicted the harms of Jim Crow. Because a "therapeutic and loosening process" served as his general aim Wright staved off what the critic Kenneth Burke called "wholly debunking" and polemical perspectives.[7] He also rejected clichéd and sentimental portraits of the Southern social order, insisting that *Black Boy* should not afford the "consolation of tears."[8] That turn of phrase, employed by Wright

in a retrospective exploration of *Native Son* (1940), echoed Burke's contemporaneous invocation of "easy consolation" to categorize literary strategies that barred "realistic naming" and as a consequence made "solace
cheap."[9] Wright's reading of Burke would considerably inform *Black
Boy*'s rhetorical orientation, for Burke's critical imperative to find a means
by which one could "accurately name and confront [one's] situation," especially through techniques such as "perspective by incongruity" and the
"comic corrective," became to a large extent Wright's.[10]

The story of Wright's familiarity with Burke's criticism predates *Black
Boy*, arguably beginning with his purchase of Burke's *Permanence and
Change: An Anatomy of Purpose* (1935) the year it was published. Burke's
examination of "language and the role of symbols in social life" attracted
readers in disparate fields, including sociology and social psychology, and
included analyses of the power of racial thinking.[11] Wright and Burke's
intellectual interplay has been seldom noted. While it is known that Burke
reflected on Wright's work in his books throughout the 1940s and early
1950s, if only sporadically and briefly, what Michel Fabre once alluded to as
Wright's "debt towards Kenneth Burke" has eluded sustained scholarly
investigation.[12] Yet undertaking such an inquiry makes heightened appreciation of Wright's facility in criticism and rhetorical theory, with "what is
being done in writing in the world," as he put it, possible, and foregrounds
his own critical and rhetorical endeavors.

The problem of race hierarchy enters the pages of *Permanence and Change*
when Burke briefly explores the situation of poor Southern whites in the early
twentieth century, focusing on the ways they endowed "distinction of color"
with rhetorical and social heft.[13] Within an economic structure that diminished social distinctions, making them subservient to the logic of the market,
"distinction of color" served as an "outstanding way of differentiating some
competitors from others," Burke argued. "Distinction of color" came in
precisely where the economic structure itself failed to provide a differentiating
principle, giving traction to white supremacy, which in certain forms could even
make "intimidation by lynching" into an "adequate solution" to economic
distress. Burke would later further this line of argument in *Rhetoric of
Motives* (1950) with support from *Black Boy* itself. According to Burke,
Wright's description of the South's racist social environments had brought
into view a society organized by monetary norms that were rivaled and dis-
placed by an ideology of racial hierarchy. Supremacist doctrines had to undergo
constant revision because they contravened the logic of monetary transaction,
but the processes by which they were revived could be difficult to discern. For
Burke, Wright's illustration of the "sullenness and thoroughness with which this

'order' can be imposed" improved understanding of the overall workings of the "deliberate cult of the irrational, the Absurd" that was the "magic of 'white supremacy'."[14]

Beginning in the mid-1930s, Burke's criticism began to carry an appeal for Wright that existed in tension with the sanctioned discourses of the Communist Party USA that were so much a part of Wright's trajectory. The party denounced racism and segregation but did not, by and large, broach the symbolic, and by extension motivational and psychological, dynamics that sustained and reproduced the racist social order. This is what Burke did when he explored "distinction of color" as a symbolic and behavioral matrix, and it very likely did not go unnoticed by Wright. Indeed *Permanence and Change* may have intensified Wright's interest in psychological approaches to social questions through its concerns with attitudes, orientations, symbols, and behavior. Wright praised its redefinition of "Marxist aesthetics in terms of a poetry of action" by which "Communism becomes a poetic conception of life, of man unfolding their personalities through action."[15] Burke modeled for Wright a kind of cultural criticism conversant with, but also at some remove from, Communist Party rhetoric. Wright noted that Burke's method of analysis allowed critics to identify subtle connections between anxieties and antagonisms in seemingly unrelated realms of activity: "Burke feels that money can be expressed in terms of religion; sex in terms of hate; etc., etc., all of which I think is very true."[16] The wide compass of Burke's rhetorical analysis, together with his predisposition toward a charitable attitude within criticism, may have helped prompt Wright's move from "rigid political concepts to more humane and psychological ones."[17]

Permanence and Change opens with a guiding supposition: although "all living things are critics," humans are capable of a further procedure, namely, the "criticism of criticism," or the power to "interpret our interpretations."[18] Although dominant interpretations, or what Burke more often termed "orientations" or "perspectives," were largely "self-perpetuating," they could also wane, making "reorientation" of one kind or another possible, and they could at times be altered by a "direct attempt to force the critical structure by shifts of perspective."[19] In the 1940s, Wright sought to make his work a lever in such a direct attempt so as to intervene in, not only comment upon, the critical structure pertaining to US race hierarchy and segregation.

Wright's attempt at reorientation in *Black Boy* relies above all on the literary construction of a figure whose dissident critical intelligence develops almost preternaturally amid a sequence of injurious environments. Wright makes his younger self, Richard, the vehicle for a "kind of consciousness" that presents scenes of the Jim Crow South through "perspective by incongruity" or "planned incongruity," central terms from Burke's *Permanence and Change*.[20] Burke's "perspective by incongruity" implied means of circumventing established and self-perpetuating orientations, the possibility of an interpretive mode alert to the limitations of all perspectives. A writer making use of "perspective by incongruity" could pose a different way into a subject ensconced in longstanding formulas, not in order to render the new perspective beyond critique, but to nevertheless invite readers to consider the limitations of their own orientations. Planned incongruity allowed Wright to merge his main character with the role of organic critic. Richard observes his surroundings, interprets his own and others' motives, and repeatedly brings everything he encounters under critical scrutiny, not least the racist social order in which he lives. In implementing perspective by incongruity, Wright traversed the boundaries of autobiography to put forward a work that was also a literary-critical gambit, a contribution to "what is being done in writing in the world" that promised a new orientation on the Jim Crow South and the national race question alike.

Planned incongruity had to do with bringing together "subjects that 'normally' belong in distinct orders," and in so doing furnish new insights, the ability to "see around the corner."[21] In *Black Boy*, the technique provides Wright with the means by which to produce *another* Jim Crow South, a representation that makes it *in and of* the modern world and that refuses to cloak its psychological harms in polemic or euphemism. In making Richard a critic capable of bringing both the quotidian and extraordinary qualities of the South's Jim Crow order into view, and of deftly handling the materials of a time and place, Wright presented an incongruous perspective. His decision was especially provocative given that in the 1940s, when the book was published, Southern black youth remained segregated and marginalized not only in fact, but also in mainstream thought, which placed them in liminal relation to dominant conceptions of the human. Wright gives Richard a critical function and psychological perspicacity incongruous with assigned infrahuman roles. Richard's unusual "kind of consciousness" renders him an interpreter of interpretations, capable of "yearning for a kind of consciousness, a mode of being that the way of life about me had said could not be, must not be, and upon which the penalty of death had been placed."[22]

Mary McCarthy understood Wright's perspective by incongruity as a purposeful "self-aggrandizement and self-dramatization."[23] Constance Webb similarly claimed that the insistence on Richard's criticality "carries to an extreme pitch the separation of the intellectual Negro seeking the full expression of his personality."[24] McCarthy and Webb each in their own way expressed interest in the techniques Wright was bringing to bear on his narrative, and they pointed to the book's planned and incongruous dimensions. For his part, Wright disclosed the following in "*Black Boy* and Reading": "The point is this: I do not believe that it is possible for a Negro boy growing up in the environment of the South today to develop that sense of objectivity that will enable him to grasp the meaning of his life."[25] Wright's pessimistic premise opened the way for a narrative experiment that veered from conventional storytelling about African American life by making intellectual separateness, as Webb noted, and the magnification of dramas of childhood and youth, as McCarthy noted, the basis for a work less invested in verisimilitude than in perspectives on segregation and race hierarchy as yet absent in American letters.

Wright had attended Burke's 1937 address to the second meeting of the Congress of American Writers, later published as "The Relation Between Literature and Science," and Burke's remarks on childhood experience read in no small measure like *Black Boy*'s working method. Burke's lecture focused in particular on the way childhood experience, or the "intimate world," later informs and interacts with the "abstract, impersonal, political and economic matter of adult experience."[26] He theorizes that this integration necessarily involves "dealing with a new situation in terms of an earlier and different situation," or what Burke calls "partial hypnosis."[27] If discrepancies between the "intimate world" and "adult experience" were common enough, and the source of many conflicts, there were occasions, Burke argues, when they could be aligned so as to produce a new critical perspective that encompassed each of them. At times, writers employed "modes of integration that give us a correct perspective, a serviceable structure of meanings and attitudes."[28] *Black Boy* seeks to integrate childhood experience with the persistent effects of segregation and racism in the adult world, making the latter not merely the context for the former, but instead the very materials that may be reinterpreted in the light of the former. Burke's address also suggests an interpretation of Wright's subtitle, "A Record of Childhood and Youth." For Burke, science could scarcely be severed from the poetic or the literary because he held "criticism" to be one of its synonyms. Not only was science a "formal style," it was also "*organized* doubt, *creative* skepticism, the converting of quizzicality into a *positive* method."[29] Read in the light of science as criticism, "record" communicates the site of a meticulous and stylized experiment, for *Black Boy* does nothing if not painstakingly gather various personalities and cultural patterns so as to subject them to creative skepticism. Immersed in but also detached from his surroundings, Richard brings his critical awareness to bear on his environment, making its component parts, including the lineaments of the racist social order, available for quizzical re-description. It is vital to recall that Wright considered other subtitles that also communicated methodical analysis, including "A Record in Anxiety," "A Study in Anxiety," and "A Chronicle of Anxiety."[30]

Burke had spoken at the first meeting of the Congress of American Writers in 1935, which was especially fraught and which Wright had also attended. The Congress had ratified the demise of the John Reed Clubs, key sites of activity and interaction for writers in the Communist Party. Wright's participation in the Chicago John Reed Club had played an important role in his trajectory as a writer. As a delegate to the proceedings, he pushed for the clubs' retention, finding himself at odds with the Communist Party leadership that sponsored the Congress. At the same meeting, Burke gave a speech that amounted to a quarrel with Communist Party rhetoric. In "Revolutionary Symbolism in America," he argued that the category of "worker" had limited efficacy beyond the immediate context of Communist Party organizing, and that "people" would do far more to expand the appeal not only of the organization but of socialist thought more generally. The worker category as a locus of symbolism could "enlist our *sympathies*, but not our *ambitions*," Burke held urging a substitution of terms such that "political alignment" could be "fused with broader cultural elements."[31] Burke's readiness to question the party's tendencies and deliver a contrarian assessment of its rhetorical policies likely struck Wright as noteworthy given his own differences with the party.

If Wright read Burke and attended his speeches in the 1930s, Burke, for his part, would by the early 1940s begin producing commentary on Wright's work.[32] He included brief but acute analyses of *Native Son* in *The Philosophy of Literary Form: Studies in Symbolic Action* (1940) and other works. Burke deemed *Native Son* "disturbingly impressive," not least because its competing impulses – that of the "Negro novelist" and the "Marxist critic" – effectively resulted in two stories, "one imagistic and the other conceptual."[33] For Burke, the well-known closing argument presented by defense attorney Boris Max on behalf of Bigger Thomas gave expression to a "conceptual" narrative put forth by Wright the Marxist critic. The imagistic story begins when Bigger kills a rat in his dilapidated tenement at the start of the novel. Before any major developments, Burke writes, readers are made to understand that "Bigger's rebirth will be attained through the killing of the 'rat' within himself." In Burke's view, this story – that of the "Negro novelist" – does not quite conform to the logic of the closing argument, effectively another story within the novel, in which Bigger instantiates social, economic and political conditions. Wright had composed a story in which "Bigger's criminal protest *as a Negro*" exceeded the bounds of the Marxist terminology of the closing argument, generating questions and a "whole new avenue to follow" regarding the "ambiguities of power." Wright copied Burke's long paragraph about *Native Son* onto a separate sheet of paper, perhaps to keep it close at hand and think more methodically about its implications.[34] *Philosophy of Literary Form* appears on a list of "books to take" Wright apparently made as he prepared to move to Paris.[35]

In the essay "Surrealism," Burke connected Wright to surrealist aesthetics. Wright's work put into practice surrealism's "principle of diversity, of centrifugality, the 'liberal' principle of 'loosing,' in contrast with the regionalisms and socialisms, that represent the principle of unity, of centripetality, the collectivist principle of 'binding.'"[36] In linking Wright to surrealism, Burke intimated that the "principle of diversity" challenged the collective ordering of "race" by making it difficult to see racial categories as self-same and self-evident. The centrifugal dynamic in *Black Boy* at least partly explains the portrayal of Richard's criticality, which deflects racial categorization, and tends to move away from rather than toward recruitment by any kind of racial thinking. Wright presents an orientation and concomitant terminology not susceptible to racialization, and therefore one through which his main character can all the better discern racial ideologies and their effects. In addition to contravening the rules of "race," Wright also presented philosophical stances in *Black Boy* that Burke found convincing. Indeed, in both correspondence and published work, Burke implied the compatibility of Wright's methods of inquiry with his own critical procedures. The "sense of the world that was mine and mine alone," as Wright put it, confirmed something of Burke's own experience.[37] "Whatever indignities and fears I have suffered," Burke reflected in relation to Wright's work, "I have always had the feeling that I suffered them as an individual."[38] The theoretical point Burke extracted from his reading of *Black Boy*, and which he credited Wright with revealing in memorable ways, was that the "problem of repair," the work of contending with the effects of adverse circumstances and situations, arose in the first instance as an "individual problem."

When Burke commented approvingly on *Black Boy* was he responding to elements of his own criticism in refracted form? Any attempt at an answer to this question must examine a pivotal moment of enunciation in *Black Boy*: the "tolerant of all and yet critical" attitude Richard acquires "towards life."[39] This attitude, which Wright also describes as a predisposition to be "skeptical of everything while seeking everything," pervades the book such that Richard's ability to navigate the maze of Jim Crow injustice and trying domestic environments comes to depend upon how adeptly he can protect and sustain his "tolerant of all and yet critical" attitude. Because it is neither caustic nor naïve, but rather "tolerant of all yet critical," the attitude ascribed to him may be understood as an extension of Burke's discussions of the limits of polemic and euphemism. In his invocation of the term "attitude," but more importantly in the *type* of attitude he embeds throughout the book, Wright brings into circulation rhetorical tendencies validated throughout Burke's corpus.[40] Wright does not employ what Burke called a "polemical-debunking" frame as he presents different scenes of the Southern social order. To do so would be to fuel invective, which for Wright seems as misguided as resorting to clichés about the Jim Crow South.[41] As if heeding Burke's warning "against too great reliance on the conveniences of moral indignation," Wright makes the subjects of segregation and racial hierarchy unavailable for polemic. But what they lose polemically they gain in relevance to a more consequential story about modern living.[42]

Despite oppression, demoralization, and fear, Richard does not indulge in resignation. Instead of resigning himself to his conditions he continually revives quizzicality about his circumstances and the world at large. Resignation cannot achieve a narrative foothold in Wright's text, at least not for long, because his planned incongruity places a premium on what Burke called a "comic frame," which "tells the mind that it must equip itself to accurately name and confront its situation."[43] In Burke's lexicon, planned incongruity was closely aligned the "comic frame," "comic ambivalence," or the "comic corrective," which helped make a person a "student of himself" by harnessing a "*maximum consciousness*."[44] The comic frame had critical functions for thinking through the alienating dimensions of modern life. Without denying materialistic factors in human interaction, the comic frame posited "human life as a project in 'composition.'"[45] Eluding the cynicism of polemic and euphemistic approaches to alienation, Richard's "emotional distance" helps to give his observations a diagnostic character, an attribute of Burke's comic frame.[46] Listening in on the conversation of a group of older black boys in one scene, Richard exercises his growing diagnostic capabilities, attaching short descriptors to the verbal play of the boys. "Them white folks sure scared of us, though," one boy says, to which Richard appends, "Sober statement of an old problem." Later, "Man you reckon these white folks is ever gonna change?" "Timid questioning hope," Richard deduces.[47] As in other scenes, Richard exhibits a sensibility that recalls Burke's inclination to "transcend or transmute our irritation, frustration, and anger with ourselves, other people, and social institutions by becoming interested in them."[48] It is worth noting that just as Wright's critical and imaginative writings represented everyday rhetorical gestures and patterns, such as the dialogue among the boys, Burke's criticism was known for analyzing the rhetoric of both formal literature and ordinary speech.

Richard's proclaimed "emotional distance," closely connected to his reluctance to conform to the religious belief system of his elders, leads to the question of what "attitude toward God and the suffering in the world" he will adopt.[49] Richard makes suffering elemental to his thinking, but because he cannot "feel weak or lost in a cosmic manner," he refuses to submit to religious creeds.[50] "My faith, such as it was, was welded to the common realities of life, anchored in the sensations of my body and what my mind could grasp, and nothing could ever shake this faith, and surely not my fear of an invisible power."[51] The orientation of Wright's book recasts suffering by steering clear of a *cosmic* approach to feelings of weakness and loss. Richard elevates the "common realities of life," snubbing the "cosmic," and it follows that all he experiences and witnesses, including the persistent threat of racial violence and the degradations of segregation, come to form part of the common. Richard trades the cosmic for the common, which can then serve as the basis for what Burke called a "faith" that assimilates everything to the "realities of life," bringing all circumstances and situations within the realm of interpretation.[52] Richard becomes relieved of "cosmic images of dread" as he begins to contend with "reality, quivering daily before me."[53] By making scrutiny of the "common realities of life" central to his work Wright not only emphasizes the common, but he also draws attention to the perspectival and interpretive character of experience generally.[54]

Tragedy, according to Burke, "deals with the cosmic man, whereas comedy deals with *man in society*."[55] Reworking the "comic," and making it a resource for navigating the common realities of life and arriving at novel orientations, Burke presents a concept that diverges from the "humorous" and turns on the possibility of effective "attitudes toward history." Wright, also seeking new attitudes, installs planned incongruity as the governing dynamic of his work, giving *Black Boy* its broadly "comic" – man in society – tendency. The book renders "all attitudes and theories with a kind of comic allowance for their contradictions and for the confusion which their mutually exclusive presence creates," as Frederick Hoffmann wrote in regard to Burke's work, and in so doing performs an "ever-increasing renunciation of the desire for easy clarification."[56]

Burke's comic mode seeks to transcend the "competitive ambition" so much a part of the modern world not so much by "excoriating" it as by "'appreciating' it."[57] Perspective by incongruity furthers the comic mode, for it provides ways of appreciating, and developing charitable understanding of, a range of perspectives. In *Black Boy*, Richard is ever more capable of a "tolerant yet critical" attitude marked by an avoidance of dogmatism and reluctance to anathemize individuals or situations. He thus exemplifies a comic mode, which in no way seeks to minimize the racist social order, but on the contrary, emerges as an experiment in writing, a corrective to much existing work on the South and race hierarchy. The situation of segregation and race hierarchy becomes available such that their harms, confusions, and terrors can be appreciated in ways that predominant discourses do not allow. Along the way, Wright presents a range of scenes of the Jim Crow South in *Black Boy* as a national story by which Americans can become observers of themselves – the crux of the comic mode. As in Burke, Wright's inclination is to implicate everyone, including himself, within his critical ambit. For Wright, the comic mode may have seemed especially important for writing about racism since the vast scope it allowed countered the practice of relegating race hierarchy to the margins of criticism, and also because it also invited readers into a kind of deliberation regardless of their affiliations and cultural locations through its anti-dogmatic orientation. In *Black Boy* Wright set as his task an experimental work in which his writing became the site of inquiry, quizzicality and charitable understanding, ingredients for the attenuation of antagonism and therefore productive of community with others. He met his goal, at least insofar as "we feel secure in the hands of a conscious – in fact, self-conscious – storyteller, and as a result we respond in the detached, admiring way that spectators view the smooth unraveling of an aesthetic product," in the words of one critic.[58] Put otherwise, Wright produces a work of appreciation for the racist social order on the view that without such appreciation viable means of addressing its power cannot be devised.

In a seeming nod to Burke's "Literature as Equipment for Living," Wright, in the unpublished essay "Towards the Conquest of Ourselves," envisions expressive works and criticism that can serve as "instruments for our living."[59] Too "much of Negro artistic expression has been designed, wittingly or not, to bolster our feelings of defeat and hurt here at home," Wright wrote, but "we have to speak loudly and honestly to find out how human we are." Attending more to "crossed-up feelings" would make possible "a new way to make our lives known to America." Wright regarded the identification of psychological dynamics and patterns essential for making individuals students of themselves and, by extension, for expanding the self-reflexivity of groups. Toward this end, *Black Boy*'s emphasis on psychological maladies serves not to promote feelings of defeat but rather to acknowledge them as a step in their undoing. Richard refers to some around him who "solve the problem of being black by transferring their hatred of themselves to others with a black skin."[60] Scarcely free of psychological disturbance himself,

Richard is for much of the book beset with anxiety and apprehensive about his "inability to adjust myself to the white world," which "had already shattered a part of the structure of my personality."[61] The imperative in *Black Boy* is to bring psychosocial problems to the surface and to make them the "common realities of life." *Black Boy* thus corresponds to what Wright argues in his introduction to *Black Metropolis*, where blacks emerge as modern subjects who share in the "glorious hopes of the West," absorbing "all of its anxieties, its corruptions, its psychological maladies."[62]

In Wright's use of "anxiety," also evident in "A Study in Anxiety," among the subtitles considered for *Black Boy*, psychological disturbance and black life in the American North and South alike are brought into the same conceptual plane. "Anxiety" and cognate terms provide Wright with common abstractions by which to make black life part of "modern living." Burke reminds readers in *Permanence and Change* that "abstraction means literally a 'drawing from'," and that planned incongruity accomplishes much of its work "whenever a similar strain can be found in dissimilar events."[63] The Jim Crow conditions and Southern scenes Wright presents become fragments of the modern world in no small part because they reveal neurotic patterns. Wright adopts what Burke called "Freud's formula," wherein "everybody was abnormal, hence it followed that it was normal to be abnormal."[64] Along these lines, in *Attitudes toward History* the comic frame becomes a "method of study" that "provides a rationale for locating the irrational and the non-rational" in a given situation, and in turn encouraging "critical formulations that enable us to size up the important factors in reality" and "adopt workable attitudes toward them."[65] Evaluating responses to *Black Boy*, Wright seemed frustrated above all by the reluctance to grant that he had written the Jim Crow South into the modern by portraying a repository of modern cultural patterns, a place as riven by psychosocial problems as any. By presenting the Jim Crow South as a space of "modern living" replete with psychological ills, Wright sought to dramatize instances of anxiety and neurotic symptomology that called for remedies.

Throughout *Black Boy* and in large part because of his preoccupation with modern anxiety, Wright lends the category "black boy," and all that it implicates, what Burke called "new regions of inference."[66] Just as navigating life in the Jim Crow South often leaves Richard "near the edge of nervous collapse," so too does the book characterize "modern living" for Southern blacks as "one long, quiet, continuously contained dream of terror, tension and anxiety."[67] If "hunger" would remain among the keywords of *Black Boy*, then Wright's reliance on *anxiety* and related terms arguably does more to revise the meanings that collect around racial hierarchy and segregation. Wright's expanded range of inference works in the service of what Burke, in

"Calling the Tune," called "humanization."[68] In that essay Burke identified literary strategies organized primarily in terms of "idealization, or humanization" as those that allowed a writer "simultaneously to 'be himself' and to act as public spokesman for his patrons, or customers." Such writers drew upon the vast array of resources available to them, not least the "retrospective recovery of key situations in our past history."

In *Black Boy*, Wright's careful deployment of moments from his own past dramatizes the need for a broader reckoning with the national racial order. Ralph Ellison addresses this tactic when he notes Wright's capacity to "reveal to both Negroes and whites those problems of a psychological and emotional nature which arise between them when they strive for mutual understanding."[69] Attending to those problems meant acknowledging the intractable psychological character of racial antagonism itself, and having the temerity to ask, as Wright has Richard ask, "What was it that made the hate of whites for blacks so steady, seemingly so woven into the texture of things?"[70] The often unsettling episodes >Wright gathers in *Black Boy* collectively form his bid to speak unsentimentally on behalf of the nation about disenfranchised Southern blacks whose situation becomes emblematic of modern anxiety. All the while, Wright creates a work integrated with national life through its "tolerant of all and yet critical" orientation.

Ellison also understood *Black Boy* as a work thoroughly related to "what is being done in writing in the world," as his essay, "Richard Wright's Blues," demonstrates. His early drafts give an even greater indication that he recognized its broader ramifications, lending support to a vision of Wright as an artist "dedicated to modernism," as Werner Sollors has argued.[71] Wright had produced a "statement of man's relationship to his total world: only the self-blinded will limit its meaning to its immediate political incidents. These form only the play within the play, in which the conscience of America is trapped 'like a patient etherized upon a table.'"[72] In gesturing at Wright's modernist commitments, Ellison implicitly urged an emphasis on the critical and experimental character of *Black Boy*. In a not dissimilar way, Jerry W. Ward Jr. writes of the book that it "transcends the limits of simplistic correspondence between historical fact and narration to achieve a necessary language for projecting the ambiguities of human existence."[73] That language and those ambiguities emerge in large measure through the structuring incongruity – a crystalline awareness amid the deprivation, violence and the somber consistency of Jim Crow regulation – that Wright presses into narrative service.

Wright's capacity to project the "ambiguities of human existence," nurtured in part through his fluency in Burke's criticism, brought his work within the realm of existentialism. By the late 1940s, when many critics noted how the "Existentialists explain Wright," Constance Webb was among the few positing an alternative critical scenario: "Wright explains the Existentialists."[74] In suggesting that Wright served as a resource for existentialist thinkers, Webb may have had in mind the ways attitudes in *Black Boy* recur in Simone de Beauvoir's delineations of existentialism. Bringing Wright into her treatise on *The Ethics of Ambiguity* (1947), Beauvoir describes existentialist ethics as the defiance of coercive and oppressive structures. "During the war," she writes, "when Negro leaders were asked to drop their own claims for the sake of the general interest, Richard Wright refused; he thought that even at a time of war, his cause had to be defended."[75] Yet such opposition was not reducible to negation. In her view, Wright enacted existentialist ethics because such an ethics proceeds "without foundering" in what she calls the "anguish of pure negation."[76] Beauvoir contends that "what happens to me by means of others depends upon me as regards its meaning," a view that shares something of the quizzical, comic – man in society – thinking found throughout *Black Boy*.[77] Beauvoir's vision of existentialism was prefigured in Wright's attempt at a critical venture that would name a "situation already demoralized by inaccuracy" while also pursuing a "therapeutic and loosening process."[78]

Very much in line with Beauvoir, the Howard University scholar Arthur P. Davis argued that *Black Boy* could not be reconciled with the "typical American optimism" by which "we have fooled ourselves that things are not really as bad as they seem."[79] According to Davis, "*Black Boy* rudely kicks this frail prop from under us, dumping us unceremoniously on the ground of ugly reality. And we do not like it."[80] Wright did not founder in pure negation nor did he allow his work to shore up the "typical American optimism." Burke, in his parsing of the "polemical-debunking" frame and the penchant for euphemism, had identified the very poles cited by Beauvoir and Davis as the ones Wright skillfully eludes. If planned incongruity afforded Wright a method of studying the Jim Crow South while avoiding the cynicism of polemical-debunking frames, which placed a higher premium on "winning an argument than in understanding a process," then the result was a philosophical reflex that complemented mid-twentieth-century existentialism.[81] Wright indicated as much, intimating that his thinking was its own existentialist vernacular, as when he told C. L. R. James that "everything he read in Kierkegaard he had known before."[82] The fluency Wright acquired over many years in Burke's critical idiom contributed to this philosophical dispensation. He appeared to subscribe to Burke's view that "our lives and our histories are constantly in the making," such that even when the "materials of experience are established, we are poetic in our rearrangement of them."[83]

Despite his disappointment with initial responses to *Black Boy*, Wright valued some later commentary on his work. "One of the best reviews," Wright noted in his journal, came from Lionel Trilling.[84] Trilling understood the book as an "exercise of the author's moral and intellectual power" that undoubtedly drew upon, but could not be limited to, its biographical and sociological materials.[85] According to Trilling, Wright had not added to the store of "autobiographical or reportorial or fictional accounts of misery and oppression," because the "author does not wholly identify himself with his painful experience, does not, therefore, make himself a mere object of the reader's consciousness, does not make himself that different kind of human being, a 'sufferer.'" Wright instead presented an unanticipated figure: "the same kind of person as the reader, as complex, as free." Disarmingly, Wright produced a personality that navigated tense modern environments that were perhaps unlike but not altogether different from those of his readers and, startlingly, given prevailing representational practices, he made a "black boy" the repository of an unmistakably involved and taut psychological disposition. Trilling thus affirmed – even if he did not exactly name – the planned incongruity Wright introduced into his work, suggesting that the "objectivity which comes from refusing to be an object" in *Black Boy* was above all a literary-theoretic maneuver.[86]

Other reviewers emphasized Wright's psychological acuity. Isidor Schneider would write in *New Masses* about Wright's "keen observations of the neurotic behavior patterns produced by the race tensions in America."[87] Similarly, Patsy Graves, in *Opportunity*, described Wright's book as an overdue account of the "psychic wounds inflicted upon Negroes by the contradictions in our society."[88] In the words of Mary McCarthy, *Black Boy* treated the "neurotic pattern of I-and-They" at the core of racial domination.[89] In her view, the "suffering, hunger, beatings, insults, slights [and] injuries" all lent evidence to the "pressure of neurotic exploitation" throughout the Jim Crow social order.

Through planned incongruity, Wright endows Richard with a perspective "designed to 'remoralize'," to borrow from Burke, "by accurately naming a situation already demoralized by inaccuracy."[90] Wright's titles, and not only his subtitles, tell the story of *Black Boy* as re-moralization. Wright encountered misgivings about his first choice of title – *American Hunger* – from the Book-of-the-Month Club, which made the book one of its selections. Originally designed to encompass two parts, one covering his childhood and youth and another his Chicago years, *American Hunger* was truncated. Its new incarnation, limited to the Southern years, would be called *Black Boy*. Yet *American Hunger* as a title already registered Wright's planned incongruity, for it is as a budding critic that Richard can gather insights and render them American. Reminiscent of such titles as *American Humor: A Study of the National Character* (1931) by Constance Rourke, as well as culture and personality studies that made the analysis of national character a primary orientation, Wright's original title points toward the theme of national neglect. If Richard often goes hungry, so too are Southern blacks by custom starved of inclusion as equals in the nation.

According to Wright, the new title would signal national neglect and broach the subject of racism in a more immediate and vernacular way. Of the title of *Black Boy*, he wrote, "It is honest. Straight. And many people say it to themselves and wonder how he lives. *Black Boy* seems to me to be not only a title, but also a kind of heading of the whole general theme."[91] The title thus refers to the central figure of the narrative, but also communicates Wright's understanding of segregated sociality and racial hierarchy as modes of "modern living," not marginal or aberrant patterns, which he wanted his readers to appreciate in the fullness of their reach. This was the purpose and the appeal of the planned incongruity he adopted. If readers came to the book already thinking "how bad this life was," they would perhaps eventually regard the title as implicating black and white, South and North, as something activated and made essential within an entire cultural matrix, by the time they put it down. In his description of the title as a broad metaphor as in the comic orientation he chose for his book, then, Wright was involved in the "exercise of the author's moral and intellectual power," as Trilling argued, and one could add in the furthering of certain conceptual and theoretic procedures. Wright had achieved his aim if it became ever more evident that his story had everything to do with the wide expanse of "modern living," or as the psychiatrist Fredric Wertham put it, if it was regarded as emblematic of "American civilization" and "modern civilization in general."[92]

Notes

1. Richard Wright, journal entry, March 8, 1945. Richard Wright Papers, Beinecke Rare Book and Manuscript Library, Yale University.
2. Reprinted in *The Flowers of Friendship: Letters Written to Gertrude Stein*, ed. Donald Clifford Gallup (New York: Knopf, 1953), 380.
3. Ibid., 380.
4. Wright, journal entry, March 8, 1945.
5. Ibid.
6. Richard Wright to Philip Wylie (October 10, 1944). Reprinted in Michel Fabre, *Richard Wright: Books and Writers* (Jackson: University Press of Mississippi, 1990), 192.

7. Kenneth Burke, *Attitudes toward History*, 3rd ed. (Berkeley: University of California Press, 1984), 166.

8. Richard Wright, "How 'Bigger' Was Born" in *Native Son* (New York: HarperCollins, 2005), 454. First printed in 1940.

9. Kenneth Burke "Literature as Equipment for Living." Reprinted in Kenneth Burke, *Perspectives by Incongruity*, ed. Stanley Edgar Hyman (Bloomington: Indiana University Press, 1964), 105. First published in 1937.

10. William H. Rueckert, *Encounters with Kenneth Burke* (Urbana: University of Illinois Press, 1994), 119.

11. Louis Wirth, "A Review of '*Permanence and Change*.'" Reprinted in *Critical Responses to Kenneth Burke, 1924–1966*, ed. William Rueckert (Minneapolis: University of Minnesota Press, 1969), 104. First published in 1937.

12. Michel Fabre, "Wright's First Hundred Books," *The World of Richard Wright* (Jackson: University of Mississippi Press, 1985), 23. An exception to the relative dearth of work on literary and philosophical cross-pollination between Burke and Wright is Eugene Miller's important but mostly neglected *The Voice of a Native Son: The Art of Richard Wright* (Jackson: University of Mississippi Press, 1990). See chapter 3, "The Uses of Kenneth Burke."

13. Kenneth Burke, *Permanence and Change: An Anatomy of Purpose*, 3rd ed. (Berkeley: University of California Press, 1984), 15.

14. Kenneth Burke, *Rhetoric of Motives* (New York: Prentice-Hall, 1950), 259.

15. Fabre, *Richard Wright: Books and Writers*, 20.

16. Richard Wright, journal entry, January 7, 1945. Richard Wright Papers, Beinecke Rare Book and Manuscript Library, Yale University.

17. Richard Wright, "Writing From the Left," draft, n.d., Richard Wright Papers, Beinecke Rare Book and Manuscript Library, Yale University. For more on Wright and mid-twentieth century psychological thought, see Jay Garcia, *Psychology Comes to Harlem: Rethinking the Race Question in Twentieth Century America* (Baltimore: The Johns Hopkins University Press, 2012).

18. Burke, *Permanence and Change*, 5–6.

19. Ibid., 169.

20. Richard Wright, *Black Boy* (New York: HarperCollins, 1991), 169. First published in 1945.

21. Kenneth Burke, "Surrealism," in *New Directions in Prose and Poetry* (New York: Kraus Reprint Corporation, 1967), 575. First published in 1940.

22. Ibid.

23. Mary McCarthy, "Portrait of a Typical Negro?" in *Black Boy (American Hunger): A Casebook*, ed. William L. Andrews and Douglas Taylor (New York: Oxford University Press, 2003), 43. First published in 1945.

24. Constance Webb, "What Next for Richard Wright?," *Phylon* 10:2 (1949), 163.

25. Richard Wright, "*Black Boy* and Reading" in *Conversations with Richard Wright*, ed. Keneth Kinnamon and Michel Fabre (Jackson: University Press of Mississippi, 1993), 82. First published 1945. It was also here that Wright noted the wide reading he did while composing *Black Boy*, referring to works that "endlessly modified my attitude."

26. Kenneth Burke, "The Relation Between Literature and Science," *The Writer in a Changing World*, ed. Henry Hart (New York: Equinox, 1937), 159.

27. Ibid., 166.

28. Ibid., 170.

29. Ibid., 158.

30. Michel Fabre, *The Unfinished Quest of Richard Wright*, 2nd ed. (Urbana: University of Illinois Press, 1993), 578.

31. Kenneth Burke, "Revolutionary Symbolism in America," *American Writers' Congress*, ed. Henry Hart (New York: International Publishers, 1935), 89, 91.

32. It was also in these years that Wright and Burke were both associate editors of the literary publication *Direction*, which had ties to the League of American Writers. See Michael Denning, *The Cultural Front: The Laboring of American Culture in the Twentieth Century* (New York: Verso, 1996), 194.

33. Kenneth Burke, "Foreword," *Philosophy of Literary Form: Studies in Symbolic Form*, 3rd ed. (Berkeley: University of California, 1974), x.

34. Fabre, *Richard Wright: Books and Writers*, 20.

35. Ibid., 265.

36. Burke, "Surrealism," 575.

37. Wright, *Black Boy*, 100.

38. Kenneth Burke to Ralph Ellison. December 16, 1945. Ralph Ellison Papers, Library of Congress.

39. Wright, *Black Boy*, 100.

40. It was upon the concept of *attitudes* – not *history* – that Burke insisted the accent should fall in his title. See Kenneth Burke, "Introduction," *Attitudes toward History* [1955].

41. Ibid., 167.

42. Ibid., 174.

43. Rueckert, *Encounters with Kenneth Burke*, 119.

44. Burke, *Attitudes toward History*, 171.

45. Ibid., 167, 173.

46. Ibid., 113.

47. Wright, *Black Boy*, 93.

48. Timothy W. Crusius, *Kenneth Burke and the Conversation after Philosophy* (Carbondale: Southern Illinois University Press, 1999), 199.

49. Wright, *Black Boy*, 115.

50. Ibid.

51. Ibid.

52. Burke, *Permanence and Change*, 133.

53. Wright, *Black Boy*, 122.

54. For a persuasive argument that emphasizes how terms related to the common, including communism, were central to Burke's lexicon, if also later banished "in part because of Burke's own self-censorship," see Denning, *The Cultural Front*, 437.

55. Burke, *Attitudes toward History*, 42.

56. Frederick J. Hoffman, *Freudianism and the Literary Mind* (New York: Grove Press, 1957), 104.

57. Kenneth Burke, *A Grammar of Motives* (Berkeley: University of California Press, 1969 [1945]), *xvii*.

58. Marjorie Smelstor, "Richard Wright's Beckoning Descent and Ascent," in *Richard Wright: Myths and Realities*, ed. C. James Trotman (New York: Garland, 1988), 97.

59. Wright, "Towards the Conquest of Ourselves," draft, n.d., Richard Wright Papers, Beinecke Rare Book and Manuscript Library, Yale University. In "How 'Bigger' Was Born," Wright similarly writes that, as time passed, writing *Native Son* "became a necessity ... the writing of it turned into a way of living for me." See "How 'Bigger' Was Born," 448.
60. Wright, *Black Boy*, 253.
61. Ibid., 201.
62. Wright, "Introduction," *Black Metropolis*, xxv.
63. Burke, *Permanence and Change*, 104
64. Ibid., 127.
65. Burke, *Attitudes toward History*, 214.
66. Burke, *Permanence and Change*, 103.
67. Wright, *Black Boy*, 95, 253.
68. Kenneth Burke, "The Calling of the Tune," *The Kenyon Review* 1:3 (1939), 275.
69. Ralph Ellison, "Richard Wright's Blues," *The Antioch Review* 5:2 (1945), 198.
70. Wright, *Black Boy*, 164.
71. Werner Sollors, "Modernization as Adultery: Richard Wright, Zora Neal Hurston, and American Culture of the 1930s and 1940s," *African American Writing: A Literary Approach* (Philadelphia: Temple University Press, 2016), 134.
72. Ralph Ellison, "Wright's Blues: The Tragedy of Consciousness," draft, n.d., Ralph Ellison Papers, Library of Congress.
73. Jerry W. Ward Jr., "Introduction," *Black Boy*, xvi.
74. Webb, "What Next for Richard Wright?," 163.
75. Simone de Beauvoir, *The Ethics of Ambiguity*, trans. Bernard Frechtman, 2nd ed. (New York: Kensington, 1964), 89.
76. Ibid., 68.
77. Ibid., 82.
78. Richard Wright to Philip Wylie (October 10, 1944). Reprinted in Michel Fabre, *Richard Wright: Books and Writers* (Jackson: University Press of Mississippi, 1990), 192.
79. Arthur P. Davis, Review of *Black Boy*, *Journal of Negro Education* 14:4 (Autumn 1945), 589.
80. The most public instance of someone not liking *Black Boy* was surely that of Mississippi Senator Theodore Bilbo, who denounced the book on the floor of the Senate as the "dirtiest, filthiest, lousiest, most obscene piece of writing I have ever seen in print." The Southern segregationist described Wright's work as a "damnable lie from beginning to end," "practically all fiction," and called for the book to be banned. Bilbo also considered it essential in assessing *Black Boy* to tell his fellow senators that Wright resides in "Brooklyn, N.Y., where he is living with a white woman and is living happily, he says." See Theodore Bilbo, "Remarks about *Black Boy* Made before the U.S. Senate," in *Understanding Richard Wright's Black Boy*, ed. Robert Felgar (Westport: Greenwood, 1998), 147–148.
81. Burke, *Attitudes toward History*, 327.
82. C. L. R. James, "Black Studies and the Contemporary Student," in *At the Rendezvous of Victory: Selected Writings* (London: Allison and Busby, 1984), 195. First published in 1969.

83. Burke, *Permanence and Change*, 218.
84. Richard Wright, journal entry, April 4, 1945. Richard Wright Papers, Beinecke Rare Book and Manuscript Library, Yale University.
85. Lionel Trilling, "A Tragic Situation" in *Richard Wright's Black Boy (American Hunger): A Casebook*, 38. First published in 1945.
86. Ibid., 39.
87. Isidor Schneider, "One Apart," *New Masses* 55 (1945), 23.
88. Patsy Graves, "Opportunity" in *Richard Wright: The Critical Reception*, ed. John M. Reilly (New York: Burt Franklin, 1978), 173. First published in 1945.
89. McCarthy, "Portrait of a Typical Negro?," 203.
90. Burke, *Attitudes toward History*, 309.
91. Richard Wright to Paul Reynolds, August 10, 1944. Quoted in Fabre, *The Unfinished Quest*, 254.
92. Fredric Wertham, Review of *Black Boy*, *Journal of Clinical Psychopathology* 6 (1945): 643.

3

NATHANIEL F. MILLS

Marxism, Communism, and Richard Wright's Depression-Era Work

Richard Wright's commercial and critical success made him the most well-known Communist writer of the late 1930s and early 1940s, a position that also made him a prime target for postwar critics who argued that investments in Marxist thought and the Communist left diminished the aesthetic sophistication and political creativity of African American literature. In 1949, James Baldwin defined Wright's *Native Son* (1940) as a "protest novel" that dismisses "niceties of style or characterization" in favor of abstractions like "the good of society" and that depicts human reality only in reductive formulas drawn from politics or sociology.[1] Ralph Ellison echoed Baldwin in "The World and the Jug" (1963/1964), finding that *Native Son* neglects African American culture and transforms black individuals into ideological types: "How awful that Wright found the facile answers of Marxism before he learned to use literature as a means for discovering the forms of American Negro humanity."[2]

This dichotomy of protest and art limned by Baldwin and Ellison became so hegemonic in the Cold War era that even Wright had recourse to it.[3] At the conclusion of his contribution to *The God That Failed* (1950), a collection of ex-Communist testimonials, Wright associates his art with political disillusion: disabused of his hopes for Communist activism, he elects to use literature to explore and advocate for "the inexpressibly human."[4] Bill Mullen explains this as Wright's attempt to retroactively redefine the intellectual influences on his major late 1930s works from the vantage point of his mid-1940s break from the left.[5] However, Wright's echo of Baldwin and Ellison's assumptions is a reminder of how the postwar devaluation of "protest" would long shape critical understandings of African American literature and, ironically, Wright's own achievements.

Zora Neale Hurston, in her review of *Uncle Tom's Children* (1938), made a companion argument to Baldwin and Ellison's. For Hurston, Wright's fiction devalued Southern black life and culture because he espoused didactic Communist distortions of the South as "[a] dismal, hopeless section ruled by brutish hatred and nothing else." Leftism, Hurston charges, kept Wright from recognizing the cultural richness and sustaining positivity of black life. "One hopes that Mr. Wright will find in Negro life a vehicle for his talents," she concludes.[6] Hurston's critique has often been validated in scholarly discussions of Wright,[7] which William Maxwell argues has had the effect of "steering Wright to the fringes of folk-minded African-American canons and institutionalizing a scare story about the Old Left's violence to black writing's vernacular ingredient."[8] A political reformulation of many of Hurston's conclusions can be seen in Harold Cruse's influential *The Crisis of the Negro Intellectual* (1967), which uses Wright as evidence that Jewish American Communists co-opted autonomous black political and cultural expression. Wright, Cruse charges, "was so ideologically blinded by the smog of Jewish-Marxist nationalism that he was unable to see his *own* clearly." For Cruse, the ruses of "vulgar Marxism" and "Communist Party propaganda" prevented Wright from engaging the "values" and "revolutionary significance" of African American culture.[9]

Despite their prominence, such negative evaluations of Wright's Depression-era work neglect the specific uses it makes of Marxism and Communism. Wright's Marxism does not function as didactic exhortation removed from the particularities of African American reality; rather, Wright draws from Marxism's philosophy of history in his fiction to produce a Marxist aesthetic attuned to the cultural resources and political capacities of African Americans. In this chapter, I argue that Wright uses historical materialism, Marxism's signature theory of history as spelled out in canonical statements like *The Communist Manifesto* (1848), as an organizing frame for his writings. In this manner, Marxist theory leads Wright to represent African American experience as rich with sources of cultural resilience, such as vernacular communal knowledge and traditional religious sensibilities, that furnish revolutionary political consciousness and empowerment.

Historical materialism plots history as driven by class struggle – active resistance to economic exploitation and social domination on the part of the exploited and dominated – through successive modes of economic production (feudalism, capitalism) toward communism, a socioeconomic condition free from material and political inequity.[10] The exploited laboring class in a given mode of production is positioned, by virtue of its complexly subordinate role in both production and society, to overthrow the social and economic structures of the present and advance history into a new phase. The basic assumptions and narrative structure of historical materialism guide the emplotment of modern African American history in *Twelve Million Black Voices* (1941), the character arcs of the protagonists in "Bright and Morning Star" (1938) and "Fire and Cloud" (1938), and the delineation of Bigger Thomas's subjectivity in *Native*

Son (1940). In these works, African Americans access transformative political agency because Wright sets African American culture and lived experience within a historical narrative form in which oppressed groups and their practices have the potential to catalyze progressive temporal change.

My identification of Marxist historical form as a thematic and theoretical frame in Wright's work is influenced by Caroline Levine's theorization of form itself. Levine holds that form, as a general principle of organization and utility, is a structuring feature of both social and literary ontology. Thus closing formalism's distance between literary form and social reality, Levine argues that a given form provides "particular constraints and possibilities" – what Levine terms *affordances* – for organizing, illuminating, or changing social reality.[11] Marxism's theory of history, as a form, thus affords particular possibilities for representing African Americans not as beaten down by racism and capitalism, but as empowered to act against those oppressions.

Of course, criticisms of Marxism have long since identified the liabilities of its narrative of history. Its teleology of progress and emphasis on the role of economic developments in creating conditions for historical change make Marxism's historical narrative susceptible to regressive misapplications, a susceptibility that can be read as a constraint of the form itself: it can imply that social and cultural practices are either merely extraneous to, or straightforward undifferentiated reflections of, primary economic processes; it can dismiss the immediacy of socioeconomic suffering as only a passing phase; and it can subordinate political agency to abstract processes of historical determination. Wright's Depression-era work, however, is cognizant of these constraints and the potentially self-defeating consequences of plotting African American experience within a Marxist historical narrative. In his writing, therefore, he designs endings that suspend neat political resolution, thereby refusing to allegorize revolutionary progress as an historically inevitable, teleologically assured narrative end. By identifying historical tendencies while insisting on the necessity of strategic action and organization to realize the progressive movement of those tendencies, Wright operates, without flattening or simplifying, historical materialism's complex dialectic of objective processes and subjective agency.

That necessity of willed political action to effect historical change is operative in Wright's work through his depictions of Communist political work. In "Bright and Morning Star," "Fire and Cloud," and *Native Son*, the Communist Party does not preach propaganda to the reader, but is depicted as, and valued to the extent that it operates as, an enabling vehicle for black political struggle. Communism, in other words, is a signifier of and banner for African American agency. In "How 'Bigger' Was Born," his 1940 essay on the composition of *Native Son*, Wright uses the figure of Lenin both to signal Marxism's insistence on the role of action in putting history into motion, and to locate that revolutionary will and capacity within African American experiences of alienation and oppression in the modern United States. In his implementations of Marxism and Communism as, respectively, an enabling historical narrative and an ethic of agency, Wright defines blackness as something much more politically and culturally significant than a passive index of "brutish hatred and nothing else."

Wright's Depression-era work thus does not abandon what Ellison called "discovering the forms of American Negro humanity" for Marxism's "facile answers." Wright in fact pursued something very like that discovery, if one understands it free from the Cold War ideological implications of Ellison's dichotomy of black "humanity" and Marxist "answers." Wright used Marxism to depict blackness not in simple terms of deprivation or victimhood, as Ellison, Baldwin, and Hurston variously suggested, but as culturally sustained and capable of effecting revolutionary historical progress. To adapt Henry Louis Gates Jr.'s influential theory of the African American text as the "Talking Book," an effort to make "the text of Western letters" express the "individual and collective voices" of African Americans, Wright makes Marxism talk about and through African American sociopolitical experiences and cultural outlooks.[12]

Wright became affiliated with the Communist Party of the United States in 1933 after joining the Chicago chapter of the John Reed Club, a party institution for fostering working class writers. He broke from the party in the mid-1940s, less from any change in his radical convictions than in response to the party's uncritical support of the US war effort and retreat from domestic anti-racist and anti-capitalist activism.[13] The party was aligned with an international Communist movement inspired by and loosely directed from Soviet Russia, but Brian Dolinar explains that the party "promoted several cultural organizations to draw black cultural workers into its orbit" during the Depression. Closely aligned with but not beholden to the party, therefore, was what Dolinar terms the "black cultural front," a network of institutions that encouraged the political and cultural expression of African Americans.[14]

Wright often complained about party tendencies toward anti-intellectualism and dogmatism, but he played active roles in the party's literary infrastructure. For instance, he served on the editorial board for the Chicago John Reed Club's journal *Left Front*. He objected when the party dissolved the clubs in 1935, but he still participated in the newly formed League of American Writers. When he moved to New York in 1937, he joined the editorial staff of *Challenge* and helped re-launch it as *New Challenge*, a publication more in line with party discourse. He also worked as a reporter for the *Daily Worker*, the party's main newspaper.[15] Wright's activities did not compromise his autonomy Lawrence Jackson notes that Wright "conduct[ed] his art with characteristic independence," and Mark Naison explains that the "considerable prestige" the party gained from Wright's association provided him with latitude: if Wright benefited from the support of party institutions, the party in turn was "[willing] to tolerate a certain amount of heterodoxy in order to keep a valued black artist within its fold."[16]

Wright also studied Marxist theory and its intellectual contexts. Margaret Walker, a close friend of Wright's in the 1930s, described how he "read Communist pamphlets first, then plunged into the recommended books ... He studied the history of revolution – Russian, French, and American – read Marx's *Communist Manifesto*, and learned to analyze the plight of black people in Marxist terms." He directed Walker herself toward works like Marx's *Capital*, John Reed's *Ten Days That Shook the World*, and the writings of Friedrich Nietzsche and Adam Smith.[17] Wright's self-education in Marxism was eclectic, expansive, and driven by his own intellectual and literary aims.

One work in particular influenced Wright: Joseph Stalin's *Marxism and the National Question* (1913), which Wright called "a most politically sensitive volume that revealed a new way of looking upon lost and beaten peoples."[18] Stalin argued that an effective approach to international revolutionary politics must recognize the right of a nation to self-determination, to "arrange its life according to its own will."[19] The sovereignty of a nation, both in terms of its external relationships and its internal culture, must be respected. An espousal of national autonomy in the name of international proletarian revolution seems paradoxical, but Stalin's historical materialist understanding of the ontology of the nation makes national self-determination an important catalyst in the development toward the international eclipse of capitalism. A nation is "subject to the law of change" and "a historical category belonging to ... the epoch of rising capitalism."[20] As such, the development of nations within history – understood in the Marxist sense as a dialectical progression through modes of production, from feudalism to capitalism to communism – is the condition for the growth of the political acumen of the proletariat of each nation. Nationalist and anti-colonial politics are thus linked, sequentially and dialectically, to international anti-capitalism: as capitalism develops, nations develop their cultural distinctiveness and institutional structures, and nationalist political movements encourage "the free development of the intellectual forces of the proletariat of subject nations." Stalin suggests that workers come to an awareness of their world-historical revolutionary agency through national cultural channels, and holds that Marxists must oppose the oppression of national, political, and cultural autonomy: "There can be no possibility of a full development of the intellectual faculties of the Tatar or of the Jewish worker if he is not allowed to use his native language at meetings and lectures, and if his schools are closed down."[21] Stalin thus positions the development of national identities and cultures as a necessary step toward the emergence of an international proletariat that will usher in the historical transition to communism.

Stalin's argument influenced the Communist Party's Black Belt Thesis.[22] Crafted in 1928 and officially in effect until 1935, this policy of the international Communist movement held that African Americans in the US South constituted an oppressed nation with the right to self-determination. Consequently – and this is a point that has been obscured by Harold Cruse's influential postwar reevaluation of black encounters with Communism – American Communism read black culture as a positive expression of national consciousness and revolutionary practice. This validation remained in place even after the party formally moved away from African American self-determination as part of its shift to the coalitional anti-fascist Popular Front in 1935. For instance, "some of the first serious jazz critics got their start writing for *The Daily Worker* and other Communist publications," Robin Kelley writes. "The Communist press became one of the biggest promoters of black theater, music, dance, and the plastic arts."[23] In light of its role in elevating African American culture within the discourse of the left, Stalin's text, William Maxwell explains, "won [Wright] totally to Communism" a commitment that, for Wright, "became a source for the recognition of African-American folk culture."[24]

Stalin's text implies that the particular or "national" experiences and cultural traditions of African Americans are located within a temporal progression toward self-emancipation and the transcendence of racial and national difference. By situating national development on a historical materialist timeline, Stalin suggests how one could reframe the journey of black people within American history as one moving ever closer to an exit from that history. In other words, rather than a disorienting *non*-movement from one kind of servitude to another and from one site of marginalization to another (from slavery to Jim Crow, from sharecropping to industrial labor, from the rural South to the urban North), Marxist historical form could re-plot black history as a purposive movement through successive modes of production, from Southern agricultural feudalism to Northern urban capitalism toward, eventually, international communism. African American cultural traditions and folk knowledge could be rendered not as essentialized or fixed expressions outside history, but as fluid vehicles of revolutionary consciousness shifting in time with material developments. Marxism could shift the temporality of blackness from stasis to becoming, redefining blackness in terms of African Americans' cultural resources and own active efforts toward freedom.

Wright pursued this project in *Twelve Million Black Voices*. This photojournalistic text narrates black history in the collective voice of the folk, tracking the journey of African Americans from slavery through emancipation and the Great Migration to the emergence of a new generation proletarianized by industrial labor and radicalized by left-wing activism during the Depression. This narrative is organized by historical materialist understandings of trajectory and causation, with progressions between modes of production catalyzed by economic shifts and reflected in new forms of sociopolitical and cultural awareness. The Civil War is a war between the "Lords of the Lands" and the "Bosses of the Buildings," and causes like abolition are superstructural reflections of that underlying economic conflict. The Great Migration emerges from the overproduction of Southern cotton, the global expansion of the cotton market, and the automation of labor: dispossessed from the economic means of production of Jim Crow feudalism, African Americans migrate to the North. Wright explores how this transition occasions the loss of traditional ways of life and their reinvention in modern cities. As "[t]he sands of our simple folk lives run out on the cold city pavements," the "children" of the older generations evince "strange moods": desires for the material comforts of modernity from which they have been alienated, and an "eagerness to fight." Just as the dialectic of capitalism in *The Communist Manifesto* destroys older sociocultural forms but, in so doing, facilitates the formation of the revolutionary proletariat across cultural lines, the death of Wright's feudal folk becomes the birth of a new generation ready to participate in the negation of capitalism: "hundreds of thousands of us are moving into the sphere of conscious history."[25]

Marxism thus leads Wright to conceive of black life as more than the negations of oppression. In *Twelve Million Black Voices*, African American music, dance, verbal expressions, and religious traditions reflect economic changes, but this is not a vulgar devaluation of the cultural in favor of the economic. Rather, these practices develop within Marxism's historical time and serve as African Americans' own adaptive conduits for the expression of cultural sustenance and sociopolitical aspiration. Wright's use of Marxism, then, entails a celebration of the particularity and resourcefulness of black culture and historical experience. Combining black folk cultural and Marxist idioms, Wright rewrites a history of apparently ceaseless toil, exploitation, and abuse as one instead defined by African Americans' self-driven progress, however irregular and halting, *through* those experiences. Wright's use of historical materialism can be said to romanticize – and perhaps aggrandize –

suffering as a catalyst for African American agency. As discussed above, the dialectic of historical materialism can locate oppression in a privileged conceptual relation to liberation. However, Wright nonetheless dislodges the apparent inevitability of racial and economic oppression by putting it in historical motion: taking the apparently recurring experience of African Americans' perpetual servitude under various names (slavery, Jim Crow, industrial labor), Wright temporalizes it *as* history, as a trajectory toward temporal difference and social change driven by African American efforts.

Accordingly, Wright held that black writers must use Marxist theory to scan African American culture for resources that could inform that agency. In "Blueprint for Negro Writing" (1937), Wright calls for black writers to see "society as something becoming rather than as something fixed and admired." This "Marxist conception of reality and society" – that is, social reality temporalized within Marxist historical form – enables the black writer to represent the political acumen and agency of the black masses within history. This approach requires close attention to forms of black culture (music, folklore), which, combined with vernacular guidance passed on within the community, have constituted "the channels through which the racial wisdom flowed." Historical reality, and black cultural parsings of that reality, are equally fluid: as history progresses, "racial wisdom" develops as an explication of that progress. The black community's proprietary cultural resources, because culturally particular, thus carry "nationalist implications" and tend to be manifested in a racially exclusive "expression of group-feeling." Wright famously argues that black writers must "transcend" this tendency, but this does not mean that black culture can be ignored as the inadequate other of Marxism. Rather, writers must transcend nationalist "group-feeling" in a dialectical sense, understanding African American culture as in fact offering articulations of historical materialist realities and identifying, within it, usable expressions of revolutionary consciousness. Using historical materialist language, Wright explains that black culture contains "those vital beginnings of a recognition of value in life as it is *lived*, a recognition that marks the emergence of a new culture in the shell of the old. And at the moment this process starts, at the moment when a people begin to realize a *meaning* in their suffering, the civilization that engenders that suffering is doomed."[26]

In "Bright and Morning Star," Wright stages a synthesis of Marxism, Communism, and African American lived experience. Sue, an elderly African American woman, is involved with a cell of Communist operatives in a small Southern town. Her sons Johnny-Boy and Sug, and Johnny-Boy's lover, a white woman named Reva, are members of the party. They learn that the sheriff has planted an informant in the party who has discovered the location of a planned meeting. Sue finds out that Booker, a white Communist, is the informant, but not before he gets the names of party members from her. At the same time, Johnny-Boy is captured and tortured by the sheriff's men to compel him to give up names. To stop Booker from revealing the names to the sheriff, Sue goes to the sheriff with the pretense of bringing a winding sheet to carry home her soon-to-be-killed son. But under the sheet she conceals a pistol that she uses to kill Booker, surprising the other whites, who then kill her and Johnny-Boy.

As the story opens, Sue sees "the silent rush of a bright shaft of yellow that swung from the airplane beacon in far off Memphis." The beacon temporarily illuminates the landscape of the Jim Crow South while also suggestively destroying it: the beacon is "cutting through the rainy dark ... like a gleaming sword."[27] The beacon symbolizes the forward-moving trajectory of history, and its spatial relationship to the story's setting encodes the temporal relationship of feudalism to capitalism. The beacon shines from a site of modern capitalism that is "far off," yet its temporary illumination of the present scene registers the future eclipse of Jim Crow, a future of which the party's interracial collaboration furnishes glimpses. The beacon indicates how the party's actions are working to realize history's tendency toward the destruction of a benighted, feudal mode of production: that destruction might still be far off, but its already in the works.

Sue's friendship with Reva has demystified Southern race relations. Sue previously accepted subservience to the "mountain" of whiteness, but her friendship with this white woman has de-fetishized white supremacy and allowed Sue to own her folk-derived, organic human strength: "If in the early days of her life the white mountain had driven her back from the earth, then in her last days Reva's love was drawing her toward it, like the beacon that swung through the night outside."[28] The beacon here signals a progressive historical tendency in Aunt Sue's simultaneous recovery of her cultural strength and cooperation with radical whites: both draw her, and history itself, closer toward the future.

Sue's political radicalism recasts her former religious faith: "The wrongs and sufferings of black men had taken the place of Him nailed to the Cross; the meager beginnings of the party had become another Resurrection."[29] The messianic promise of Christianity expresses a powerful utopian longing that nonetheless, for Wright, tends to sacrifice human agency to theological fictions. When Bigger Thomas is in jail in *Native Son*, for instance, Reverend Hammond and Bigger's pious mother can offer him nothing more than a Christianity defined by the kinds of misreadings implied by Marxist historical form. Their faith naturalizes suffering and relegates sociopolitical desires to imaginary fulfillment "beyond this world."[30] However, Sue has transcended her faith in the dialectical manner Wright described in "Blueprint": her Marxism has not supplanted but materialized her culturally embedded faith, turning it from an ideology of passivity to a source of practice. As Sue goes to shoot Booker, she looks back at her home: "The lamp glowed in her window, and the yellow beacon that swung every few seconds seemed to feed it with light."[31] Black folk identity, symbolically located in Aunt Sue's domestic space, and the progressive tendency of Marxist history represented by the beacon, "feed" each other and become visible, in Sue's retrospective glance, as combined catalysts for her forward motion. As Sue leaves to partake in the process of moving history past Jim Crow through her political agency, she is following a trajectory inherent in black culture yet newly illuminated by Marxist historical theory.

However, the ending undercuts this triumphant narrative buildup. Sue personifies the black folk's movement, through its own cultural channels, into historical agency, but the climax of the story does not allegorize any straightforward revolutionary victory. Sue and Johnny-Boy are killed, and as Gregory Meyerson shrewdly points out, Sue fails to send a warning to the other party members that the sheriff has discovered their meeting location and is planning to trap them; her act, in fact, will probably lead to the destruction of the local party.[32] The ending fails as an allegory of revolution because such a resolution would imply the historical inevitability of revolutionary transcendence, an inevitability that would function, like Reverend Hammond's Christianity, to occlude the necessity of active commitment. Wright's story ends by reminding the reader that Marxism's abstract principles of historical determination enable but do not *ensure* progress. Such progress occurs unevenly through class struggle, through the contingent messiness and occasional failures of situated strategies and actions. The distance in the ending between the figurative and the literal, between the glimpsed possibility of a neat allegorical resolution and the actual errors and unpredictable outcomes of agency that close the narrative, furnishes an autocritique of the story's recourse to Marxism: Marxist historical form identifies resources for struggle and tendencies toward historical transcendence but automates no messianic guarantees.

Wright does not mechanically impose Marxist historical theory and Communist strategy on African American experience, but stages a reciprocally informing encounter in which leftist precepts are themselves modified from the perspective of African American experience. When Johnny-Boy tells his mother that someone has leaked the location of the meeting, Sue suspects white comrades like Booker who have recently joined because she's known the black members all her life. Johnny-Boy objects to her reasoning, insisting that racial difference is nothing but a ruse by which capital and Jim Crow divide the masses. "Ah cant see white n Ah cant see black," he tells Sue. "Ah sees rich men n Ah sees po men." Sue worries that his strictly by-the-book Marxist line on race is itself an ideological delusion: "She knew his faith; it was deep ... But he believes so hard hes blind."[33] Sue's experiential knowledge of the workings of racial difference is an example of what Wright in "Blueprint" terms the "racial wisdom" of African Americans. Sue turns out to be correct, and Booker's name informs the reader of how her suspicion is an epistemologically reliable product of African American historical experience: like Booker T. Washington, Booker makes ostensibly progressive overtures while being compromised by a functional role *within* Jim Crow. The knowledge won from experience and passed down through the black community revises the leftist tendency to abstract race from considerations of class conflict.

Wright's representation of the Communist Party in "Bright and Morning Star" thus implies its obligation to work without any dogmatic blinders and to incorporate African American experiential knowledge in its revolutionary strategy. In "Fire and Cloud," for instance, the party advocates organized action as an alternative to the temptation to passively acquiesce to a fantasy of inevitable historical change. Dan Taylor is a black preacher in a Southern town that's suffering a food shortage. Taylor must decide whether to risk his own standing with the Jim Crow establishment, his family's safety, and his own life in order to join a protest march organized by local Communists. His wife urges him not to join because of the impact it will have on their son's future: "Don do nothin wrong! Its fer Jimmy Ahm astin!" At a meeting of his congregation, Deacon Smith urges Taylor to "[w]ait n see how things come out!" Both insist that change will result magically from Taylor's inaction, thus enjoining passivity and the deferral of liberation. Sacrificing the uncertain risks of action to the myth of a future determined entirely by objective processes – in other words, waiting – cancels the possibility of change and prolongs present suffering indefinitely. "Ahm tireda waitin," Taylor responds. After a group of whites beat Taylor to intimidate him from joining the protest, Taylor tells Jimmy: "All mah life Ah done tried n cant do nothin!"[34] His efforts to keep his family in the good graces of the town's whites have merely perpetuated subservience: they are non-actions that keep history frozen in an intolerable present. He tells his son that, instead, they must act to set history in forward motion by joining the march.

In this story, Communist political commitment is inseparable from a culturally derived sense of African American agency. When the Communist organizers Hadley, who is white, and Green, who is black, come to persuade Taylor to join the march, they inadvertently arrive at the same time that the mayor and chief of police come to threaten Taylor. Jimmy carefully directs the Jim Crow leaders to the parlor, while leading the Communists to wait in the Bible Room. Taylor is anxious the two groups don't discover each other: "Hadley n Greens there in the Bible Room n the Chiefa Police is waitin in the parlor!" The import of this seemingly out-of-place comic scenario is to suggest the true identity of Communism as a capacity for action always-already located within black culture. In the parlor – the public site of African Americans' subservience to Jim Crow – safety is bought by refusing to act while waiting for a better tomorrow. But the image of "Reds a-waitin in the Bible Room" suggests the historically significant agency located within the "racial wisdom" and culture of the black community.[35] Taylor has to translate the utopian dreaming of Christianity – which, like common misreadings of historical materialism, is here a messianic teleology producing resignation – into action in the present. By electing to act rather than wait, Taylor sides, all at once, with the Communists, his faith, his people, and his culture.

Wright theorized this understanding of Communist activism in "How 'Bigger' Was Born." He explains that *Native Son*'s protagonist Bigger Thomas was based on an archetype of subjectivity, "the Bigger Thomas pattern," that Wright first encountered in certain Southern African Americans who channeled their frustrations into impulsive revolts against Jim Crow. Their acts of defiance emerged from a condition of being alienated from black sociocultural institutions and, at the same time, from a modernity "whose glitter came ... through the newspapers, magazines, radios, movies, and the mere imposing sight and sound of daily American life." Caught between social and cultural manifestations of two historically successive modes of production – no longer capable of being at home in the feudal South, but barred from full access to capitalist modernity – and lacking progressive leadership, these types resorted to desperate acts of violence and were often "shot, hanged, maimed, lynched, and generally hounded."[36]

In Chicago, Wright recognized this archetype manifested in the class-based revolts of militant workers who were also alienated from the fruits of capitalism. This revelation suggested that the "Bigger Thomas pattern" might not be just a mode of fruitless black desperation, but instead a general anti-capitalist subjectivity with transformative potential. Wright uses Lenin to figure this redefinition of Bigger Thomas's alienation as revolutionary awareness. He recalls "reading an interesting pamphlet telling of the friendship of Gorky and Lenin in exile. The booklet told of how Lenin and Gorky were walking down a London street. Lenin turned to Gorky and, pointing, said: 'Here is *their* Big Ben.' 'There is *their* Westminster Abbey.' 'There is *their* library.'" Wright recognizes this attitude as "the Bigger Thomas reaction" but here reinvented, with the authority of Lenin's name, as the essence of radical potential.[37]

Wright's source for this anecdote is actually Leon Trotsky's 1924 biography of Lenin (published the following year in the US), in which Lenin makes these claims to Trotsky.[38] Trotsky summarizes Lenin's point: "The invisible shadow of the shareholders of society lay, as it were, in his eyes on all human culture."[39] By pointing out how those who own the means of cultural production also own the means of economic production, Lenin materializes Bigger Thomas's cultural alienation as an expression of the general economic alienation of the exploited under capitalism. Thus framed within Marxist theory, the frustration and impulsive acts of the Bigger Thomas archetype become expressions of revolutionary consciousness and capacity. And while there were situated political reasons for Wright changing Trotsky to Gorky here, surely one motive was to allow him to project himself into the anecdote as the committed writer taking from Lenin a lesson he would implement in his fiction.[40]

Wright thus depicts Communist commitment solely in terms of interracial collaboration and black agency, or as the impulses of the "Bigger Thomas reaction" organized as political interventions. In *Native Son*, Jan Erlone initially attempts to introduce Bigger to the finer points of Communist policy by giving him "some pamphlets," but neither Bigger nor the reader ever read their contents. Instead, when Bigger forges a ransom note from the Communists to try to extort money from the Daltons, who haven't yet discovered Mary Dalton's body in their furnace, he includes "one of those signs, like the ones he had seen on the Communist pamphlets. He wondered how they were made. There was a hammer and a round kind of knife."[41] Bigger's use of the hammer and sickle sign thus doesn't signify any specific party line; rather, it ornaments one of the first manifestations, however here misguided, of Bigger's agency.

Similarly, Bigger's education by the Communist characters Jan and Boris Max does not instruct Bigger in party policy. Instead, they collaboratively chart the positive content and political potential of Bigger's subjectivity. Like Reva's friendship with Sue in "Bright and Morning Star," Jan's friendship with Bigger allows Bigger to transcend his instinctual suspicion of whites and begin to see white Communists as allies and interlocutors who can acknowledge his experiences *as* the experiences of a capable human subject rather than as mere products of oppression. After Max asks Bigger about his life, desires, and motivations, Bigger realizes that "he had talked of his own accord, prodded by excitement, by a curiosity about his own feelings." Jan and Max not only recognize Bigger as a subject rather than a villain or victim, but they also allow the reader to see Bigger's subjectivity as shaped by the same objectively revolutionary impulses that motivated Lenin. When Max gives his courtroom speech, he insists that African Americans like Bigger "[feel] the capacity to be, to live, to act, to pour out the spirit of their souls into concrete and objective form with a high fervor born of their racial characteristics," but that the nation gives them no channel for the expression of this positively defined, agential, and particularly black subjective desire.[42] Max suggests that collective black experience incorporates culturally and historically molded forms of wisdom and agency that can, if politically organized, propel history forward. Cathy Bergin thus argues that the Communists in *Native Son* validate a "particular model of black subjectivity," shaped in part by the period's "Communist discourses of black rage," that "threatens the boundaries of racist power structures." Communism in *Native Son* is, she writes, a "humanist and flexible discourse of radical recognition" attuned to the particularities of African American historical experience.[43]

Wright's achievement as a Marxist thinker and Communist writer, therefore, was to make both influences adumbrate a purposive and positive African American identity within a history marked by dislocation, alienation, and servitude. His break with the Communist Party was not a renunciation of that achievement. Michel Fabre explains that when Wright left the Communist movement in the mid-1940s, he wasn't renouncing the Marxist structure of his thought or his general commitment to revolutionary activism. Rather, he had come to feel that "the socialism practiced by the American Communist Party did not give enough attention to the fight against racism and the development of the individual" – both fundamental components of his Depression-era work.[44] Despite the caricatures of his 1930s leftism offered by critical evaluations, Wright's work of the period is shaped by the formal and theoretical utility of Marxism and Communism for advancing African American communal and subjective concerns.

Notes

1. James Baldwin, *Notes of a Native Son* (Boston: Beacon Press, 2012), 18–19.
2. Ralph Ellison, "The World and the Jug," in John Callahan, ed., *The Collected Essays of Ralph Ellison* (New York: Modern Library, 2003), 167.
3. Thomas Hill Schaub writes that postwar liberal critics "used discussion of the novel as a vehicle for their political and cultural values." Disillusioned with Communism and newly committed to American values, these critics aligned literary naturalism with totalitarian tendencies and instead valued ethical ambiguity, aesthetic experimentation, and the internal complexities of individual human experience. Lionel Trilling's *The Liberal Imagination* (1950) positioned Henry James as the sophisticated practitioner of the latter kind of fiction, and Theodore Dreiser as representative of the naïveté and formulaic simplicity of the former. This dichotomy, Michael Nowlin argues, elevated the postwar critical stock of Ellison and Baldwin at the expense of Wright's. See Thomas Hill Schaub, *American Fiction in the Cold War* (Madison: University of Wisconsin Press, 1991), 28; Michael Nowlin, "Ralph Ellison, James Baldwin, and the Liberal Imagination," *Arizona Quarterly* 60, no. 2 (2004): 118.

4. Richard Wright, "Richard Wright," in Richard H. Crossman, ed., *The God That Failed* (New York: Columbia University Press, 2001), 162.

5. Bill V. Mullen, *Popular Fronts: Chicago and African-American Cultural Politics, 1935–46* (Urbana: University of Illinois Press, 1999), 19–43.

6. Zora Neale Hurston, "Stories of Conflict," *The Saturday Review*, April 2, 1938, 32.

7. Richard King, for example, argues that for Wright, the "traditional black culture of the South was an inadequate vehicle for black progress in the United States" because it was historically eclipsed. See Richard H. King, *Race, Culture, and the Intellectuals: 1940–1970* (Washington, DC: Woodrow Wilson Center Press, 2004), 138.

8. William J. Maxwell, *New Negro, Old Left: African-American Writing and Communism between the Wars* (New York: Columbia University Press, 1999), 156–157.

9. Harold Cruse, *The Crisis of the Negro Intellectual: A Historical Analysis of the Failure of Black Leadership* (New York: New York Review of Books, 2005), 182, 188, 189.

10. Throughout this essay, "communism" refers to the post-class future Marxism positions as the endpoint of its materialist history. "Communism" and other capitalized variations refer to the actual institutions of the Communist movement in the mid-twentieth century, particularly the Communist Party of the United States.

11. Caroline Levine, *Forms: Whole, Rhythm, Hierarchy, Network* (Princeton: Princeton University Press, 2015), 6.

12. Henry Louis Gates Jr., *The Signifying Monkey: A Theory of African-American Literary Criticism* (New York: Oxford University Press, 1988), 131.

13. Hazel Rowley, *Richard Wright: The Life and Times* (New York: Henry Holt and Company, 2001), 74–80, 263–264, 291–295.

14. Brian Dolinar, *The Black Cultural Front: Black Writers and Artists of the Depression Generation* (Jackson: University Press of Mississippi, 2012), 3, 7–8.

15. Michel Fabre, *The Unfinished Quest of Richard Wright* (Urbana: University of Illinois Press, 1993), 102–151.

16. Lawrence P. Jackson, *The Indignant Generation: A Narrative History of African American Writers and Critics, 1934–1960* (Princeton: Princeton University Press, 2011), 60; Mark Naison, *Communists in Harlem during the Depression* (Urbana: University of Illinois Press, 1983), 210.

17. Margaret Walker, *Richard Wright: Daemonic Genius: A Portrait of the Man, a Critical Look at His Work* (New York: Amistad Press, 1988), 63, 73–74.

18. Richard Wright, *Black Boy (American Hunger): The Restored Text* (New York: Perennial Classics, 1998), 335.

19. Joseph Stalin, *Marxism and the National Question*, in *Marxism and the National Question: Selected Writings and Speeches* (New York: International Publishers, 1942), 23.

20. Ibid., 12, 17.

21. Ibid., 21.

22. Anthony Dawahare, *Nationalism, Marxism, and African American Literature between the Wars: A New Pandora's Box* (Jackson: University Press of Mississippi, 2003), 74.

23. Robin D.G. Kelley, *Freedom Dreams: The Black Radical Imagination* (Boston: Beacon Press, 2002), 50–51. See also Dawahare, *Nationalism, Marxism, and African American Literature between the Wars*, 89–91.

24. Maxwell, *New Negro, Old Left*, 162, 165.

25. Wright, *Twelve Million Black Voices* (New York: Basic Books, 2008), 26–27, 136, 147.

26. Wright, "Blueprint for Negro Writing," *New Challenge* 2 (Fall 1937): 55, 60, 55–56, 58, 57.

27. Wright, *Uncle Tom's Children* (New York: Perennial, 2004), 221.

28. Ibid., 229.

29. Ibid., 225.

30. Richard Wright, *Native Son: The Original 1940 Text* (New York: Perennial, 2003), 263.

31. Wright, *Uncle Tom's Children*, 253–254.

32. Gregory Meyerson, "Aunt Sue's Mistake: False Consciousness in Richard Wright's 'Bright and Morning Star,'" *Reconstruction* 8, no. 4 (2008): http://reconstruction.eserver.org/Issues/084/meyerson.shtml.

33. Wright, *Uncle Tom's Children*, 234, 233.

34. Ibid., 187, 191, 209.

35. Ibid., 164, 169.

36. Wright, "How 'Bigger' Was Born," in *Native Son: The Original 1940 Text* (New York: Perennial, 2003), xii, xiii, xi.

37. Ibid., xvii.

38. The proper attribution of this anecdote to Trotsky, rather than a pamphlet about Lenin and Gorky, has been generally overlooked. Richard Bucci's study guide is the only source I know of that tracks this misattribution. See Bucci, Richard Wright's *Native Son, MAXnotes* (Piscataway: Research & Education Association, 1996), 70–73.

39. Leon Trotsky, *Lenin* (New York: Blue Ribbon Books, 1925), 8.

40. As Bucci observes, in the wake of Trotsky's banishment from the Soviet Union in 1928, any "favorable reference" to his work by a Communist Party writer could entail unwanted scrutiny by the Soviet-aligned party. See Bucci, *Richard Wright's Native Son*, 72–73.

41. Richard Wright, *Native Son*, 79, 167.

42. Ibid., 333, 366. I explore Native Son's correlation of Communism and subjectivity at length in *Ragged Revolutionaries: The Lumpenproletariat and African American Marxism in Depression-Era Literature* (Amherst: University of Massachusetts Press, 2017).

43. Cathy Bergin, *"Bitter with the Past but Sweet with the Dream": Communism in the African American Imaginary* (Leiden: Brill, 2015), 91, 98–99, 109.

44. Michel Fabre, *Unfinished Quest*, 231.

4

ROBERT B. STEPTO

Rhythms of Race in Richard Wright's "Big Boy Leaves Home"

Richard Wright is one of the truly extraordinary African American writers of the mid-twentieth century, but one whose work is rarely thought to invoke modern American musical forms. In comparison to Langston Hughes, where's the blues in Wright's work? In comparison to Ralph Ellison, where's the Jazz?

In "Big Boy Leaves Home" (1936), which Wright appropriately described as a novella, Wright is quite attentive to music in his own heartfelt way. In particular, in writing about Big Boy somehow surviving a day full of shootings (in which two of his best friends die) and a night in which another friend, Bobo, is dismembered and burned, Wright composes what Ralph Ellison would memorably describe as Wright's "Negro blues."[1] In his essay, "Richard Wright's Blues" (1945), Ellison explains, "The Blues is an impulse to keep the painful details and episodes of a brutal experience alive in one's aching consciousness, to finger its jagged grain ... "(46). As readers of "Big Boy Leaves Home," we are beset by the "brutal experience" that is alive in Big Boy's "aching consciousness," which was something Wright could no doubt imagine because his own boyhood had been crammed with violence and catastrophe. So, where's the blues in Wright's work? It's not literally in the lyrics that are occasionally sung; it's in the nearly autobiographical moments when Wright creates Big Boy and presents (to quote Ellison again) a "chronicle of personal catastrophe expressed lyrically" (46).

While Negro blues permeates "Big Boy Leaves Home" in this most particular way, it is not the only American musical tradition present in the story. Big Boy and his brethren sing, chant, and shout black songs both sacred and profane, and indeed feel free to do so as long as they are momentarily young men roaming and enjoying nature's promise. White music also rings sharp notes in the story, beginning with lines from the Broadway hit, "Is It True What They Say About Dixie?"

Whatever Southern white fantasy world that show tune conveys is thoroughly obliterated when the burning of Bobo begins and the white song

74

repeatedly sung is instead a lynch song, "We'll hang ever nigger t a sour apple tree ..." (54) What we see here is Wright having a conversation with real American musical traditions from the *outside*, which had real meaning for real people in the South. Furthermore, Wright is creating music *inside* "Big Boy Leaves Home" itself by alternating prose forms and repeating key words and images in ways that form what I'm calling "race rhythms," as when words like "boy" and "Big Boy" appear and reappear and even seem to glare at each other.

In this chapter, I will discuss five songs (black and white) in "Big Boy Leaves Home," noting how each has its own racial rhythm and character. Then I will observe –and in that sense, listen to – the rhythms Wright creates with the prose changes and key word repetitions just described. In all, we see Wright, in his first published story, being responsible to his Negro self and to the "voiceless Negro boys" with whom he felt a deep kinship.

I

"Big Boy Leaves Home" begins with lyrics from "Is It True What They Say About Dixie?," a 1936 song written by Broadway legends Irving Caesar, Sammy Lerner, and Gerald Marks. It was a huge hit that year for Jimmy Dorsey and his orchestra, with Bob Eberle on vocal, the same year Richard Wright completed and published "Big Boy Leaves Home," and prefaced it with these lyrics from the Broadway song:

> *Is it true what they say about Dixie?*
> *Does the sun really shine all the time?*
> *Do sweet magnolias blossom at everybody's door?*
> *Do folks keep eating 'possum, till they can't eat no more?*
> *Is it true what they say about Swanee?*
> *Is a dream by that stream so sublime?*
> *Do they laugh, do they love, like they say in ev'ry song? ...*
> *If it's true, that's where I belong.* (16)

Beginning with this mythic fantasy about the South is a way of announcing that "Big Boy Leaves Home" is going to tell a very different story – a story that is about leaving, not belonging. Wright no doubt heard the repetition of "they" in this song and said to himself, "It all depends on who the 'they' is! Let me tell you about another 'they'!" The mention of "magnolias" is like-wise suggestive. He certainly knew that the magnolia is Mississippi's state flower, but he was hardly interested in extolling that. One great mischievous touch in the story is Wright making clear that Will drives a Magnolia Express

Company truck; it is a Magnolia truck that carts Big Boy away from the mob and the South. In this tale, that is why that magnolia is "sweet!"

Directly after "Is It True What They Say About Dixie," we "hear" Big Boy and the boys singing

Yo mama don wear no drawers ...

Clearly, the voice rose out of the woods, and died away. Like an echo another voice caught it up:

Ah seena when she pulled em off ...

Another, shrill, cracking, adolescent:

N she washed 'em in alcohol ...

Then a quartet of voices, blending in harmony, floated high above the tree tops:

N she hung 'em out in the hall ... (17)²

The song in itself introduces another "they," a "quartet" of adolescent boys playing hooky from school and having such a good time that they just might do something stupid, like frolic in Jim Harvey's swimming hole. Soon after, they hear a train's whistle, and they begin to "chant, pounding bare heels in the grass" (19):

> *Dis train boun fo Glory*
> *Dis train, Oh Hallelujah*
> *Dis train boun fo Glory*
> *Dis train, Oh Hallelujah*
> *Dis train boun fo Glory*
> *Ef yuh no need fer fret er worry*
> *Dis train, Oh Hallelujah*
> *Dis train ...* (19)

This song is as sacred as their first song was profane. It confirms that while the boys can be boys and be a bit naughty, they are also conversant with the lyrics and harmonies of their black spiritual community. The train bound for glory is a homecoming train, Heaven bound. Part of Wright's point is that the boys joyously sing of homecoming just moments into the day when three of them will be killed. And we might ask, do any of those boys reach home? Is Big Boy even remotely bound for glory when he leaves home in Will's truck?

As the boys approach Harvey's property, they talk about being hungry and soon chant a song about pie, meat, and bread that ends with these lines:

> *Ah wanna go t town*
> *Towns too far*
> *Ah wanna ketch a car*

> *Cars too fas*
> *Ah fall n break mah ass*
> *Ahll understand it better bye n bye ...* (22)

This is the song that brings them to the barbed-wire fence they have to climb over to get to Harvey's swimming hole. The danger of the situation and the whole question as to whether they understand what they are doing is pre-figured in the last lines of the chant. This is a key moment in the story when the song tells us something about the boys' circumstances and anticipates the violence that will beset them.

Just before the white mob captures Bobo, Big Boy hears their dogs and their voices. Then someone starts singing:

> "We'll hang ever nigger t a sour apple tree ... " (54)

The song seemingly enables the mob to grab Bobo and to rope and chain him. Right thereafter, female voices are heard ("Jack! Jack! Don leave me! Ah wanna see im!" [55]). When the mob song starts up again, the women sing as well and make the song "round and full"(55). The song is even more horrifying as it becomes melodious and in harmony with nature.

"We'll hang ever nigger t a sour apple tree ... " is a southern, neo-Confederate, Jim Crow revision of the lyric Boston Union Army soldiers added to "John Brown's Body" during the Civil War: "We'll hang Jeff Davis to a sour apple tree." John Stauffer and Benjamin Soskis also inform us that in the final weeks of the war, freedmen sang the John Brown song and included this verse: "We'll hang Jeff Davis to a sour apple tree/On Canaan's happy shore!"[3] What Wright knew about this song's history is unknown; perhaps hearing the Jim Crow version was a terrifying event in his Mississippi childhood. But in having the white mob here sing of hanging "ever nigger," Wright, the young black author, exposes such behavior and exerts authorial control of such events. Wright and Big Boy may live on if the lynch song is "mastered" in his pages.

Wright's structuring and shaping of "Big Boy Leaves Home" with the five songs just discussed is a remarkable feature of his storytelling. We begin with "Is It True What They Say About Dixie?" and end with a quite particular "they" singing "We'll hang ever nigger t a sour apple tree ... " The two songs bookend the novella and speak to each other as the two "white" songs in the story. In between, we find the three songs the "quartet" of black boys sing and chant. Each of their songs tells us something about the boys and their situation, and each presents a form of black creative folk expression. Even so, we cannot help but note that all this black creativity is barricaded between the Southern fantasy show tune from the North and the vicious lynch song from the South. That in itself proclaims what Wright has to say about what is true about Dixie and the state of the nation in the 1930s.

II

The prose changes in "Big Boy Leaves Home" involve abrupt shifts from a vernacular or folk English to standard English and back. Readers hear these as rhythmic shifts between black and white English, as in the confrontation at the swimming hole between the boys and Jim Harvey. But Wright is up to something more complicated and subtle: he's announcing and contending that he is a young, black, Southern-born writer who is conversant in both languages and who is at home in both languages.

Most often in "Big Boy Leaves Home," the prose changes are shifts from the spoken or sung to the written. The story begins in just that way. Here again are the first three lines:

> "YO MAMA don wear no drawers ..."
>> Clearly the voice rose out of the woods, and
> Died away. Like an echo another voice caught it up:
> Ah seena when she pulled em off ...

The back and forth of the two voices occurs five times. As Wright's line enjambment and italics emphasize, two voices are telling this story.

Big Boy's return home after Jim Harvey murders Lester and Buck, and Big Boy's retaliative killing of Harvey, is a huge turn in the story that is made all the more vivid by the prose changes. Big Boy's first moments home are described as follows:

> Panting, he stumbled through the doorway.
> "Lawd, Big Boy, whuts wrong wid yuh?"
> His mother stood gaping in the middle of the floor. Big Boy flopped wordlessly onto a stool, almost toppling over. Pots simmered on the stove. The kitchen smelled of food cooking.
> "Whuts the matter, Big Boy?"
> Mutely, he looked at her. Then he burst into tears. She came and felt the scratches on his face.
> "Whut happened t yuh, Big Boy? Somebody been botherin yuh?"
> "They after me, Ma! They after me ... "
> "Who!"
> "Ah ... Ah ... We ... "
> "Big Boy, whuts wrong wid yuh?"
> "He killed Lester n Buck," he muttered simply.   (35)

The passage begins in a standard English in part because Big Boy is physically home but not yet truly home. Nor is he fully in conversation with his mother. Note that when he finally begins to answer her questions, it takes him a moment to speak, as she does, in the vernacular of home. In this short passage, Big Boy's name appears no less than five times. While the repetition expresses his mother's anxiety, it also reminds us that the name is a term of endearment, part of the vernacular of home. Big Boy has come home to that as well.

Big Boy's brief time at home comprises Part III of the novella. In Part IV, after each family member gives him something to sustain him (notably, his mother wraps up some of the food mentioned already), he flees to one of the kilns he and his buddies built the summer before, hoping to hide safely there until he can climb aboard Will's Chicago-bound truck in the morning. He sings no songs, there is no one to talk to or with. But standard and vernacular prose shifts are still telling the story. Before Big Boy even reaches the kilns, he has these thoughts:

> He veered off the track and trotted over the crest of a hill, following Bullard'sRoad. His feet slipped and slid in the dust. He kept his eyes straight ahead, fearing every clump of shrubbery, every tree. He wished it were night. If he could only get to the kilns without meeting anyone. Suddenly a thought came to him like a blow. He recalled hearing the old folks tell tales of blood-hounds, and fear made him run slower. None of them had thought of that. Spose blood-houns wuz put on his trail? Lawd! Spose a whole pack of em, foamin n howlin, tore im t pieces? He went limp and his feet dragged. Yeah, thas whut they wuz gonna send after im, blood-houns! N then thered be no way fer im t dodge! Why hadn't Pa let im take tha shotgun? He stopped. He oughta go back n git tha shotgun. And then when the mob came he would take some with him. (46)

While some readers might question why the language of fear suddenly becomes a vernacular black English, Wright's point is that Big Boy is black and fears for his life because he is black and has killed a white man – while standing naked right in front of the white man's white woman. The words rushing into his head must indicate all that. This isn't just a dark moment for Big Boy – it is a black moment. Even more to the point, this is for Big Boy a blues moment, and true to the blues, what we "hear" is Big Boy's howling at us "'bout his Situation"

Note that Big Boy's howl brings him to wishing he had Pa's shotgun. If he had it, he'd for sure take down some of mob with him. This anticipates precisely how Silas deals with the white men coming on to him at the end of "Long Black Song" (1938), one of the three novellas appearing with "Big

Boy Leaves Home" in the original edition of *Uncle Tom's Children* (1938). We might say it also anticipates Wright's "Note on Jim Crow Blues" that prefaces Josh White's *Southern Exposure: An Album of Jim Crow Blues* (1940). In that note, Wright expressly praises the album for containing "the fighting blues." Big Boy's telling us what he'd do with Pa's shotgun is "fighting blues" indeed!

When the mob nears, Big Boy hears the white men talking to each other. This occasions prose shifts in which, at first, the vernacular English is white speech and the standard English is Wright's narrator describing Big Boy:

> He heard footsteps. Then voices came again, low and far away this time.
> "Seen anybody?"
> "Naw. Yuh?"
> "Naw."
> "Yuh reckon they got erway?"
> "Ah dunno. Its hard t tell."
> "Gawddam them sonofabitchin niggers!"
> "We oughta kill ever black bastard in this country!"
> "Waal, Jim got two of em, anyhow."
> "But Bertha said there wuz *fo!*"
> "Where in hell they hidin?"
> "She said one of em wuz named Big Boy, or something like tha." (52)

The white men are coming; they know his name. Big Boy hears them guffaw about driving his Ma and Pa out of their shack and burning it down. The next paragraph begins in the narrator's standard English but soon reaches for the vernacular of Big Boy's blues voice presented before:

> Big Boy eased to the edge and peeped. He saw a white man with a gun slung over his shoulder running down the slope. Wuz they gonna search the hill? Lawd, there wuz no way fer im t git erway now; he wuz caught! He shoulda knowed theyd git im here. (52)

As matters monstrously proceed and Bobo is found, mutilated, and burned, the shifts back and forth between the American languages of that dreadful moment convey the cacophony of the horror and violence. Wright has fully brought us to a point in the story where the shifts from vernacular to standard English are no longer just about the inner and shared lives of black folk. The shifts are not a rhythm of race communion; they are rhythms of race hate and race warfare. Much of what is significant here in terms of language is that both blacks and whites are presented in vernaculars. Wright may be suggesting that the races share something; after all, words like "erway" and "wuz" appear in both race vernaculars. But what they share is hardly about support or endearment. That the standard English voice is solely the narrator's voice – Wright's voice, we may say – reminds us of how important it was for Wright to declare his authorial control of this novella and of his own life story. Big Boy can leave home and maybe get to Chicago because Wright has already accomplished that.

III

"Big Boy Leaves Home" is full of word repetitions that create rhythms of race within the black community and certainly at key moments between the blacks and whites. Note, for example, the repetition of Big Boy's name when his friends fondly address him in their happiest moments and also, as observed before, the repeat of his name in his mother's wail of concern. Big Boy, Big Boy, Big Boy is a race rhythm, a black race rhythm, expressing endearment while notably challenging what white people mean when they call a black boy or man a boy. We see all of this in the repetitions marking the exchange between Big Boy and Jim Harvey at the swimming hole. After Big Boy strikes Harvey with the barrel of Harvey's gun, Bobo says to Big Boy,

> "C'mon, *Big Boy*, les go!"
> Breathing hard the white man got up and faced *Big Boy*. His lips were trembling, his neck and chin wet with blood. He spoke quietly.
> "Give me that gun, *boy*!"
> *Big Boy* leveled the rifle and backed away.
> The white man advanced.
> "*Boy*, I say give me that gun!"
> Bobo had the clothes in his arms.
> "Run, *Big Boy*, run!"
> The man came at *Big Boy*.
> "Ahll kill yuh; Ahll kill yuh!" said *Big Boy*.
> His fingers fumbled for the trigger. (32; italics added)

As the added italics help make clear, the repetition or exchange, if you will, between "Big Boy" and "boy" in itself embodies the raucous racial rhythm of the confrontation. Partly because of that, this is one of the moments when we first begin to wonder what Wright is fully suggesting in naming Big Boy "Big Boy." How big is he or will he be? How is he not the white man's boy but still a colored boy?

"Neck" is another word that repeats and resonates in each part of the story. Early on, notably after the boys have climbed over a barbed-wire fence, Buck, Lester, and Bobo decide to "get" Big Boy, and they grab him "about the neck, arms, and legs, bearing him to the ground." (23) Soon, Big Boy manages to get Bobo by the neck and twist his head to the ground. Bobo is in real pain and yells, Hes got aholda mah neck!" (23) This sets off a rhythm:

> Big Boy squeezed Bobo's neck ... yuh hurtin mah neck! ... Tell them others a git t hell offa me or Ahma break your neck ... hhes ggot mmah nneck ... N Ahma break it too ... hhhes got mah nnneck ... Grab his neck, Bobo ... Ah cant ... To save Bobo, Lester and Buck got up and ran to a safe distance. Big Boy released Bobo, who staggered to his feet, slobbering and trying to stretch a crick out of his neck ... Shucks, nigger, yuh almos broke mah neck ... yuh almos broke mah neck, man.   (24–25)

Grabbing Bobo by the neck and torturing him is how Big Boy gets free from everybody on top of him. Of course, this ominously portends the end of the story when Big Boy gets free of the white mob arguably because the mob has Bobo "by the neck" and is preoccupied with lynching him. Cavorting and wrestling by day has become mayhem and murder by night. It all began when the four boys crossed the fence and got closer to Harvey's swimming hole.

When the white mob arrives near the kiln where Big Boy is hiding, Big Boy is in the midst of exclaiming another "fighting blues" about wiping out "the whole bunch." Notably, he declares that he will get them one by one by the neck.

> He caught one by the neck and choked him long and hard, choked him till his tongue and eyes popped out ... When he had finished with one, another came. He choked him too.   (51).

What ends these wild thoughts is the first sound of the white men yelling for each other. With that intrusion, Big Boy, we are told, "snatched his fingers from the white man's neck and looked over the fields" (51).

The white mob does not get Big Boy, by the neck or otherwise, most likely because Big Boy is able to stay in hiding after he kills the one bloodhound that discovers him in the kiln. How does he kill him? By the neck.

> Instinctively, he fumbled for the throat as he felt the dog twisting between his knees. The dog snarled, long and low, as though gathering strength. Big Boy's hands traveled swiftly along the dog's back, groping for the throat. He felt the dognails again and saw green eyes, but his fingers had found the throat.   (58–59)

Right as the dog dies, Big Boy hears "shouts and footsteps above him going past." The mob would have heard the scuffle if it had come by only moments before. Big Boy saves his own neck by strangling the dog.

The repetition of neck "events" is a major thread in "Big Boy Leaves Home," with the episodes involving Big Boy and Bobo, and Big Boy and the dog obviously bookending the novella. As the story develops from black boys cavorting, sometimes hurtfully, to white mob scenes, the repetition becomes a rhythm of race. Race is even a factor in Big Boy's killing the dog: we know why the dog was let loose to search for Big Boy and why Big Boy must close his fingers and push "his full weight on the dog's throat." In having real and imagined violence expressed in these specific terms, Wright is creating an environment of race violence in which the actual murders of Bobo, Lester, and Buck are not aberrations but part of a whole.

Many trains are mentioned over the course of "Big Boy Leaves Home," whenever Big Boy and the other boys hear the sound of them. The sounds are rhythmic with the chug-chug of the engines, the clatter of the cars, and the wails of the whistles. These are, in Ellison's words, "blues-tempered echoes of trains." They are race rhythms in the specific sense that the sounds invariably prompt the boys to dream and yearn for freedom, for heading North. In the first pages of the story, they hear a train:

> In the distance a train whistled mournfully.
> "There goes number fo!"
> "Hittin on all six!"
> "Highballin it down the line!"
> "Boun fer up Noth, Lawd, boun fer up Noth"
> They began to chant, pounding bare heels in the grass.   (19)

Immediately, they sing "*Dis train boun fo Glory*," a freedom and home-coming song that is as sacred as it secular. Notably, each boy exclaims in this passage; they form a choir. They know exactly which train it is – the number four – and where it is headed. At least three more trains in the story are named by number, this being a strong indication of how certain specific trains run through the thoughts and yearnings of Wright's burdened black folk.

The next train coming through is the number seven. It occasions the last conversation the boys have before the white woman, Bertha, suddenly appears at the edge of the swimming hole:

> Far away a train whistled.
> "There goes number seven!"

"Headin fer up Noth!"

"Blazin it down the line!

"Lawd, Ahm goin Noth some day."

"Me too, man."

"They say colored folks up Noth is got ekual rights."

They grew pensive. A black winged butterfly hovered at the water's edge.
A bee droned. From somewhere came the sweet scent of honeysuckles. Dimly
they could hear sparrows twittering in the woods. They rolled from side to side,
letting sunshine dry their skins and warm their blood. They plucked blades of
grass and chewed them.   (28–29)

The passage begins much as the first one did with the train identified
and its speed and destination exclaimed. But when the boys actually
speak of themselves going North and having rights, they grow pensive
and enter the last idyllic, pastoral moment of their lives. Bees ...
sparrows ... sunshine: Wright is unsparing in letting us know that all
this simple beauty in life is near for the boys just before Buck and Lester
are shot dead.

There are no trains in the section of the story where Big Boy runs home
after killing Jim Harvey. But when he must choose between running
through streets or down the railroad tracks, he decides on the tracks.
That in itself expresses a hope that, one way or another, the railroad will
help him get away, and indeed, he does reach home. After everyone agrees
that Big Boy should hide in the kilns and wait for Will's northbound truck
in the morning – it having been argued that the white folks would surely be
looking for him near the trains – he departs: "He made for the railroad,
running straight toward the sunset" (45). Hopefully, the track path that got
him home safely will take him back into the hills. He does make it to the
kilns in the hills, but not before he hears a train (notably a train without
a name or number) approaching: "As he turned from the road across
a plowed field he heard the train roaring at his heels. He ran faster, gripped
in terror" (46).

The kiln hole offers refuge and Big Boy soon hears a train he knows
about, the number nine. He hears it "far away and mournful" (48). While
the number four train led the boys to sing of being bound for glory, the
number nine's music for the moment is the blues. In the midst of all that, Big
Boy recalls his friends and the summer days when they dug the kilns and
built fires and made steam whistles and fantasized about Big Boy being
Casey Jones speeding on the Southern Pacific, while "Bobo had number two
on the Santa Fe, Buck wuz on the Illinoy Central. Lester the Nickel Plate"
(48). Four boys, four points of the migration compass, four trains to get

them elsewhere. Train number nine gives a blues rhythm to his loneliness; Big Boy remembers each friend and begins to worry about Bobo. Where is he?

The last train Big Boy hears is the number twelve. Its bells and whistles are part of the cacophony of sounds pressing in on him and flattening him. Much of the noise is mob noise: dog noise (one dog has found the snake Big Boy killed) and white folk noise, in particular, someone singing: "*We'll hang ever nigger t a sour apple tree* ... " (54). Right thereafter, someone in the mob screams, "WE GOT IM! WE GOT IM!" (54). And yes, with the help of the dogs, they got Bobo. Clearly, Big Boy hears the wail of a train he knows (the number twelve!) and knows that it is not going to save him – or Bobo. The black spirituals and even the blues "sung" before by the trains are now overwhelmed by the white mob song, sung once again after Bobo is caught. Wright tells us that the white women now lend their voices to "*We'll hang ever nigger t a sour apple tree* ... " Yet another part of the race rhythm of this white song is that a hound dog's howl floats "full into the night" – "At each lull of the song" (55).

The trains rumbling through "Big Boy Leaves Home" help tell and "race" the rhythm of the story. Most particularly, the trains Big Boy and others know at least by number – 4, 7, 9, 12 – both give them hope and tell them that they should not hope for too much. In 1936, Richard Wright is clearly building into this story a commentary on the black migration North.

IV

Lyrics from the show tune "Is It True What They Say About Dixie?" preface "Big Boy Leaves Home" but never are sung in the course of the story. What we "hear" instead are the songs Big Boy and his brethren sing and cling to in order to survive the horrors of Southern life. Each song declares what is really true about Dixie. Even the white lynch song is a truer portrayal of Southern realities than what the show tune claims to present.

Wright is aware that people live with rhythms as well as words. That is a key reason why he confronts the show tune with "real" songs of the South, as opposed to mounting a tart reply in his own voice. This is also why he is attentive to the prose shifts and word repetitions that present the rhythms of endearment and confrontation that are so basic to black life. In all, what is true about Dixie for Wright is a "blues tempered" tale full of "raucous racial rhythm."

Notes

1. Ralph Ellison, "Richard Wright's Blues," in William L. Andrews and Douglas Taylor, eds., Richard *Wright's* Black Boy {American Hunger): A Casebook (Oxford: Oxford University Press, 2003), 46. All future page references in my chapter are to this publication of Ellison's essay. Other very helpful essays on Wright and the Blues include John McCluskey, "Two Steppin': Richard Wright's Encounter with Blue-Jazz," *American Literature*, 55:3, 1983; William Ferris, "Richard Wright and the Blues," *Mississippi Quarterly*, 61:4, Fall 2008; and Shawn Salvant, "*Black Boy's* Blues Refrain," *Southern Quarterly*, 46:2, Winter 2009.
2. Richard Wright, "Big Boy Leaves Home," the first novella in Wright's *Uncle Tom's Children* (1940) (New York: Harper Perennial Edition, 1991); all page references in this chapter are to this Harper Perennial Edition.
3. John Stauffer and Benjamin Soskis, *The Battle Hymn of the Republic: A Biography of the Song That Marches On* (Oxford: Oxford University Press, 2013), 13.

5

GENE ANDREW JARRETT

Sincere Art and Honest Science

Richard Wright and the Chicago School of Sociology

Early on in Richard Wright's career, when he was a member of the Communist John Reed Club, one of the first sociologists he'd ever met was Louis Wirth, a professor in the Department of Sociology at the University of Chicago and an expert on the urban enclaves of Jewish communities. How Wright came to learn of the professor was serendipitous. In January 1933, he had visited a welfare office on Chicago's South Side and there met a caseworker appointed by the Cook County Public Welfare Office. She was Mary Wirth, Louis Wirth's wife. As she built a rapport with Wright, she ascertained his interests in psychology and sociology, and recommended that he find time to meet her husband – which he eventually did a few months later. Wright dropped by Wirth's department office and knocked. Horace R. Cayton Jr., one of only a handful of African Americans studying sociology at the doctoral level at the university, opened the door.[1] Cayton recalled the encounter vividly:

> I opened the door and there was a short brown-skinned Negro, and I said, "Hello. What do you want?" He looked like an undergraduate, so I was perhaps condescending in a polite fashion, and, of course, he was also colored. He said, "My name is Richard Wright. Mrs. Wirth made an appointment for me to see Dr. Wirth." That made me a little more respectful. I told him to come in. "Mrs. Wirth said that her husband might help me. I want to be a writer."[2]

When Wright finally came to meet with Wirth during this occasion, the professor supplied the fledgling writer a sociology reading list. Reading the slew of books was equivalent to a crash course; it was a belated undergraduate introduction of the twenty-four-year-old man to the academic discipline of sociology. Moreover, Wright and Cayton grew to be colleagues, if not close friends. Over the next decade, Wright increasingly devoted his energies to scouring sociological scholarship; adopted this information to sharpen the societal analysis of his bestselling fiction like *Uncle Tom's*

Children (1938) and *Native Son* (1940); and socialized more often with the academic community of Chicago's urban sociologists.

When the opportunity thus presented itself for Wright to pen an introduction to *Black Metropolis: A Study of Negro Life in a Northern City*, scheduled for release in 1945 and edited by Cayton and St. Clair Drake, a fellow African American doctoral classmate, he seized it. Several months before the book's release – the afternoon of January 1, 1945 – Wright invited Drake and Cayton, along with Lawrence Reddick, an acquaintance who was also curator at Harlem's Schomburg Center, to spend time with him in his Brooklyn apartment. As on other occasions, the meeting turned into a serious intellectual debate; this time, it revolved around the sociological accuracy of studies of African American life.[3] Over the course of their discussion, Wright sensed Drake's skepticism that literature and sociology could hold value in relation to one another. Drake resisted Wright's countervailing opinion that these two different modes of intellectual activity could be combined to great effect.[4] Drake's reservations were not seeking to "protect" "scientific integrity," as Wright would later put it. Rather, they were amounting to a "fierce rejection of art, of intuitive perception, of emotion," to illuminate the "hard real world."[5]

The introduction Wright would eventually write for *Black Metropolis* squarely addresses this issue. "Chicago is the city from which the most incisive and radical Negro thought has come," he writes. "There is an open and raw beauty about that city that seems either to kill or endow one with the spirit of life."[6] In this tradition of progressive intellectual work, he imagined wedding the statistics of empirical research with the putative truths forged through fiction. Literature and sociology could work together to paint a remarkably nuanced and vivid picture of the urban conditions and challenges faced by African Americans. Wright's ability to apply sociology to literature was demonstrated in the stance he took during his prior debate with Drake: "I found that sincere art and honest science were not far apart, that each could enrich the other."[7]

This sort of collaboration – or rather, the perception of this collaboration – resonated in studies of American literature a decade after Wright synthesized his ideas in *Black Metropolis*. According to David J. Alworth, the notion that "imaginative literature" could "participate in the production of sociological knowledge" crystallized in mid-twentieth-century scholarship on the literature of the American Renaissance. Alworth maintains, for instance, that Erving Goffman's *The Presentation of Self in Everyday Life* (1956) "makes the compelling case for reading imaginative literature as a means of apprehending sociality" or "as a repository of sociological data." In this sense, Herman Melville was an author who assumed "empirical authority" and turned out to be "as systematic as a sociologist." This characterization is consistent with historical evidence that a "porous boundary" existed between literature and sociology before the latter emerged as an academic discipline at the turn of the twentieth century, most notably with the establishment of the American Sociological Society in 1905.[8]

Wright belonged to a long line of American writers who incorporated sociological analysis or rhetoric in their literary writings. As a critic, he likewise embraced a viewpoint that appreciated literature's sociological potential. Nonetheless, the limitations of sociology as he knew it during his time, especially with respect to this discipline's academic treatment of African American experiences, concerned him. Of course, his expression was not as pointed as the cynicism of Ralph Ellison. Mainly through nonfiction, Ellison took to task sociologists and social critics who perpetuated pathological myths about African Americans. Ranging from his now-legendary 1944 review of Gunnar Myrdal's *An American Dilemma: The Negro Problem and Modern Democracy* to his incisive 1954 essay "Change the Joke and Slip the Yoke," Ellison condemned how much Robert Ezra Park, the preeminent faculty member in the Department of Sociology at the University of Chicago from 1913 to 1933, and Irving Howe, a famous social critic, had oversimplified African American "personalities" in their writings. Ironically, as evidenced in his 1945 review of Wright's *Black Boy*, Ellison did not entirely oppose the sociological speculation that a cohesive black folk consciousness had been deteriorating amid modern industrialization. Still, he trenchantly exposed the "inherent racial bias" of this school of thought.[9]

A preponderance of literary evidence shows that, over the course of his career, Wright tended to admire urban sociology, in contrast to the degree that Ellison – and, later, African American sociologists Albert Murray and Joyce A. Ladner – were willing to impugn the field's reputation. Wright's concerns, I argue, had less to do with the consequences of racial condescension among white sociologists than with the lack of articulation between what he had called "sincere art" and "honest science." Reminiscent of the early concerns of W. E. B. Du Bois and the African American sociologists of his generation, Wright's desire for a faithfully multidimensional image of African American life sought to balance an artistic sensibility, which could capture the nuances of human experience, with empirical acumen, which could attend to potential thematic patterns discernible within raw data. Wright's introduction to *Black Metropolis* offers a critique of sociological studies of African American experiences, albeit subtly, with an eye toward limning that interdisciplinary balance. In general, he sought to explain what literature could bring to sociology. But he did so against the specific backdrop of explaining how and why this social science, especially through its institutional rearing in Chicago, had informed his own creative writing, as recent scholars have widely noted.[10]

The Sociology of Race

The story of sociology's rise as an academic discipline of the social sciences, especially where issues of race are concerned, tends to refer to the era between World War I and World War II, when Park made his mark. Yet, as Aldon D. Morris has asserted, "the first school of scientific sociology in the United States" began not in Chicago but "by a black professor located in a historically black university in the South" – namely, Du Bois.[11] Du Bois developed (especially through his learning at the University of Berlin from 1892 to 1894) a specialty in quantitative and empirical methodologies, and sought to apply them in a decidedly scientific approach to human behavior and racial inequality.

Toward this end, Du Bois set the tone for a loosely defined "school" orbiting around Atlanta University. African American social scientists and thinkers such as Du Bois, his mentor Alexander Crummell, and Atlanta University alumnus and trustee Richard Wright Sr. (no relation to Richard Wright, the writer) embarked in the late 1890s on trying to prove three main ideas: first, that race was socially constructed; second, that the social environment precipitated or exacerbated racial inequality; and, third, that sociology must avoid the scientific racism in which African Americans were assumed to be biologically and culturally inferior. Du Bois's 1899 publication of *The Philadelphia Negro* was the emblem of this school. The book served as the first major empirical sociology of African American urban life in its investigation of Philadelphia's Seventh Ward through surveys, archival research, and ethnographic statistics. "The Du Bois-Atlanta school of sociology," Morris concludes, "was guided by a scholarly principle: sociological and economic factors were hypothesized to be the main causes of racial inequality that relegated black people to the bottom of the social order."[12]

A couple of decades after Du Bois affirmed his methodological approach to sociology and race, Park emerged with his own. The record shows that Park was quite aware of Du Bois's scholarship. Park had referred to Du Bois's exceptional *The Souls of Black Folk* (1903) in his coursework on race at the University of Chicago. He had cited *Philadelphia Negro* and Du Bois's 1920 literary work *Darkwater: Voices from Within the Veil* in the bibliography of his own *Introduction to the Science of Sociology* (1921), co-edited with Ernest Burgess.[13] He was also likely quite conscious of Du Bois's political leadership. In 1905, Park agreed to serve as the director of public relations at Tuskegee Institute and as a ghostwriter for its founder, Booker T.

Washington, whose notorious belief in the manual training of the Negro put him at odds with Du Bois's aspirational creed of higher education and the Talented Tenth. The so-called Wizard of Tuskegee and the Chicago sociologist shared a redemptive vision of slavery as a peculiar institution that supposedly civilized African Americans and ameliorated relations between slaveholders and slaves. They also shared the idea that subsequent eras of cultural and political modernity did not necessarily liberate African Americans from "the workings of a predetermined race relations cycle that changed gradually and was not amenable to human intervention."[14] What the Du Bois-Atlanta school and Park concluded about African Americans diverged in remarkable ways.

Park sought to guide sociology toward a comprehensive approach to the evolution and function of human society. He tried to examine "urban experience, migration, social institutions and neighborhoods, race and questions of cultural assimilation, ghettoes, and delinquency."[15] A focal topic was the challenge faced by ethnic or racial minorities in assimilating to or defying the norms of American society. African Americans constituted a subject for the methodological development of sociology as an academic field during its "growing orientation toward realism, empiricism, and hard facts."[16] Mainstream sociological studies of the city at the time attempted to produce rich data sets about African American social, cultural, political, and economic conditions. Chicago was where Park and his departmental colleagues investigated the social and empirical dynamics of race.

In the first half of the twentieth century, the close association that existed between cities and African American lives justified the sociological approach to Chicago. Quite marked was the link of race to the city: tens of thousands of African Americans were living below ground, in cellars. Yet the link was also symbolic. Stereotypical images of African Americans automatically conjured up the city, and not infrequently vice versa, in the public imagination. The racially unequal distribution of economic resources led to "racialized spatial trends," suggesting that "more undervalued black labor poured" into cities, where these citizens believed they could seek "an escape from Jim Crow and a chance to participate in the militarized industrialism of the 1940s." The city's systemic segregation by race indicated "both a special exercise of power and a means for urban capitalism's expansion in a post-crisis atmosphere."[17] African Americans were polarized into neighborhoods where the quality of housing conditions was poor, even as the high costs of these rentals were supposed to signify higher standards of living. In addition to these unfair circumstances, the systemic denial of African Americans' access to adequate labor opportunities and protective unions sucked them into an unending whirlpool of poverty and malaise.

Between circa 1915, when the Great Migration from the South was in full swing, to 1927, the year of Wright's own arrival in Chicago, the African American population had swelled from 40,000 to more than twice that amount. In the meantime, it became "the most residentially segregated city in the nation."[18] The Great Depression also afflicted Chicago, especially the South Side, as devastatingly as it had any of the other urban areas with massive African American populations and unemployment (such as Harlem). Chicago provided the ideal source of stories and data to drive creative and scientific thought alike. The city gave rise to what would informally be called the Chicago School of Sociology.

The school was not without its flaws. As suggested before in the comparison of Du Bois to Park, the school consistently featured "a hierarchical relationship that defined white sociologists as cultivated experts and authorities in relation to black subjects."[19] Racial condescension characterized the Chicago School's perspective on Chicago itself, demonstrating that it would perpetuate the racism that Du Bois tried to mitigate in his own work decades earlier. Park attributed the cultural traits of people of African descent to their innate qualities, which distinguished them irreconcilably from those of Anglo-European descent. He could not "conceive two races farther removed from each other in temperament and tradition than the Anglo-Saxon and the Negro." The record shows, according to Aldon D. Morris, that the racial Darwinism of Park's depiction of African Americans, regardless of intention, ingrained sociological narratives of alienation: African Americans became a population without a "cultural homeland," their African heritage utterly deleted by slavery, their "dark complexion" and "tropical temperament" the main traces of their difference.[20]

Wright's Introduction to Chicago Sociology

After Wright's initial meeting in the spring of 1933 with Louis Wirth and Cayton, he proceeded to build his network of sociologists while slowly learning methodological nuances. When he was elected secretary of the John Reed Club in September, he inaugurated a lecture program that met on Saturdays. Wright had invited Wirth, along with other "progressive social scientists as guest lecturers," to the club.[21] The other guests included Burgess, a faculty member in the Department of Sociology, to lecture on the nature of art in Russia, in addition to Melville Herskovits, an anthropologist educated at the University of Chicago and Columbia University who went on to become a professor at Northwestern University. Wright gravitated to the individuals, institutions, and literature of the Chicago region; he was deeply aware of, yet invigorated by, the exclusivity of Chicago-area social scientists. Note that the deficiency of Wright's own academic credentials didn't at all diminish Cayton's admiration for him. In Cayton's mind, Wright was one "poetic little Negro" with whom he desired to spend more time after their first meeting in Wirth's office. By April 1934, the "evident thoroughness with which Wright had done the reading" of the sociology books "astounded" Wirth.[22]

Over the next decade, Wright continued to immerse himself in the academic community of sociologists. In April 1941, thanks to Cayton's arrangement, Wright met one of this community's most consequential leaders in Robert E. Park. Wright remembered the encounter:

> I recall clearly my walking into the living room of the community center that evening and being greeted by an infirm white haired old gentleman who insisted, with the aid of his cane, (he was southerner) upon rising from his chair to greet me, I urged him to remain seated, "I rise in your honor, sir," Dr. Park said.[23]

Then, the elder man exclaimed, "How in hell did you happen?"[24] A legendary and retired white sociologist, aged seventy-seven, was hailing the authority of a thirty-three-year-old African American writer on the rise. But the irony of this supplication emerged precisely from the former's insuppressible disbelief that the latter could defy the odds of professional failure. (In fairness, Wright's probable marveling at his own survival reciprocated Park's disbelief.) Fellow, mostly white, sociologists would have likewise prognosticated misery for an African American who had migrated, like Wright, from the Black Belt to Chicago in search of a better world.

During the same month of his visit with Park, Wright was still meeting with Wirth to learn more about advancements in sociology. Now closer to the aptitude of a University of Chicago sociology major (albeit seven years after receiving that very first sociology reading list), Wright was interpreting texts by E. Franklin Frazier on the African American family; Charles M. Raussig on the historical relation of rum to slavery and rebellion; Elizabeth Lawson on African American history; Cayton and George S. Mitchell on race, labor, and unions; Arthur F. Raper and Ira de A. Reid on sharecroppers; and Wirth himself on urban life.[25] Against the backdrop of this education, Wright continued to enter and engage the Chicago School's alternately casual and formal inner circles. The occasions ranged from regularly talking shop with Cayton and Drake to being invited by Cayton to address the Institute of Psychoanalysis in April 1943, only shortly afterward to embark on a southward journey to fulfill a speaking engagement, arranged by

Johnson, at Fisk University.[26] Wright was a non-academic yet an academic insider at the same time.

Wright's Literary Move to Sociology

Wright enjoyed rather anointed status when the opportunity arrived at the turn of 1944 for him to contribute to *Black Metropolis*. By then he had begun to infuse his creative writing with what he had learned in sociology, which had made a deep impression on him in his articulation of "neurotic behavior and crime to environment."[27] Over the course of his life, his interests in racial and criminal sociology combined with those in criminal psychopathology, which inspired him to investigate Freudian psychoanalysis.[28] Wright identi- fied Park, Wirth, and Robert Redfield as the scholars who pioneered the link of sociology to anthropology and psychology for generations of faculty and students at the University of Chicago. Their "scientific volumes," as Wright once put it, were "brilliantly characterized by insight and feeling."[29] Other studies, marked by "slavish devotion to figures, charts, graphs, and sterile scientific techniques," failed to illustrate the many dimensions of urban life he personally experienced as one of the millions of African Americans who journeyed from the South to the North during and in the decade after World War I.[30]

Rigorous scholarship and harrowing experience framed Wright's own comprehension of sociology. Unsurprisingly, they shaped his published fic- tion. *Native Son* follows a young black man caught in a terrifying dilemma after he panics and kills a white woman. Set in 1930s Chicago, the novel details the destitution and desperation experienced by many urban African Americans. Given that Mary Dalton for a time was supposed to represent an objective observer of Bigger Thomas, her language imports the sociological discourse that had typified the academic literature that Wright had been reading the previous decade. In a way, her figuration works to indict the limitations of this discourse. As Cynthia H. Tolentino points out, "Mary uses the language and tropes of social science closely associated with her school – the University of Chicago, the institutional base for the Chicago School sociologists and a key site for the knowledge production of race during the early-twentieth century." Tolentino goes on to say, therefore, that given Mary's role "as part of the University of Chicago social science discourse" and "how ineffectual her interpretation of race is when seen from Bigger's perspective," it is arguably the case that "Bigger's murder of Mary also represents an attempt to kill off that discourse." The testimonies buttressing the case against Bigger in the novel's concluding court scene depict the racist prejudices of academic sociology. A "psychiatric attaché of the police department" and a psychology professor, for example, comment on the latent criminality and sexuality they suspect Bigger has embodied for a long time.[31] *Native Son* may be regarded as the closest Wright came to echoing the cynical perceptions of urban sociology's purported discrimination against African Americans.

In addition to Wright's published fiction, one could also look at his unpublished work, such as his draft of a lengthy manuscript, close to 1,000 pages, titled *Black Hope*. In such "crude condition" that, incidentally, he would never publish it as a refined novel during his lifetime, *Black Hope* centered on the lives of a young, light-skinned, racially mixed woman who graduated from the University of Chicago and became a social worker, and a brown-skinned man (not unlike Wright himself) who rejected a post-office job to become a writer. Wright uses the struggle of the couple to stay together as a case study for more than just the controversial attribution of social and economic success to the lightness of skin color. This storyline also captures the actual and philosophical challenges that African Americans encountered in their quest for happiness and the meaning of life. One could explore the relationship between Wright's abandonment of the manuscript and his experimental focus on the exploitation of female domestic workers.[32]

Five years after the release of *Native Son*, Wright published "The Man Who Lived Underground" (1945), which also bore sociological imprints. While hiding in the city sewers, accused of a crime he did not commit, an African American man realizes the inherent guilt of humanity. When he tries to confess, the police inform him that the criminal has already been apprehended. He then takes the police on a seemingly mad journey underground, and he is shot and left for dead. In the most abstract sense, the novella recalls *Native Son* in depicting the attempted survival of an African American man alleged to have murdered a white woman. His navigations beneath the city streets allegorize the struggle of African Americans as they negotiated the incriminating hazards of urban life. Ellison would adopt the urban vision that Wright provides in "The Man Who Lived Underground" in the marvelous novel he published seven years later, *Invisible Man* (1952). Despite the ultimate and well-documented differences between how Wright and Ellison convey the tragedies of African American life, both shared an understanding that "segregation and subterranean living" in the "Fordist city" symbolized two sides of the same proverbial coin for African Americans.[33]

The various depictions of urban life in Wright's published fiction invite comparisons to what Thomas Heise has called "the context of Chicago's black-belt slum that had come under such intensive sociological scrutiny in the recent past."[34] At the same time, these scenes indicate the visceral potency that Wright's memories of his own traumatic life brought to his literary imagination. In his introduction to *Black Metropolis*, he insists that the images he rendered so vividly in literature were as convincing as sociological data:

> If, in reading my novel, *Native Son*, you doubted the reality of Bigger Thomas, then examine the delinquency rates cited in this book [*Black Metropolis*]; if, in reading my autobiography, *Black Boy*, you doubted the picture of family life shown there, then study the figures on family disorganization given here.[35]

By the time Wright wrote this introduction, he had been on an intellectual journey that, as he puts it in *Black Boy*, had once "veered from fiction proper into the field of psychology and sociology."[36] The intellectual growth depicted in *Black Boy* correlates almost perfectly with the kinship of writing and sociology in his actual life. His memory of his own inspired autodidacticism, his romanticized avidity for the Western literary canon (including Gertrude Stein, Stephen Crane, and Fyodor Dostoevsky), recalls with equal fervor how he consumed scientific literature. Both genres of writing provided him the insight and language he needed to explain the peculiarities of his own behavior and of his family's habits. "I studied tables of figures relating population density to insanity," he remembers in *Black Boy*, "relating housing to disease, relating school and recreational opportunities to crime, relating various forms of neurotic behavior to environment, relating racial insecurities to the conflicts between whites and blacks."[37] Readings of sociological data went hand in hand with literary art during the formative years of his intellectual life.

Wright on the Art and Science of Sociology

In his introduction to *Black Metropolis*, Wright seeks to theorize the relation of sociology to literature, while noting the academic shadow that Park's legacy had cast over the book. Park's recent death, on February 7, 1944, compelled Cayton and Drake to dedicate the book to his memory. They recognized his influence not only over their alma mater, but also over Tuskegee University and Fisk University, two historically black institutions where Park, in their eyes, proved that he was truly an "American scholar and friend of the Negro people," a pioneer who proved, in the context of "civilized man," one could see that "[u]rban life and culture are more varied, subtle and complicated, but the fundamental motives are in both instances the same."[38] The full apparatus of sociological study – the investigative teams, the generating and curating of data, the funding from the Work Projects Administration – was brought to bear on analyzing the entire community of Chicago's South Side. One could say that Cayton and Drake were facing a methodological conundrum: they were producing their study not only because of Park's influence but also despite it. Like Wright – and, farther back, Du Bois – they sought to dissuade sociologists and lay readers alike from reducing African American personalities to frightening racial pathologies. But the critique that Park merited was counterbalanced by an unavoidable respect that the pioneer instilled.

Divided into four parts, *Black Metropolis* is unquestionably comprehensive in research and outlook. First, it explores the phenomena of the Great Migration and subsequent racial conflicts in the first half of the twentieth century. Next, it explains the myths and realities of the racial "color line" to guide an analysis of African Americans in the Chicago "ghetto," and the consequences they faced in breaking the "job ceiling" and leveraging labor unions and political representation. Third, it documents the powerful role the press and the church played in African American urban communities; the development of African American–owned businesses; and the prospects of style, sexuality, and family across socioeconomic strata – that is, from the "upper" to the "lower" classes. Finally, it lays the groundwork for future conceptual and methodological approaches to African American urban life. The book is replete with tabulations of the Chicago populace according to race, ethnicity, place of birth, employment, the press, businesses, education, churches, and social clubs. Geographical maps as well as statistical charts and graphs are located throughout. Cayton and Drake produced nothing less than a remarkable study designed to advance sociological thought for generations to come.

For Wright, *Black Metropolis* was noteworthy for its "research and scientific achievement," for deploying facts to dispel the fictions of African American life in Chicago.[39] His fascination with the book had as much to do with the object of study as with its critical methods and methodology. In his introduction, Wright unites himself with Drake and Cayton by claiming that they were transplanted in Chicago; that they, as fellow African Americans, "feel personally identified with the material in this book." Therefore, he believed that they, like himself, could only succumb to the uncontrollable environmental forces that gripped African Americans down the socioeconomic ladder. "And there in that great iron city," Wright reflects, "that impersonal, mechanical city, amid the steam, the smoke, the snowy winds, the blistering suns; there in that self-conscious city, that city so deadly dramatic and stimulating, we caught whispers of the meanings that life could have, and we were pushed and pounded by facts too big for us."[40] Despite his voracious reading of both sociology and literature, the environment was uninterpretable; he "did not know what [his] story was" until he "stumbled upon science" and "discovered some of the meanings of the environment that battered and taunted [him]."⁴¹ Certainly, the word "science" was his euphemism for urban sociology. Yet it was also an allusion to a very specific brand of the academic discipline that, he knew, could come only out of the Chicago School of Sociology.

Unmistakably, Wright gestures to the Department of Sociology at the University of Chicago, particularly the "huge mountain of facts piled up" there. Wright goes on to say that the data informed his nonfiction, including the 1941 photo-documentary *Twelve Million Black Voices*, about the modern roots and history of the oppression of African Americans in the United States, and his autobiography *Black Boy*. The information also enhanced his fiction, namely, the 1938 short story collection *Uncle Tom's Cabin*, which features six novellas depicting especially how violence can be deployed to terrorize and coerce, if not kill, African Americans, and the novel *Native Son*. Together, these literary works showed how sociology inspired his vision of the "forces that molded the urban Negro's body and soul."⁴² Against all odds, Wright's own success as a creative writer turned out serendipitously to justify his admission to a university where he was "never a student" and "it [was] doubtful if [he] could have passed the entrance examination."⁴³ Yet he was intelligent and creative enough to realize that art and science had to go hand in hand in any compelling portrait of Chicago.

Wright's introduction to *Black Metropolis* marks his attempt at publishing an academic essay. The results are mixed. A handful of pages into it, he admits what he intends to do: "Hence, at the risk of sounding didactic, I will try to show that there is a problem facing us, a bigger one than even that of the Negro, a problem of which the Negro problem is a small but a highly symbolically important part."⁴⁴ The feared didacticism does come across in the essay, resonating insofar as any academic publication, with its usual intellectual identification with particular traditions of education and scholarship, by definition aims to instruct scholarly readers and serve as a touchstone for future teachers. But the pedagogic tone is the least of the essay's problems. At its core, the essay seeks to prove that the so-called Negro Problem was a byproduct, a phase, of the universal "hunger" shared by all people in the Western world: they have struggled against "the life of industrialization which has pounded their lives to meaninglessness, which has reduced them to appendages to machines," while rejecting "the shaky, class foundations of their society."⁴⁵

Structurally concentric, Wright's introduction is an essay within an essay. The internal essay is a self-interested study of the longstanding class and capitalist foundations of the Negro Problem, an emphasis predicted by his well-publicized Communist leanings and whose emphasis on "hunger" helps set up the title of *American Hunger*, the autobiography published posthumously in 1977 that was intended to be a continuous second volume to *Black Boy*. The enveloping essay seeks to praise *Black Metropolis* as "working within the compass of the most normal ideas and moral imperatives of the West" that Wright had just illustrated.[46] What the reader encounters, then, is an introduction by turns erudite in its allusions to a vast range of historical events and canonical authors and thinkers of Western literature.[47] But it is also a disjointed and inefficient mode of argumentation that turns his history of Western "hunger" from feudalism to the present into a speculative detour, and his recurring allusions to it into distractions. More compelling are Wright's claims that *Black Metropolis* provides a sociological paradigm for showing "how *any* human beings [*sic*] can become mangled, how *any* personalities [*sic*] can become distorted when men are caught in the psychological trap of being emotionally committed to the living of a life of freedom which denied them."[48] Put in these terms, the book has the philosophical potential to broaden the emphasis on African Americans in Chicago to address the experiences of racial oppression in an American urban environment.

Black Metropolis does not beg readers to recognize the fact of the Negro Problem. "The hour is too late to argue if there *is* a Negro problem or not," Wright insists. Rather, the book supports and extends Myrdal's *An American Dilemma*, which details the brutal obstacles faced by African Americans, but which also espouses hope for progress based on faith in a national creed of individualism and democracy.[49] Where *Black Metropolis* differs is in its call for action. Mindful of the "ultimate aspirations of the Negro," the book seeks to apprise many readers of "the facts of urban Negro life," of how these facts attest to the common ambition for a better life, regardless of race.[50] But it goes further by encouraging readers to apply Cayton and Drake's book in their own special ways: whether in individual reflection and activity, in the agitation expected of an organized group, or in a "political party."

Expansive and relevant, Wright's imagination of the practical outcomes affirms that *Black Metropolis* could deepen our insight to the sociological contexts of African American communities. The contexts include "peculiar personality formations," "the highest rates of hyper-tension," the interregional "differential" of "psychological damage" across the African diaspora, and the incrimination of urban African American populations. These hypotheses may serve to inscribe again and regard as essential the same sort of racial myths that a thoroughgoing sociological study of race, region, and class like *Black Metropolis* has been seeking to dismantle. At one point, Wright sounds like an exoticist when he says that "the full weight of the

Western mind has yet to be brought to bear upon this forgotten jungle of black life that lies just across the street or next door or around the corner from white Americans."[51] But the point is well taken that the sociology as it is depicted in *Black Metropolis* "is not a volume of mere facts" but a way forward "for other workers, black and white, to paint in the shadings, the background, to make three-dimensional the personalities caught in this Sargasso of racial subjugation."[52] Sincere art and honest science could be the tools with which these "workers" could conduct this illustration, in a collective pursuit of racial progress and equality.

Notes

1. The other African Americans studying sociology were St. Clair Drake, of Cayton's own generation; and the scholars Charles S. Johnson and E. Franklin Frazier, of the previous one.
2. Cayton and Wright, quoted in Toru Kiuchi and Yoshinobu Hakutani, *Richard Wright: A Documented Chronology, 1908–1960* (Jefferson: McFarland & Company, 2014), 41.
3. The scene is depicted in Hazel Rowley, *Richard Wright: The Life and Times* (Chicago: University of Chicago Press, 2001), 299–300.
4. Ironically, Drake's influence, Robert E. Park, had been on record a couple of decades earlier legitimizing the racial sociology and psychology of African American literature. In 1923, Park published an essay seeking to document the reflection of "Negro race consciousness" in "race literature," which ideally "could advance notions of scientific objectivity." Park's rendition of the racial psyche in African American literature of the turn of the century, including Paul Laurence Dunbar's, is oversimplified and stereotypical. For more, see Cynthia H. Tolentino, *America's Experts: Race and the Fictions of Sociology* (Minneapolis: University of Minnesota Press, 2009), 1–3.
5. Quoted in Rowley, *Richard Wright*, 300.
6. Richard Wright, "Introduction" in *Black Metropolis: A Study of Negro Life in a Northern City*, edited by St. Clair Drake and Horace R. Cayton (New York: Harcourt, Brace and Co., 1945), xvii.
7. Ibid., xviii.
8. David J. Alworth, "Melville in the Asylum: Literature, Sociology, Reading," *American Literary History* 26.2 (2014): 234–261; quotations on 235, 238, 246.
9. Kenneth W. Warren, *So Black and Blue: Ralph Ellison and the Occasion of Criticism* (Chicago: University of Chicago Press, 2003), 84. For more information about Ellison's critique of sociology and the social sciences, see chapters three, "Of Southern Strategies," and four, "To Move without Moving: Reconstructing the Fictions of Sociology."
10. These scholars include Christopher Douglas, Thomas Heise, Hazel Rowley, and Cynthia Tolentino.
11. Aldon D. Morris, *The Scholar Denied: W.E.B. Du Bois and the Birth of Modern Sociology* (Oakland: University of California Press, 2015), 1.
12. Ibid., 58.

13. Ibid., 137–138.
14. Ibid., 128.
15. Christopher Douglas, "Richard Wright, Robert Park, and the Literature of Sociology" in *A Genealogy of Literary Multiculturalism* (Ithaca: Cornell University Press, 2009), 68.
16. Ibid., 69.
17. Thomas Heise, "The Black Underground: Urban Riots, the Black Underclass, and the Work of Richard Wright and Ralph Ellison, 1940s–1950s," in *Urban Underworlds: A Geography of Twentieth-Century American Literature and Culture* (New Brunswick: Rutgers University Press, 2011), 131.
18. Rowley, Richard Wright, 53.
19. Tolentino, America's Experts, 2.
20. Park, quoted in Morris, The Scholar Denied, 119, 121.
21. Douglas, "Richard Wright, Robert Park, and the Literature of Sociology," 67.
22. Qtd. in Rowley, *Richard Wright*, 81, 82.
23. Wright, quoted in Kiuchi and Hakutani, *Richard Wright*, 121.
24. Qtd. in Rowley, *Richard Wright*, 250.
25. Kiuchi and Hakutani, *Richard Wright*, 121.
26. Rowley, *Richard Wright*, 277–280.
27. Ibid., 95.
28. Ibid., 278.
29. These "scientific volumes" include Robert E. Park and Ernest W. Burgess's *The City: Suggestions for Investigation of Human Behavior in the Urban Environment* (1925), Robert Redfield's *Tepotzlan: A Mexican Village* (1930), and Louis Wirth's *The Ghetto* (1928), along with Everett V. Stonequist's *The Marginal Man: A Study in Personality and Culture Conflict*(1937), Frederick M. Thrasher's *The Gang: A Study of 1,313 Gangs in Chicago* (1927), and Harvey Zorbaugh's *The Gold Coast and the Slum: A Sociological Study of Chicago's Near North* Side (1929).
30. Wright, "Introduction," xix.
31. Tolentino, *America's Experts*, 26–27.
32. For more information on Wright's career-long writing of this novel, see Rowley, *Richard Wright*, 188–189, 277, 281, 296, 302.
33. Heise, "The Black Underground," 141, 142.
34. Ibid., 141.
35. Wright, "Introduction," xx.
36. Qtd. in Douglas, "Richard Wright, Robert Park, and the Literature of Sociology," 76.
37. Wright, *Black Boy (American Hunger): A Record of Childhood and Youth* (New York: HarperPerennial, 1993), 327.
38. St. Clair Drake and Horace R. Cayton, *Black Metropolis: A Study of Negro Life in a Northern City* (New York: Harcourt, Brace and Co., 1945), v.
39. Wright, "Introduction," xviii.
40. Ibid.
41. Ibid.
42. Ibid.
43. Ibid.
44. Ibid., xxi.

45. Ibid., xxiii–xxv.
46. Ibid., xxv.
47. The general contours of Wright's history of Western hunger include discussions of feudalism, Jim Crow, industrial and technological modernity, World War II, Hitler, and fascism. For more, see Wright, "Introduction," xx–xxiv.
48. Wright, "Introduction," xxvi.
49. Ibid., xxix.
50. Ibid., xxx.
51. Ibid., xxxi.
52. Ibid., xxix, xxxii.

6

KATHRYN S. ROBERTS

Outside Joke

Humorlessness and Masculinity in Richard Wright

This essay considers Richard Wright's humorless approach to the subject of masculinity – and specifically black masculinity – in America. By humorless, I do not refer to the author's personality – Wright was in fact warm, mild-mannered, and often funny in person[1] – nor do I imply any stylistic failing. Such has been a trap in Wright criticism since at least the midcentury. When James Baldwin declared *Native Son* "protest literature," he caricatured the older novelist as forever "locked together in a deadly, timeless battle" with his nemesis Harriet Beecher Stowe, "the one uttering merciless exhortations, the other shouting curses."[2] In a similar vein, J. Saunders Redding insisted Wright lacked "the ironic cast of mind and heart . . . he took all men and the world as he took himself: with grim seriousness."[3] But these critiques fail to capture the centrality, purpose, and flexibility of humorlessness as a stylistic mode, one that developed over the course of Wright's career. Humorlessness becomes a tool for exposing the American myths that make any representation of black men in fiction a high stakes enterprise.

I approach humor and humorlessness as complex formal features, rather than merely tonal properties, of fictional texts. Humor is a mode of indirection. It thrives on incongruity, reversal, and substitution: sacred and profane smashed together, the high brought low, aggression discharged as laughter. Humorlessness, then, might be defined as a ruthlessly direct approach, a steady look at things as they are, a seriousness that refuses to turn away from the unbearable. Wright's poem "Between the World and Me" is in this sense a tutorial on humorlessness. It evokes the experience of seeing – and then, suddenly, being – a black male body in a culture of violent white supremacy.

> And one morning while in the woods I stumbled suddenly upon the thing,
> Stumbled upon it in a grassy clearing guarded by scaly oaks and elms.
>   And the sooty details of the scene rose, thrusting themselves between the world and me . . . [4]

The "thing" is the remains of a lynching, "a design of white bones slumbering forgottenly upon a cushion of ashes," "a charred stump of a sapling pointing a blunt finger accusingly at the sky."[5] The speaker inventories the evidence of the crime – "butt-ends of cigars and cigarettes," "a whore's lipstick," "a pair of trousers stiff with black blood" – until his own eyes reach the "eye sockets of the stony skull ... "[6] Suddenly the poet is "the thing," experiencing the "bubbling hot tar" and the "baptism of gasoline" on his own flesh.[7] It is an aggressive and unflinching poem, not easily forgotten once read. It forces the reader to acknowledge the mutilated body as a speaking self rather than an inert object. And it has lived on, notably, as the title and epigraph of Ta-Nehisi Coates's 2015 epistolary memoir, which asks the Wrightian question "How do I live free in this black body?"[8]

The phrase "between the world and me" captures the bidirectional drama of vision and blindness that structures both stereotypical representations of black men in America and the experience of being black.[9] Between the gaze of the white world and a black man is the screen of stereotype, which Jeffery Leak helpfully specifies as "myths of inferiority, sexual prowess, criminality, cultural depravity, and homosexual emasculation."[10] Between the poet and the world is the knowledge of white terror against black bodies, producing a paralyzing self-consciousness. This is something like W. E. B. Du Bois's classic description of "double consciousness," but Wright tends to be more interested in the disabling features of this double vision than in its power to confer critical distance. Part of Wright's project was to represent the violent encounters between people caught in this two-way dynamic of racial fear and hatred. But his work also reaches toward forms of intimacy that bridge or escape this impasse of mutual distortion.

We might expect humor to function as a social bridge: dissolving interpersonal tension, enabling bonding. In *Black Culture and Black Consciousness*, Lawrence Levine characterizes black folk humor as both an escape valve for aggression and a mode of communal expression. He cites Henri Bergson's claim that "laughter always implies a kind of secret freemasonry, or even complicity, with other laughers, real or imaginary."[11] But Wright's approach to humor tends to add a layer of critical distance, to throw a screen of reflective analysis over everyday social relations. A scene from his first novel, written in 1934 and published posthumously as *Lawd Today!*, captures this strategy of distancing around scenes of black male laughter, and sets the pattern for further elaboration of this technique in later works. This modernist novel, which riffs on James Joyce and John Dos Passos, among others, follows a postal worker named Jake through a single day. The scene in question concludes a card game among four friends:

Bob laughed uproariously. It was a very peculiar laugh, beginning noiselessly, a sharp expulsion of breath coming from the diaphragm; an expulsion that traveled slowly upwards, holding those who heard it in suspense, and finally cracking in a loud guffaw which terminated in something resembling a pig's squeal.

. . .

Jake and Bob laughed so long that Al and Slim began laughing. And when Jake and Bob saw that they had made their opponents laugh at their *own* defeat, they laughed harder. Presently, they stopped laughing at the joke Jake had made, and began laughing because they had laughed. They paused for breath, and then they laughed at how they had laughed; and because they had laughed at how they had laughed, they laughed and laughed and laughed. Suddenly Slim's laugh turned into a violent cough.[12]

The passage begins in the style of naturalism, describing the laughing body in mechanical and animal terms, proceeds through Gertrude Stein–inspired repetition that renders the word "laugh" alien or meaningless, and concludes with melodramatic irony as the laugh turns into an ominous, consumptive cough. This experiment in style creates a sharp division between reader and represented scene. Anatomical description, repetition, and irony collaborate to ensure that reader cannot participate in the laughing freemasonry of the card game.

This is one among many scenes of black male communal laughter in Wright's fiction. The story "Big Boy Leaves Home" from *Uncle Tom's Children* (1938) begins, "Laughing easily, four black boys came out of the woods into cleared pasture."[13] The 1952 novel *The Outsider* opens with an adult recapitulation of this scene: "four masculine figures mov[ing] slowly forward shoulder to shoulder" down a snowy street on Chicago's South Side, "their gruff voices explod[ing] in jokes, laughter, and shouts."[14] Wright's humorlessness does not consist in a total avoidance of the comic. It is instead an active engagement with the elements of humor – whether representations of men laughing, comically exaggerated symbolism, or more complex formal irony – that studiously denies the reader the escape valve of laughter. What is the meaning, for Wright, of this persistent association between black men and circumscribed humor? The answer to this question evolves along with Wright's thinking about race, masculinity, and community, and the fictional techniques he developed in relation to these themes.

The strange laughter scene of *Lawd, Today!* is fairly innocuous (despite the incongruous intrusion of Slim's cough). No white characters appear in the chapter, and few in the book as a whole, which focuses on an ordinary day in the life of its lower-middle class black characters. And yet, it is as if a screen of prose stands between the represented scene and the reader's experience of it, protecting it from a potentially stereotyping gaze. This protection of black laughter is polemical, and consistent with Wright's criticism of other black writers. In a 1937 review of Zora Neale Hurston's novel *Their Eyes Were Watching God*, Wright accused her of continuing "*voluntarily* [...] the tradition which was *forced* upon the Negro in the theater, that is, the minstrel technique that makes the 'white folks' laugh. Her characters eat and laugh and cry and work and kill; they swing like a pendulum eternally in that safe and narrow orbit in which America likes to see the Negro live: between laughter and tears."[15] The humorlessness of the scene in *Lawd, Today!* is a function of Wright's desire to represent black laughter and community as a feature of ordinary life without falling into the too-easy stereotype of minstrelsy.

In *Lawd, Today!*, Wright protects black male laughter from a distorting gaze. In "Big Boy Leaves Home," his approach is precisely the opposite: Wright exaggerates the sexual imagery of racist stereotyping, calling attention to the "screen" between the world and black male subjects. The story begins in an all-black world, and the sexual imagery contributes to a feeling of Edenic innocence in the scene. The laughing adolescents emerge from the woods amid a bouquet of genital symbolism: "They walked lollingly in bare feet, beating tangled vines and bushes with long sticks."[16] The thematic importance of this sexual imagery becomes clear as the story approaches its climax. The first part of the story is charged with homoerotic intimacy and a polymorphous sexuality. The boys walk toward the mythical swimming hole, "laugh[ing] easily" (this is repeated a page later) and playing the Dozens: "*Yo Mama don wear no drawers* ... "[17] They lie in the grass, enjoying the feeling of being alive in nature and away from adult (and white) eyes.

> They fell silent, smiling, drooping the lids of their eyes softly against the sunlight.
> "Man, don the groun feel warm?"
> "Jus like bed."
> "Jeeesus, Ah could stay here ferever."
> "Me too."
> "Ah kin feel tha ol sun goin all thu me."
> "Feels like mah bones is warm."[18]

The boys test out various modes of being together, some indirectly sexual, all fully sensual. They sing about Mama's underwear, savor side-by-side the soft ground and warm sun, share fantasies of "hot peach cobbler swimmin in juice,"[19] and play-fight: "Big Boy grunted, picked up his stick, pulled to his feet, and stumbled off. [...] He ran, caught up with them, leaped upon their backs, bearing them to the ground."[20] Big Boy dares the others to take him on, and schools them in the ways of hand-to-hand combat: "When a ganga guys jump on yuh, all yuh gotta do is jus put the heat on one of them n make im tell the others t let up, see?"[21]

Between the vernacular realism of the dialogue and the symbolic charge of the imagery, Wright crafts a scene that calls to mind Barry Jenkins's 2016 film *Moonlight*, which Hilton Als pronounced "achingly alive" in its portrayal of black queerness. One of the film's early scenes echoes the intimacy and innocence of Wright's story. Confident, easy-going Kevin tries to show shy, awkward Chiron (nicknamed "Little") how to avoid getting picked on by the other boys: "See, you just gotta show them niggas you ain't soft."[22] In an undated draft of the shooting script, Jenkins's blocking captures the feeling Wright rendered in the opening scene of "Big Boy Leaves Home":

> This is anthropology, anatomical vignettes, the struggle of these two boys isolated to the simple, incomplete movements of partially glimpsed bodies.
>
> These are children. Sexuality is absent in these images and yet, the hints of something sensual, fleeting in its appearances; Kevin's cheek wedged close to Little's neck, blades of grass sticking to their skin.
>
> The boys on the ground, turning and rolling and laughing, huffing through exhausted breaths. Slowly, their voices going mute, the only sound the movement of their bodies against each other, against the grass. Physical exhaustion. The boys lie flat.
>
> Beat.
>
> Both Little and Kevin on their backs, looking skyward, chests heaving from the exertion.[23]

Jenkins's reference to "anthropology" is apt. In both Wright's story and the film, adolescent masculinity is isolated in this moment of potentiality, where sensual enjoyment can be shared without sex, and grappling between bodies results in pleasurable exhaustion. Big Boy and his friends laugh, sing, fight, fart, eat, bathe in the sun, and jump "black and naked" into swimming holes.[24] These scenes are all the more extraordinary and poignant for being mundane, given the context: 1920s Mississippi, 1980s Miami. Both narrator and camera linger on these tender moments precisely because deadly violence waits around the corner. In Wright's story, the white communal orgy of lynching looms, while the "New Jim Crow" of incarceration hangs over *Moonlight*. Humorlessness is a flexible mode, one that can look steadily at both intimacy and violence.

If these were different kinds of stories, we might read in these scenes the innocent homoeroticism that Leslie Fiedler found at the center of classic nineteenth-century American literature: a typically American "nostalgia for the infantile," continuous with the classic boys' books that "proffer chaste male love as the ultimate emotional experience."[25] But Wright's subject is not "petticoat tyranny"; rather, it is the tyranny of racism, and the violence that invades everyday life. Amid the droning of bees and butterflies, the boys glimpse a form that signals their doom.

> "Oh!"
> They looked up, their lips parting.
> "Oh!"
> A white woman, poised on the edge of the opposite embankment, stood directly in front of them, her hat in her hand and her hair lit by the sun.[26]

Jim, the companion to this ironically beatific figure, shoots Lester and Buck without a second thought. After a struggle, Big Boy manages to shoot Jim with his own gun. Anticipating arguments made by feminist critic Eve Sedgwick, Wright suggests here that masculinity is a racially charged contest between men. Predictably, Big Boy's phallic besting of the white man summons the lynch mob for a spectacular performance of black castration. The story ends with disturbing echoes of the Edenic beginning: Big Boy hides out in a hole, watching as Bobo is lynched by a singing mob. He wrestles with and strangles a dog that finds his hiding spot, a deadly replay of his playful fight with Bobo. Finally, Big Boy escapes toward the North in the truck of a family friend. This formal symmetry enhances the story's grim irony, underlining the contrast between the placid innocence of the beginning and the brutal ending.

In "Big Boy Leaves Home," as in *Lawd, Today!*, Wright fences off scenes of laughter and community with a stylistic screen. The boys in his story are surrounded by sexually symbolic imagery. Even their nicknames – Buck, Big Boy – evoke clichés about black male sexual prowess. To understand Wright's strategy here, it helps to return to *Moonlight*. As Als points out, one way Jenkins undoes our expectations about black masculinity is to eliminate the white gaze. There is not a single white person among the named characters, a structural feature that helps Jenkins avoid the clichéd images of black men that dominate the media: sexual abuse, prison initiations, gun violence, encounters with police. The camera work is often first personal, placing the viewer next to or behind Chiron and Juan, his adoptive father figure, as if we were participants in the scene. Wright's approach is nearly the inverse. Rather than a self-governing black community, he paints a black world through the lens of white racist paranoia. The result is a form of symbolic realism, calling attention to the stereotypes that govern black–white encounters.

This strategy – exaggerating the stereotypes of black masculinity for the purpose of critique – is familiar to us from poststructuralist theory. Judith Butler and Henry Lewis Gates Jr., among others, have described the critical uses of parodic repetition in queer and African American cultural practice. Wright continues this parodic exaggeration of stereotype in *The Outsider*, the novel he completed from Paris in 1952. The protagonist Cross Damon, in spite of his intellect, learning, and desire for autonomy, seems condemned to fulfill every negative stereotype of black masculinity. He rejects the bourgeois roles of husband, father, and provider, as well as the less conventional position of communist intellectual. While he fantasizes about escape into romantic love, he succeeds only in becoming a criminal, fugitive, and victim of a politically motivated assassination.

It is tempting to read *The Outsider* as a continuation of the purported deterministic naturalism of *Native Son*, an indictment of a machine-like racist society that turns even the most intelligent black men into criminals and victims. Moreover, Baldwin's criticism of *Native Son* would seem on the surface to be even truer of *The Outsider*. Baldwin accused Wright of "cut[ting] away" the "relationship that Negroes bear to one another, that depth of involvement and unspoken recognition of shared experience which creates a way of life."[27] But as the essays in this volume make clear, Wright never fully embraced the determinism of naturalism in *Native Son*, and *The Outsider* deploys humorlessness to create a structure far more complex than that which naturalism affords. In the later novel, humorlessness shifts from being a property of narration – as in *Lawd, Today!* and *Uncle Tom's Children* – to a character trait of the protagonist. Wright's critique in this novel points in two directions at once: both outside at a culture where white supremacy, patriarchy, and heteronormativity cripple human personality, and inside at the figure of the black male intellectual, whose calculating aloofness thwarts his own impulse to connect.

J. Saunders Redding wrote in a 1953 review of *The Outsider* that Cross Damon "becomes an idea, an abstraction, an evilly tormented apotheosis of soul-stuff and mind-stuff that has no true relation to the concrete circumstances the author invents for him."[28] In Book One, Cross is plagued by what his friend Joe jokingly calls the "four A's. *Alcohol. Abortions. Automobiles. And alimony.*"[29] His single mother has him locked in an Oedipal-religious vice of obligation and guilt; his wife Gladys refuses to grant a divorce; and his girlfriend Dot has entrapped him with her pregnancy, her age (she lied that she was legal), and her willingness to drag the other two women into the fray. Cross's interactions with other black people are sadistic: he beats his wife

Gladys with cold calculation, kills Joe in a desperate act of self-protection, and refuses to acknowledge his own sons.

Cross is all too aware of the ways others see him, and deft at manipulating their expectations for his own gain. Mae Henderson reads the novel as a drama in which Cross performs a series of roles, thus reflecting the instability of his racial identity.[30] In this reading, performance is the only path to freedom. Once Cross "kills" his old self and flees Chicago for New York – an act difficult not to read as an allegory for Wright's own trajectory – Cross embraces the idea that identity is a creative act, the power to "make [one's] own world" from scratch.[31] Cross is a confidence man who can spot vulnerability and desire in other people. This power allows him to alienate his wife's affections by gaslighting her: he beats her, then denies having done so, insisting she is crazy. It also allows him to manipulate white people by employing the clichéd modes of black minstrelsy. As part of his flight from his old life, Cross adopts the identity of a dead man named Lionel Lane. When he goes to City Hall to obtain Lane's birth certificate, Cross "call[s] upon his knowledge of white and black race relations" and resolves to "act convincingly the role of a subservient Negro" for the clerks.[32] The minstrel performance that follows is ironized through juxtaposition with Cross's inner monologue.

> "He told me to come up here and get the paper."
> The clerk blinked and looked annoyed. "*What?*" the clerk demanded.
> "The paper, Mister. My boss told me to come and get it."
> "What kind of paper are you talking about, boy?"
> "The one that say I was born," Cross told him as though he, in his ignorance, had to teach this white man what to do.
> The clerk smiled, then laughed: "Maybe you weren't born, boy. Are you *sure* you were?
> Cross batted his eyes stupidly. He saw that he was making this poorly paid clerk happy; his pretense of dumbness made the clerk feel superior, white.[33]

Wright imbues his protagonist with an ethnographer's or critical theorist's objectivity about the psychological, economic, and social motivations of racism. "In his role of an ignorant, frightened Negro," reasons Cross, "each white man ... would leap to supply him with a background and an identity."[34] Cross's temporary self-emasculation allows him to secure the new identity of Lionel Lane, a man vertiginously free of familial attachment or social obligation.

It is one thing to recognize – and deploy to one's advantage – the screen of stereotype between oneself and the world of white bureaucracy. It is quite another to find oneself trapped behind that screen even in more intimate relations. Cross's romance with Eva Blount founders because Cross cannot bridge the stereotypes that separate him from even the most sympathetic white people. Eva, who like Cross is caught against her will in a communist scheme, meets Cross with a desire to connect. But like the city hall clerks, Eva is quick to supply him with an identity, this time a set of romantic, primitivist assumptions about black people. When Cross admires her paintings, Eva expresses surprise that "a colored person would like nonobjective art. Your people are so realistic and drenched in life, the world . . . Colored people are so robustly healthy."[35] Desperate for a companion in her suffering, Eva sees Cross as a fellow victim of the Party's machinations. While Cross falls in love with Eva, he fears that she loves him for his "Negritude . . . the least important thing in his life."[36] Eva's ideas about Cross are so fixed that even when he confesses his murderous rampage to her, she assumes his words are the ravings of a traumatized mind and pities him without believing him, unable to reconcile the idea of Cross's healthy innocence with these heinous acts. When finally forced to confront the reality of Cross's crimes, Eva jumps out a window rather than adjust her ideas about her lover.

From the deconstructed minstrel scene in the post office, to Eva's primitivist assumptions about Cross's "health" and authenticity, Wright employs dramatic irony and interior monologue for the purpose of dark humor. Cross regards the invention of Lionel Lane as his creative act, but no one in the scene, and almost no one in the novel, recognizes it as a performance. Here the reader is "let in" on the joke of Cross's manipulative prowess, while the other characters remain outside. But the "joke" is not on the racist social world alone; rather, Wright's critique also points back toward his protagonist, and ultimately, toward himself.

Cross's dilemma with Eva raises the question of authenticity: if identity is fundamentally relational, in the sense that we are doomed to inhabit the masks that others project upon us, then does it make sense to think of an actor behind the role, a "self" behind the play of stereotype? Cross's thoughts about Eva's paintings suggest that expressive art is the location of an authentic self.

> He had the illusion, while studying them, of standing somehow at the center of Eva's ego and being captured by the private, subjective world that was hers, a world that was frightening in the stark quality of its aloneness; and he knew that it was out of a sense of aloneness that these bold, brutal images, nameless and timeless, had come with the force of compulsions.[37]

Cross yearns for contact with Eva's ego and feels a sense of kinship with her "aloneness" and "bold, brutal" forms. There is something decidedly self-reflexive about Cross's meditation on art here. Are we to assume that *The*

Outsider places us at the center of Richard Wright's ego? Or, as the passage also suggests, is this merely an "illusion" created by a talented artistic deceiver? There is plenty of evidence to support the former interpretation, and many critics have taken it up. "Cross, the leading character, is, of course, the spokesman for Wright himself," wrote one critic, while another called Cross "a dramatic projection of the Novelist Wright."[38] Cross is not the only spokesman for Wright in the novel. Others have noticed that Ely Houston, the district attorney who investigates Cross's crimes, espouses theories Wright aired elsewhere in his writings.[39] In both "Tradition and Industrialization" and "The Literature of the Negro in the United States," lectures given in the early 1950s, Wright offered sweeping accounts of modern history, focusing on the trajectory of societies from feudalism to industrialism, belief to atheism. In the latter speech, Wright argued for the exemplary status of African American experience in modern history, a conceit that Ely Houston repeats in Book Two. There are even direct linguistic echoes. Wright wrote that "The history of the Negro in America is the history of America written in vivid and bloody terms; it is the history of Western Man writ small,"[40] while Houston says of the criminal who kills without compunction, "He is the Twentieth Century writ small."[41] These insertions beg the question of whether *The Outsider* is not only humorless, but insufficiently fictional, a mere mouthpiece for Wright's own views. And yet, it is through the techniques of fiction – character, point of view, dramatic irony – that Wright launches his most searching critique his own intellectualized masculinity.

Wright repeatedly juxtaposes the hyperbolically analytical diction of Cross's free indirect discourse with the frank vernacular speech of other characters. These moments provide occasional glimpses at Cross from the outside. When Cross enters the train's dining car in Book Two, for example, Wright locks us into Cross's alienation through highly subjective imagery. The other passengers are "serried white faces floating above the tables," which Cross reads as signs to be deciphered for lurking suspicion. At the same time, he searches for connection, wondering if those faces contain the seeds of "relationship to still the howling loneliness of his heart."[42] Though Cross desires and reflects on intimacy, he doesn't seem to know what to do with it when offered. When the black waiter Bob Hunter winks at him, Cross labels the gesture a "racially fraternal greeting" and dissects its motive as a "situationally defensive solidarity that possessed no validity save that occasioned by the latent pressure of white hostility."[43] The clinical language of Cross's thoughts is thrown into relief by the waiter's banter: "Be with you in a sec. I'm the only waiter in this car. My pal took sick and got off in Cleveland. So I got my hands full of white shit."[44] This crosscutting underlines Cross's alienation from the people around him, but also relieves the reader from the stifling "closeness" of Cross's point-of-view. To put it another way: it is Cross, not Wright, who is humorless here. The moments of vernacular humor in the novel are like a wink from sly author to careful reader, a moment of knowing connection over the shoulder of the book's overbearing protagonist. While in *Lawd Today!*, humorlessness protects black communal laughter from a white gaze, here humorlessness has expanded to allow reader and narrator a common vantage point.

In *The Outsider*, laughter is not a shorthand for black community – however imperiled – but rather a marker of Cross's alienation from that community. When he first meets Bob Hunter's wife Sarah, we get a rare glimpse of Cross from the outside: "Sarah cupped her right palm under Cross's chin, cradling it gently. Then a wild roar of laughter spilled out of her; she bent double, unable to control herself."[45] When she manages to speak, Sarah explains that Cross has "the *sweetest* face I ever saw!" The interaction tells us something new: Cross's face is part of the mask that allows him to trick the City Hall clerks, charm Eva, and later evade the police. Cross realizes that he does not look like a Communist to Sarah, and that she has never met a "black intellectual."[46] But her wild laughter triggers Cross's reflexive rage: "now he felt himself being pushed more than ever into that position where he looked at others as though they were not human. He could have waved his hand and blotted them from existence with no more regret of taking human lives than if he had swatted a couple of insects."[47] Cross's masculinity is frightfully fragile: like the worst of internet trolls, he has an itch to retaliate with double murder for a woman's laughter.

Though Wright, himself a black intellectual, probably sympathized with his protagonist for enduring the laughter of others, he also pokes fun at the alternating insecurity and superiority that accompanies intellectual self-regard. "Black intellectual" is yet another mask Cross dons for the stage of the world, no more authentic than the "subservient Negro" or the "robustly healthy" colored person. In Book Four, after Cross has killed Hilton, he responds to the "provisional death sentence" pronounced by Central Committee member Blimin ("Now, *talk* for your *life!*") not with an explanation of his identity, but with a fifteen-page monologue. Wright uses the verb "to act" twice, as if Cross is taking the stage for a performance.[48] After Cross's diatribe, Menti, a Party lackey, quips, "With a gift of gab like that, you ought to be on the Central Committee."[49] Like Sarah's laughter or Bob's joke, Menti's tag deflates Cross's earnest monologue to the level of mere rhetoric. These may be Wright's words, but the joke seems to be on Cross.

Many critics have read *The Outsider* as Wright's flirtation with and disavowal of the role of Western existentialist intellectual. By killing off Cross, so the argument runs, Wright frees himself to turn to the more fruitful ground of nonfiction and solidarity with third-world writers.[50] This interpretation, while historically and politically gratifying, fails to account for the tenor of the homosocial, interracial relationship at the novel's emotional center – a relationship that is simultaneously satisfying, sadistic, and charged with *eros*. It is here that Wright's humorlessness becomes more than a mode of critique; it is a mode of being-with-intimacy that would otherwise provoke laughter or embarrassment.

Most characters in *The Outsider* conform to highly gendered types: the repressed, nagging wife; the innocent artist, too good for this world; the Communist and the Fascist with capital letters. As Stephen Michael Best astutely observes, Cross's roles alternate between "castration, on the one hand, and phallic investiture," the twin poles of masculinity available to black men in a racist, capitalist system.[51] The one exception to this insistent stereotyping is Ely Houston, the district attorney whom Cross first meets on the train from Chicago to New York.

Part of Wright's polemical humorlessness involves the collapsing of intellect and eros – a combination that evokes uncomfortable laughter from other characters. Cross, who once studied philosophy at the University of Chicago, approaches books with compulsive desire. "He even had books in bed with 'im!" jokes his friend Booker.[52] The joke reveals an important truth. Cross is conscious that "ideas had been his only sustained passion," and that "this love of them had that same sensual basis that drew him achingly to the sight of a girl's body swinging in a tight skirt on a sunny street."[53] But unlike his Chicago friends, Houston meets Cross's intellectual obsessions with a "kindred" enthusiasm.[54] While Cross feels a mundane sexual shame for desiring "woman as body of woman," there is no similar emotional backlash attending his fascination with Houston's body.

> The man had a huge head and remarkably black, unruly hair; a long, strong, too-white face; clear, wide-apart brown eyes; and a well-shaped mouth that held always a hint of a smile at its corners. His shoulders were Herculean with long arms that terminated in huge hands with delicately strong fingers. The hump on the back was prominent but not in any way as noticeable as Cross would have thought it would be, so naturally did it blend in with the man's general build.[55]

From the huge black head to the "long, strong, too-white face"; from the furtive smile to the "Herculean" shoulders; from the "huge hands" to the "delicately strong fingers"; Houston's body is both contradictory and "natural," hard and soft, frightful and alluring. When Houston knocks at Cross's compartment later in the night, desperate for more conversation with the mysterious Negro intellectual, Cross's "body seem[s] suddenly made of soft, melting wax."[56] The encounter leaves Cross yearning to embody an impenetrably phallic masculinity that is also impervious to desire: "He passed the train's huge, sighing, black engine and longed to become as uncaring and passively brutish as that monster of steel and steam that lived on coal. But, no; his was to feel all of these anxieties in his shivering flesh."[57] In this novel full of gendered stereotypes, Houston is a strange beast, representing a queer longing for sexual and intellectual fulfillment that Cross, who flees feeling for a "passively brutish" masculinity, will glimpse, but never achieve.

The Outsider begins and ends with episodes of male intimacy that are as humorless as any of the similar scenes explored in this essay, but more bizarre. The opening pages echo Wright's earlier escape narrative, "Big Boy Leaves Home": four masculine figures laugh, joke, and jostle one another. The same eroticized violence erupts again, but this time there is more of an edge. When Cross "ram[s] his bare fingers down the collar of Pink's neck," Pink shouts, "Jeesus! Your fingers're cold as *snakes*!"[58] If Big Boy's wrestling was affectionate, Cross's playful gestures are figured as something closer to rape. Chicago is freezing and Cross is a Big Boy after the fall: "They ought to call you *Mr. Death*!" cries Pink with ominous accuracy. Whereas the boys in the earlier story are hardly differentiated through long passages of unmarked dialogue (that is, until three of them are murdered), Cross, with his "ambiguous" and "detached" smile, stands apart from his companions.[59]

Cross Damon spends most of the novel alternating between the roles of victim and demon (as is worthy of his name). But after he is shot by a Party operative, Cross makes a furtive gesture toward redemption. *The Outsider* ends with Ely Houston standing over Cross on his deathbed. Cross "long[s] to see Houston" before dying, "but the face looming over him remain[s] a blob of pink," an image both ominous and feminine, suitable to Houston's strange physical hold on Cross.[60] In this final tableau, Wright alludes to both Joseph Conrad's Mr. Kurtz from *Heart of Darkness* ("It ... it was ... horrible ... "[61]) and his own autobiography. At the end of *American Hunger*, Wright vows "to build a bridge of words between me and that world outside."[62] Echoing the earlier text, Cross tells Houston: "I wish I had some way to give the meaning of my life to others ... To make a bridge from man to man ... Tell them not to come down this road ... Men hate themselves and it makes them hate others ... We must find some way of being good to ourselves ... We're strangers to ourselves."[63] With a Whitmanesque call for self-knowledge and brotherhood, Cross and Wright seek to bridge the space between man and man, between self and world, black and white. The most generous reader might find here a letter to the future, hope for an America where toxic masculinity does not force men like Cross to choose between a homosocial intellectual celibacy and "woman as body of woman," where white supremacy does not keep them running the deadly circuit of criminality and victimhood.

It is easy to identify Coates's *Between the World and Me* as an heir to Wright's formal humorlessness. Coates tips his hat to the literary patriarch as he looks forward to his own son's future. But my readings of "Big Boy Leaves Home" and *The Outsider* suggest that *Moonlight*, too, is among Richard Wright's children. Jenkins's film explores queer desire, furtively signaled in Wright's novel, with an emancipated humorlessness made possible by nearly seven decades of political change. Wright used humorlessness as a weapon, and the work of Coates and Jenkins testifies to its continued usefulness in the arsenal of anti-racism. But the flexibility of humorlessness as a formal mode deserves more nuanced recognition. Wright wielded it to protect black community from racist stereotype; to expose the white racist gaze; to reflect on his own tendency to analyze rather than participate in black community; and to dignify the impulse to connect across racial lines. Wright's work teaches us that both violence and intimacy sometimes warrant a humorless style, a steady gaze that resists the escape valve of embarrassed laughter.[64]

Notes

1. One interviewer described Wright as "affable, good tempered, quick to smile, almost gay," while another insisted he had "a broad sense of humor and laugh[ed] raucously, soft brown eyes twinkling behind rimless glasses." Keneth Kinnamon and Michel Fabre, eds., *Conversations with Richard Wright* (Jackson: University Press of Mississippi, 1993), xiii.
2. James Baldwin, "Everybody's Protest Novel," *Partisan Review* 16.6 (1949), 584.
3. J. Saunders Redding, "The Alien Land of Richard Wright," in Herbert Hill, ed., *Soon, One Morning: New Writing by American Negroes, 1940–1962* (New York: Knopf, 1963), 50.
4. Richard Wright, "Between the World and Me," in Granville Hicks, Michael Gold, Isidor Schneider, Joseph North, Paul Peters, Alan Calmer, and Joseph Freeman, eds., *Proletarian Literature in the United States: An Anthology* (New York: International Publishers, 1935), 202–203.
5. Ibid., 202.
6. Ibid., 202.
7. Ibid., 203.
8. Ta-Nehisi Coates, *Between the World and Me* (New York: Spiegel & Grau, 2015), 12.

9. Maurice Wallace's work has been essential to my understanding of how the visual mode both reveals and conceals black identity. See Maurice O. Wallace, *Constructing the Black Masculine: Identity and Ideality in African American Men's Literature and Culture, 1775–1995* (Durham: Duke University Press, 2002).

10. Jeffrey B. Leak, *Racial Myths and Masculinity in African American Literature* (Knoxville: University of Tennessee Press, 2005), xii.

11. Lawrence W. Levine, *Black Culture and Black Consciousness: Afro-American Folk Thought from Slavery to Freedom* (New York: Oxford University Press, 1977), qtd. on 359.

12. Richard Wright, *Early Works* (New York: Library of America, 1991), 87–88.

13. Ibid., 239.

14. Richard Wright, *Later Works* (New York: Library of America, 1991), 369.

15. Richard Wright, "Between Laughter and Tears," *The New Masses* (October 5, 1937), 25.

16. Wright, *Early Works*, 239.

17. Ibid., 239–240.

18. Ibid., 240.

19. Ibid., 243.

20. Ibid., 242.

21. Ibid., 245.

22. Hilton Als, "'Moonlight' Undoes Our Expectations," *The New Yorker* (October 24, 2016). www.newyorker.com/magazine/2016/10/24/moonlight-undoes-our-expectations.

23. Barry Jenkins, *Moonlight*, Shooting Script (u.d.), 15. http://www.dailyscript.com/scripts/MOONLIGHT.pdf.

24. Wright, *Early Works*, 246.

25. Leslie Fiedler, "Come Back to the Raft Ag'in, Huck Honey!" *Partisan Review* 15.6 (1948), 666.

26. Wright, *Early Works*, 248–249.

27. James Baldwin, "Many Thousands Gone," *Partisan Review* 18.6 (1951), 673.

28. J. Saunders Redding, "Review of *Eight Men*," in Robert Butler, ed., *The Critical Response to Richard Wright* (Westport: Greenwood Press, 1995), 226.

29. Richard Wright, *Later Works*, 371.

30. Mae Henderson, "Drama and Denial in the Outsider," in Henry Louis Gates Jr. and K. A. Appiah, eds., *Richard Wright: Critical Perspectives Past and Present* (New York: Amistad, 1993), 396–397.

31. Wright, *Later Works*, 526.

32. Ibid., 540.

33. Ibid., 541.

34. Ibid., 543.

35. Ibid., 590.

36. Ibid., 678.

37. Ibid., 591.

38. L.D. Reddick, "A New Richard Wright?," 232; and Kent Ruth, "An Outsider Queries Why?," 205, in John M. Reilly, ed., *Richard Wright: The Critical Reception* (New York: B. Franklin, 1978).

39. Sarah Relyea, "The Vanguard of Modernity: Richard Wright's *The Outsider*," *Texas Studies in Literature and Language* 48.3 (2006), 209.
40. Richard Wright, "The Literature of the Negro in the United States," in *Black Power: Three Books from Exile* (New York: Harper Perennial, 2008), 733.
41. Wright, *Later Works*, 673.
42. Ibid., 491.
43. Ibid., 491.
44. Ibid., 491.
45. Ibid., 555.
46. Ibid., 557.
47. Ibid., 555.
48. Ibid., 749.
49. Ibid., 765.
50. Michel Fabre, *The Unfinished Quest of Richard Wright* (New York: William Morrow, 1973), 379; John M. Reilly, "Richard Wright and the Art of Nonfiction: Stepping Out on the Stage of the World," in Gates and Appiah, *Richard Wright: Critical Perspectives*, 412.
51. Stephen Michael Best, "Richard Wright, Lynch Pedagogy, and Rethinking Black Male Agency," in Marcellus Blount and George Cunningham, eds., *Representing Black Men* (New York: Routledge, 1996), 114.
52. Wright, *Later Works*, 374.
53. Ibid., 419.
54. Ibid., 501.
55. Ibid., 498.
56. Ibid., 503.
57. Ibid., 508.
58. Ibid., 370.
59. Ibid., 371, 373.
60. Ibid., 838.
61. Ibid., 840.
62. Ibid., 365.
63. Ibid., 840.
64. Whatever there is of valuable insight in this essay owes a debt to the generous criticism of Glenda Carpio, Field Brown, and George Blaustein.

PART II

"I Choose Exile"

Wright Abroad

7

TOMMIE SHELBY

Freedom in a Godless and Unhappy World

Wright as Outsider

Richard Wright explored existentialist themes in such fictional texts as *Native Son* (1940) and "The Man Who Lived Underground" (1944). But his most fully realized and ambitious work of existentialist fiction is his second published novel *The Outsider* (1953),[1] which belongs to a tradition that includes Kierkegaard, Nietzsche, Dostoevsky, Heidegger, Camus, Beauvoir, and Sartre.[2] Wright is not, however, an unqualified celebrant of existentialism. Both in *The Outsider* and earlier fiction, his approach is critical engagement and searching dialogue with canonical works and figures in the tradition.[3]

Existentialism is less a doctrine than a philosophical tendency and literary movement. Existentialist thinkers reflect on a recurring set of themes, starting with recognizing, and coming to terms with, the fact that "existence comes before essence," as Sartre famously expressed it in "Existentialism Is a Humanism." What this means in the hands of the movement's more atheistic thinkers (which includes Wright) is that human beings, whether taken collectively or individually, have no purpose and that human existence lacks inherent significance. The question "What is the meaning of life?" is unanswerable. Or, if it has an answer, it is "nothing."

As agents involuntarily thrown into the world through birth, we make the meaning of our lives through deliberate and spontaneous choices. Meaning is an *act of will*, not something that we can be given or discover. This idea, or problem space, sets the stage for each existentialist writer to take the inescapable human predicament of *freedom* in a variety of directions. Typically, this leads to exploring questions about fear and loneliness, good and evil, creation and destruction, authenticity and identity, time and contingency, fate and mortality, and choice and responsibility, all themes Wright tackles in *The Outsider*.

Existentialists, aware as they are that the human predicament throws us back on ourselves as self-conscious subjects, give great attention to the subjective and emotional sides of life, sometimes in the form of phenomenological descriptions of the immediate objects of consciousness and perception, including the images and sounds in dreams. Wright takes up this theme primarily through the lens of psychoanalysis, adding a would-be scientific angle to his existentialist perspective. This hybrid theoretical framework allows him to pursue in depth two other common themes in his writings – family life and religion. Like Freud, Wright believes that many of our psychological maladies – including our deep sense of guilt, self-hatred, and desire to be punished – have their origin in these two spheres. Moreover, Wright's writing in *The Outsider*, like the works of many philosophers, is as much about self-clarification and self-knowledge as it is about narrative, character, and plot. Read alongside Wright's nonfiction, the novel is not only an intriguing literary and philosophical work, but a window on its author's own emotional life and strivings.

Reading *The Outsider*: Racial Pitfalls

Wright came to fame by writing powerfully about racism, black life, and radical politics. Many have therefore come to think of him as primarily a black protest writer, as one who uses his art to advance a political cause or challenge negative racial stereotypes by dramatizing the plight of black folk. I doubt that this was ever an apt way to describe Wright's literary contributions or aims (he operates in many keys, using a variety of instruments).[4] But it is a particularly inappropriate framework for understanding *The Outsider*, a work of philosophical fiction.[5]

Wright emphasizes throughout that his book is not about racial identity or racism. Cross Damon, the main character, feels himself alone in the world. His central problem is an individual one, not the "Negro problem."[6] His race does not figure in his most momentous decisions: "Militating against racial consciousness in him were the general circumstances of his upbringing which had somewhat shielded him from the more barbaric forms of white racism; ... his character had been so shaped that his decisive life struggle was a personal fight for the realization of himself" (525).

In maintaining that *The Outsider* is not principally about race relations or black identity, I am not suggesting that Wright was attempting to "transcend" race or to evade racial questions. After all, Cross is black (as are other characters in the novel) in an explicitly anti-black world where whites are in power, and his race does affect how other characters (white and black) interact with him and how the narrative unfolds. Nor do I claim that Wright was attempting to "reduce" questions of race to matters of class, as an orthodox Marxist (which Wright was not) might be tempted to do. Nor, finally, do I suppose that Wright was writing solely for white readers (as if black people can't appreciate a literary work rich with philosophical content). Rather, my point is that Wright is reflecting upon the human condition *through* black characters, representing black individuals, even those facing oppressive conditions and violent treatment, as all-too-human embodiments of universal motifs. This approach is easily misunderstood.

In a scathing review of *The Outsider*, Lorraine Hansberry described Cross Damon as "someone you will never meet on the Southside of Chicago or in Harlem. For if he is anything at all, he is the symbol of Wright's new philosophy – the glorification of nothingness."[7] This uncharitable assessment misunderstands Wright's purpose in exploring existentialist philosophy through fiction. Although Cross is not put forward as unique, he does not stand in for blacks in general or even for black men. Nor, as the ultimate antihero, is he a figure to celebrate or emulate. Cross is a character who, through an examination of his inner life and actions, enables Wright to pursue the philosophical questions that most interest him. If anything, his life is a cautionary tale, not a blueprint for living.

Wright was, moreover, writing in self-conscious opposition to the black literary tradition as he understood it.[8] He regarded no earlier black writer as a model – and, as a proletarian writer, was particularly alienated from writers of the educated black elite. He was not "pleading with white America for justice."[9] Nor was he afraid to take risks. He experimented formally and transgressed narrative conventions, feeling no need to play it safe in order to vindicate (or avoid "embarrassing") the race through his writing. It is of course true that Wright's works (including his writings in exile) are now canonical representations of the African American tradition. Yet, at the time, he was attempting to dramatically alter black letters, widening its genres, themes, and overall scope.

Living Underground

This approach was not a radical break from Wright's earlier writings. It was already evident in his novella "The Man Who Lived Underground," widely regarded as the precursor to *The Outsider*.[10] Fred Daniels, having been falsely accused of murder, escapes from police custody, flees to an underground passageway in the sewer system of an unnamed city, and is transformed by his experiences and choices there. He becomes a self-conscious rebel against social convention, refusing to recognize the authority of God, law, or mammon: "Maybe *any*thing's right, he mumbled. Yes, if the world as men had made it was right, then anything else was right, any act a man took to satisfy himself, murder, theft, torture."[11]

Wright uses the ordinary idea of guilt as criminal offense to explore a greater loss of innocence and a more profound sense of guilt, one comparable to the Christian idea of original sin, where everyone is "guilty" whether or not they have actually done anything wrong. Wright also dramatizes Daniels' sense of dread and solipsism by placing him alone in a pitch-black underground cave, where he must face his deepest fears (including his own mortality). He loses all sense of time, and even forgets his own name and why he came to be there in the first place. Daniels' experience underground is a confrontation with the absurd and with an acute sense of the meaninglessness of modern social life.

Daniels is also black, and "The Man Who Lived Underground" does touch on racial themes.[12] But their significance to the text should not be exaggerated. For instance, Wright studiously avoids mentioning the racial identity of the watchman, who commits suicide after being accused of Daniels' crimes and tortured by the police. The watchman serves as Daniels' doppelgänger, as does a dead baby of unspecified race who also foreshadows his demise. In fact, Wright emphasizes that the watchman, whatever his race, is treated the same way as Daniels: "Those were the same policemen who had beaten him, had made him sign that paper when he had been too tired and sick to care. Now, they were doing the same thing to the watchman."[13] The police are not, in this instance, intent on pinning the murder of a white woman on a black man: "You're free, free as air. Now go home and forget it. It was all a mistake. We caught the guy who did the Peabody job. He wasn't colored at all. He was an Eyetalian."[14] When the police do ultimately kill Daniels, they do so, not only because he is black or might expose their attempts to frame him, but also, and more importantly, because they can't fully understand his childlike declarations or frighteningly opaque motives. They also resent what he and others like him represent – a threat to the repressive mechanisms of social control that it is law enforcement's job to uphold:

> "What did you shoot him for, Lawson?"
> "I had to."
> "Why?"
> "You've got to shoot his kind. They'd wreck things."[15]

Although Wright is a militant anti-racist, "The Man Who Lived Underground" is not a racial allegory, a celebration of the black world below and an indictment of the white world above. At one point while Daniels is still underground and surreptitiously observing the activities of those aboveground, the sight of black parishioners singing hymns in church gives him not comfort or pride, but an impulse to laugh, striking him as "abysmally obscene."[16] He is gripped by a feeling of "nothingness" while watching the singers "groveling and begging for something they could never get" – namely, relief from a crippling and overwhelming sense of guilt.[17] When Daniels ascends from his cave to tell others of his newfound enlightenment, the black churchgoers physically throw him out of the church, regarding him as "drunk" and "crazy," even threatening to call the police.[18] Episodes like this, not infrequent in Wright's writings, are attempts to demonstrate the limits of religious consciousness.

Living without God

Though many existentialists write, in part, to advance a political cause, *The Outsider* is not agitprop or a defense of any political ideology. It is about the individual quest for meaning and freedom in a world without a god to love and guide us.

In Nietzsche's *Thus Spoke Zarathustra,* the protagonist begins his journey by exchanging words with a devoutly religious man. After taking leave of him, Zarathustra says to himself, "Could it be possible! This old saint in the woods has not yet heard the news that *God is dead!*"[19] Similarly for Cross, a person cannot be truly modern – cannot deal honestly with the human predicament from a scientific perspective – unless he or she is willing to live without God or religious myths: "[Cross] disliked most strongly all men of religion because he felt that they could take for granted an interpretation of the world that his sense of life made impossible. The priest was secure and walked the earth with a divine mandate, while Cross's mere breathing was an act of audacity, a confounding wonder at the daily mystery of himself" (494).

This stance raises the pressing question of how to distinguish right from wrong. If there are no sacred commandments promulgated by a deity, then human beings have to figure out on their own how to treat one another and how to live. To be driven by mere libidinal desire or caprice is to live like an animal, which is an undignified way for a free being to move about the world. Our capacity to deliberate and choose, like our mortality, is inescapable, and so we are responsible for our actions and are appropriately judged for how we use our freedom. But on the basis of what principles can we decide how to live, and what gives these principles their authority? The character of Cross Damon is the vehicle through which Wright explores these questions: "Cross had to discover what was good or evil through his own actions which were more exacting than the edicts of any God because it was he alone who had to bear the brunt of their consequences with a sense of absoluteness made intolerable by knowing that this life of his was all he had and would ever have" (494).

Fear is a primitive emotional response, as basic as any human reaction to the world we inhabit. Prior to the development of science and industry, Cross contends, humans were irrationally ruled by religious myths and a belief in magic, which provided some psychological comfort in a dangerous world. As we have come to better understand our surroundings and gained some measure of control over our environment through technology, the terrifying frontier is the human mind itself, which remains opaque even – or perhaps especially – to the person whose mind it is. Our fear turns itself inward, toward the subjective dimension of life, and becomes *dread*. Claudia Tate describes the meaning of dread in the work of Kierkegaard as "not simply fear but a dynamical emotional force which both attracts and repels man's desire for possibility, for freedom, and, ultimately, for desire itself; and, on the other, [as] the fear of possibility, of freedom, and, ultimately, of desire."[20] Dread is the starting point of Cross's journey, and the title of *The Outsider*'s first book. But its full significance cannot be grasped without examining Wright's reliance on psychoanalytic theory, which illuminates the depth of Cross's challenge.

Living without Happiness

In *Civilization and Its Discontents* (1930), Freud attempts to understand the peculiar form of melancholia characteristic of modern persons. The early "Enlightenment" worldview held that the inner workings of the human mind were largely if not entirely transparent to introspection. The mental life of the subject was believed to be largely under the agent's control, primarily through the faculty of reason. Freud developed a dramatically different view: an image of the psyche as an obscure sphere of complex forces mostly unavailable to direct introspection. Those impulses or ideas that do come to consciousness often mislead the subject about their true nature or origins. And many of these mental forces cannot be brought under the control or direction of reason.

Freud, unlike Weber and Marx, considered the problem of discontent as a perennial and permanent feature of the human condition. Weber thought that rationalization and bureaucratic domination make it difficult for people to be happy in the modern world. Marx thought that unhappiness is the result of economic exploitation and alienation, which will be overcome by a socialist revolution. Against these views, Freud insisted that human unhappiness is not new; nor, try as we might, can we triumph over it.

If there were no regulation of social interaction, individuals would be able to advance their interests limited only by the power they possess. Freud argued that the power of the community (whether it takes the form of informal association or the state) is said to be "right" or "legitimate" in opposition to the individual's power, which is regarded as a mere arbitrary force with no claim to be respected. Civilization is built upon the renunciation of libidinal (primarily sexual) and aggressive instincts. This frustration of natural human drives places the individual in perpetual and irresolvable conflict with the demands of social life. The agents of civilization – elders, teachers, clergy, and legislators – must struggle to maintain control over the inherently rebellious individual. This social control is partly achieved through brute force – police and prisons. But it is also achieved (though imperfectly) through the processes of socialization that take place in families, schools, and religious institutions. We each cultivate a "conscience" to tame and police our antisocial instincts. In effect, we learn to develop a moral sensibility, through which we *restrain ourselves* from acting on our natural instincts. The price we pay for our moral development is a loss of contentment through a heightened sense of guilt.

The superego is the internalization of parental and societal authority. Before the appearance of the superego (and the loss of innocence it brings in its wake), guilt is simply anxiety about being caught by a parental figure. But after it emerges, the distinction between *doing* something wrong and *desiring* to do something wrong disappears, since nothing can be hidden from the superego – not even "evil" thoughts. The superego punishes the ego for its forbidden wishes and deeds with the sense of guilt, calling for further renunciations of instinct through the threat of a guilty conscience.

Importantly, our sense of guilt can be *unconscious*. Thus, much of the sense of guilt produced by the demands of civilization and social life may not be recognized as such by the subject. When the guilty conscience resides in the unconscious we feel a sort of general melancholia or dissatisfaction in life. Each individual must thus find his or her own way to survive the resulting and inevitable discontent.

This is the existential and psychological context – a life without God or happiness – in which we must understand Cross and his decisions. He is in lonely rebellion against authority and social demands, trying to overcome his deep sense of malaise. What makes Cross special – that is, atypical – is that socialization has only partially tamed him. He confronts the human predicament with eyes open, without the consolations of religion *or* political ideology.

Cross as Outsider

Cross's mother names him after the crucifixion of Jesus (391), and his sense of dread is also from her legacy (385, 489). This "baleful gift" is not a matter of genetic inheritance but a consequence of the strict Christian ethics that shaped his conscience. Despite his mother's efforts to repress his natural instincts, Cross is bursting with forbidden desire. He fears this force within him, and the result is a deep sense of self-hatred that shapes the rest of his existence: "As he descended the stairs, his mother's scolding [in response to learning Cross had impregnated his underage mistress] intensified his mood of self-loathing, a mood that had been his longer than he could recall, a mood that had been growing deeper with the increasing complexity of the events of his life" (384).

Cross, who had been a philosophy major at the University of Chicago, is an atheist. His atheism is not merely or even mostly about nonbelief. It is deeper. It's about his unwillingness to submit to the dictates of another being, whether earthly or divine. Neither reason nor desire would allow it. As an intellectual, he is also keenly aware that "there [is] no cure for his malady" (388). He was once a prodigious reader of serious and challenging books but then stopped reading altogether. "Ideas had been his only sustained passion, but he knew that his love of them had that same sensual basis that drew him achingly to the sight of a girl's body swinging in a tight skirt along a sunny street" (419). Having abandoned his studies, he mostly gets drunk with friends and seeks casual sex.

Though he has a solid job at the post office, Cross is under severe economic constraints. Worse, he finds himself pressured to marry Dot, a girl he impregnated but does not love; if he does not, he will be charged with statutory rape. He's estranged from his wife Gladys (who refuses to grant a divorce) and has three sons whom he financially supports but rarely sees. Once Gladys discovers his situation – despite Cross's diabolical plot to conceal it from her – she demands that he sign over their house and car and take out a large loan against his future salary, to ensure that she and the children will be financially secure if he's convicted. Feeling trapped, Cross yields to Gladys's demands. These circumstances set the stage for Wright's primary concern: the psychological ramifications of deliberately choosing to live as an outsider.

Wright uses the term "outsider" in a variety of ways to refer to a diverse set of characters – blacks in general (though they are also said, by district attorney Ely Houston, to be "insiders" who are "gifted with a double vision" [500]), Gladys, Houston himself, Communists, and Eva Blount (the only woman Cross ever loves). Wright's first use of the term suggests that he means people who are stigmatized and excluded in society and who cope with their marginalization through minor acts of defiance, without stepping too far out of line or even understanding their transgressions as such (396). But the outsider that Wright is most interested in is the completely alienated yet enlightened and self-conscious rebel: "Were there not somewhere in this world rebels with whom he [Cross] could feel at home, men who were outsiders not because they had been born black and poor, but because they had thought their way through the many veils of illusion?" (396).

Cross comes into his own as an outsider after a subway crash that leaves him largely uninjured but kills several others, including another black man of roughly Cross's build. Mistaking him for the dead man, the authorities conclude that Cross has died in the accident. Cross has to decide whether to allow his family, friends, and coworkers to believe that he is dead, which would solve his most pressing problems but also incur a number of personal costs. He would be leaving his mother and sons behind, all of whom he loves and would miss. Nonetheless, this is the path he ultimately chooses. To demonstrate his commitment to this new life, Wright has Cross murder one of his closest friends (Joe Thomas) to avoid having his plan thwarted.

Thus Cross elects to "die" and is reborn of his own choice (he earlier considers and rejects suicide as an option). Like Jesus Christ, he perishes only to be resurrected, though not to save all humankind but only himself. He breaks all ties to his past and unburdens himself of all existing commitments and relationships. He is not bound, as most are, by tradition but is in every way free. He can fashion his life and identity however he chooses. He can even rename himself ("Lionel Lane"), which he does after moving from Chicago to New York City to begin his new life. Such self-naming might seem a trivial thing or a mere practical exigency but for Cross it is a symbolic expression of freedom. It reflects his struggle against his mother, the initial shaper of his superego. He resents her having given birth to him, raising him in accordance with an austere moral code, and naming him using Christian iconography. To choose his own name is an act of rebellion.

A fortuitous event bequeaths to him the thing he most wanted: "All of his life he had been hankering after his personal freedom, and now freedom was knocking at his door, begging him to come out" (454). The task before him is to figure out what kind of man he wants to be ("he would have to imagine this thing out, dream it out, invent it, like a writer constructing a tale" [456]), and to do so without a guide or model.[21]

Cross's choice is not politically motivated but rather an attempt to find personal satisfaction in the affirmation of a truly free existence. Nor does his race figure in his deliberations: "There was no racial tone to his reactions; he was just a man, *any* man who had had an opportunity to flee and had seized upon it" (455). However, we should note the conception of freedom Cross operates with: to do whatever one likes without being encumbered by one's past or commitments. We should also note the limits of what this freedom can deliver. While Cross is "free," this freedom does not erase his dread: "He was empty, face to face with a sense of dread more intense than anything he had ever felt before. He was alone. He was not only without friends, their hopes, their fears, and loves, to buoy him up, but he was a man tossed back upon himself when that self meant only a hope of hope" (471).

So what does "Lionel Lane" do with his newfound freedom? He lives as a thoroughgoing *nihilist* – an atheist who is fundamentally amoral and who, through his choices, self-consciously imposes order and normative significance on an inherently meaningless life and world.[22] "[Cross] passed the train's huge, sighing, black engine and longed to become as uncaring and passively brutish as that monster of steel and steam that lived on coal" (508). Cross lies, betrays, steals, invades others' privacy, commits adultery, covets another's wife, and refuses to honor his mother. Mostly, he kills or indirectly causes others to die. As murder is considered the greatest wrong one can do to another human being (showing disrespect to God might be worse), an existentialist meditation on killing gives Wright a perfect opportunity to think about the rational basis for a purely secular ethics. Cross desires to act on an unrestrained libido and to be free from the surveillance and punishment of his superego. Though he does not believe in God, he chooses to become a "little god" himself, deciding by a pure act of will what is right and wrong; judging others and dispensing punishment; and treating others either as obstacles to the achievement of his aims or objects to be used to satisfy his cravings.

Playing God

Cross throws his lot in with a group of Communists – black and white, men and women, all outsiders like him. He moves into the Greenwich Village apartment of a Communist Party Central Committee member, Gilbert (or "Gil") Blount, and his artist wife Eva. Despite their aggressive attempts to recruit him, Cross refuses to join the party or accept its ideology. He finds Marxist theory useful for analyzing modern industrial society, but cannot accept the Communists' failure to respect human subjectivity, privacy, and personal freedom, or the way they use people as mere means to political goals.

Gil and Eva's landlord, Langley Herndon, is a retired real estate broker, and a fascist. He particularly hates blacks and is outraged to find that a Negro now lives in his building. (Gil hopes to turn this irrational hatred to his advantage and use Cross as bait in his fight against fascism.) Cross is ambivalent about fascism as well. Fascists recognize, if only dimly, that capitalism is a doomed economic system and that anomie threatens us all.

Yet Cross cannot tolerate the emphasis on blood, soil, God, and tradition. Nor can he abide the fascist conviction that might makes right.

Cross hates Blount and Herndon, both for who they are as people and for what they represent. So when he happens upon the two of them in a bloody fight, he spontaneously decides to beat them to death. What do these two dark figures represent? Underneath the ideologies of communism and fascism is a naked will to power. This is not about sovereign or institutional power but interpersonal power: "It was power, not just the exercise of bureaucratic control, but personal power to be wielded directly upon the lives and bodies of others" (583).

Cross's impulse to kill Herndon and Blount is described as "imperious" (612), and it quickly dawns on him that he isn't very different from either man: "He too had acted like a little god. He had stood amidst those red and flickering shadows, tense and consumed with cold rage, and had judged them and had found them guilty of insulting his sense of life and had carried out a sentence of death upon them" (616). His condemnation of Blount and Herndon is also a self-indictment; he possesses the same impulses that he despises in others. Yet his motives remain partially opaque. To help him make sense of his choices and fully grasp why he had become a monster, he needs the mutual understanding and self-clarification that can only come through someone similar, another outsider.

Initially, district attorney Houston merely speculates as to the motives of the murderer, relying on his own instincts as an outsider: "Such a killer, if he existed, would have to, for psychological reasons, be akin to both of them, wouldn't he? At least he'd have to *understand* them" (671; original emphasis). This murderer, neither a Communist nor a fascist, would be moved by a different philosophy of life – "that no ideas are necessary to justify his acts" (671). Houston claims that he and Cross have the same lawless impulses that drive men like Blount and Herndon, except they don't act on them. Of course, Cross has acted on them, more than once, which Houston later discovers but cannot prove.

Cross's vast existentialist personal library back in Chicago is the clue Houston needs to unlock Cross's motives. He knows then that Cross is one of those who "wallowed in guilty thought" (820). Wright, relying on the Freudian idea of sublimation, suggests that these philosophical ideas are a mere rationalization for the forbidden desires of the men haunted by them. Existentialism functions analogously to Communist and fascist ideas in the lives of similar men: "For Cross had had no party, no myths, no tradition, no race, no soil, no culture, and no ideas – except perhaps the idea that ideas in themselves were, at best, dubious!" (775).

Eventually, Cross recognizes that he's a hypocrite, repudiates nihilism, and regrets his amoral choices: "He was not Lionel Lane. He was nothing, nobody ... He had tossed his humanity to the winds, and now he wanted it back" (679). Even setting aside the murders, he has violated numerous freely made commitments – obligations to his spouse, children, friends, and lovers. He betrays them so that he can unburden himself and follow his base desires, rationalizing his treachery by calling it "freedom." In the end, Cross realizes that no one can find freedom or meaning in life alone. Each needs others, which means creating and keeping commitments.

In a final and desperate attempt at redemption, Cross confesses everything to Eva, hoping that she, as a fellow outsider, might understand, forgive, and still love him. But she is horrified and responds by committing suicide. Ultimately, the Communists figure out that Cross is a killer and hunt him down. As he lays dying in a hospital room, Houston is eager to find out why Cross chose to live this way. He learns that Cross sought freedom but went about it all wrong: "I wish I had some way to give the meaning of my life to others ... To make a bridge from man to man ... Starting from scratch every time is ... is no good. Tell them not to come down this road ... Men hate themselves and it makes them hate others" (840).

Meursault, Bigger, and Wright

In the autumn of 1947, Wright read Albert Camus's *L'Étranger*, which was first translated into English by Stuart Gilbert with the title "The Outsider" (later editions were titled "The Stranger"). In his journal, Wright wrote "What is of course really interesting in this book is the use of fiction to express a philosophical point of view."[23] Although he had already tried his hand at this genre before with "The Man Who Lived Underground," Wright was clearly influenced, and perhaps provoked, by Camus's book, and a systematic comparison of Cross with Meursault would, I think, prove illuminating.[24] Here I mention just a few things to enhance our appreciation of Wright's contributions to existentialist philosophical fiction.

Both Cross and Meursault commit senseless murders without giving the matter much thought and without feeling any regret. Meursault, however, does not kill from passion – neither love nor hate nor fear. He doesn't kill because of any ideals. He just does it, and without much thought for the consequences. He shoots four bullets into a man ("the Arab"), "and it was like knocking four quick times on the door of unhappiness."[25]

Meursault, like Cross, is highly intelligent, observant, and in rebellion against society. Though his revolt is somewhat quieter, he too feels himself free to act on his instincts rather than follow social rules. He's not interested in politics or social justice causes. He is driven by sexual desire and other physical needs, like sleep and food. He doesn't believe in God and has no patience for religion. Even after he has been condemned to death, he refuses to turn to religion for solace. He regards his life as absurd, as having no real meaning, whether long or short, peaceful or violent. As a result, he doesn't think of his life choices as particularly momentous or in need of justification; he simply acts. Yet at the end of his life, though facing the guillotine, Meursault (unlike Cross) is actually happy, in part because society hates him and others like him, which Meursault takes perverse comfort in – "For everything to be consummated, for me to feel less alone, I had only to wish that there be a large crowd of spectators the day of my execution and that they greet me with cries of hate."[26]

When Houston finally confronts Cross with his crimes, he makes the following charge: "Last night you stood there in my office and committed the greatest and last crime of all. You did not bat your eye when I told you that your mother was dead. It hurt you, yes; I could see it, but you rode it out. Boy, you had killed your mother long, long ago ... " The accusation would be peculiar if not for the fact that Wright is here making a pretty direct reference to the character Meursault, who is ultimately convicted of murder because he reacted without grief to the death of his mother. The prosecutor accuses Meursault of "burying his mother with crime in his heart!" (96). Perhaps when Cross attributes his dread to his mother what he is really saying is that he blames her for forcing him, by giving birth to him and teaching him Christian morals, to live a life of meaninglessness and dread.

Cross can also be usefully compared to Wright's most famous literary character, Bigger Thomas. While Cross is a well-read, articulate black intellectual, Bigger has had limited formal education and struggles to convey his thoughts to others. Bigger isn't married and doesn't have children, so he has fewer commitments. But in other ways, the characters are similar. Both are, first and foremost, rebels – individuals striving for freedom and meaning in a world that cannot accept or understand them. Both suffer from deep existential loneliness and dread/fear (Book One of *Native Son* is called "Fear"). Bigger and Cross are men with tremendous pride (self-respect) and a fighting spirit. Both are extremely self-reflective, which is not to say that either understands himself entirely. Neither is inclined to accept or is motivated by a political ideology. Both develop personal relationships with Communists, but neither actually joins the party or any other political organization. Each needs another "outsider" to help him understand himself and to feel understood – defense attorney Max (for Bigger) and district attorney Houston (for Cross) – and this mutual recognition is supplied by someone white.

Perhaps most important for our purposes is Bigger and Cross's shared attitudes toward religious belief, mortality, and conventional morality. Though Bigger and Cross are both raised by a mother who is intensely religious, neither has any interest in or respect for religion. Though facing execution, and showered with his mother's pleas for him to turn to God, Bigger denies the existence of a deity, the efficacy of prayer, the reality of "souls," and the existence of life after death.[27] When Bigger's attorney Max asks Bigger why he didn't seek a sense of "home" in black churches, he replies, "I wanted to be happy in this world, not out of it. I didn't want that kind of happiness."[28] Bigger embraces the outlook similar to that of a nihilist, using deception and violence to achieve his aims without regret or repentance. And he is willing to go to great lengths, including killing those he ostensibly cares about, to save himself.

Cross and Bigger are brutal murderers. Yet what is most interesting to Wright about them is not that they kill or how they kill but *why* they kill. They do it not only out of pride, desire, hatred, or fear but also to realize a primitive sense of freedom that civilization, try as it might, can never fully extinguish. To take hold of that freedom is a basic existential act beyond good and evil but also, for the sake of social life, necessarily condemned and punished, with all the psychological anguish this imposes on the actor. Understood in this way, Bigger's last words are somewhat less mysterious: "What I killed for must've been good! ... When a man kills, it's for something .... I didn't know I was really alive in this world until I felt things hard enough to kill for 'em."[29]

Why would Wright develop two characters who are so unsympathetic, with whom few (if any) readers can fully identify, and whom most detest? Part of the answer has to do with the philosophical and psychological questions Wright explores in these novels, as already discussed. But it is also clear that Wright, an outsider himself, *could* identify with them, at least in part. And he thought that others, if they were fully honest with themselves, could see a bit of themselves in Bigger and Cross too.

Shortly after the publication of Native Son, Wright delivered a lecture at Columbia University titled "How 'Bigger' Was Born," included as an essay in subsequent editions of the novel.[30] Wright explains that Bigger represents a personality type he became familiar with during his time in the South and in Chicago. There are, he insists, millions of "Biggers," some black, some white. Biggers are "bad," violent, and unremorseful. Their violence can be directed toward oppressors or the oppressed (consider Bigger's murder of his girlfriend Bessie or Cross's murder of Joe Thomas). Biggers take what they want without regard for whether their actions are right or wrong. They are not afraid of conflict, not even violent confrontation, and are prepared to risk their lives to satisfy their desires. Biggers are willing, even eager, to break social rules and taboos and prepared to suffer the consequences if necessary. But they are also, Wright notes, prone to depression and mental illness. And their lives typically come to violent ends. Despite this remarkably grim characterization, Wright confesses he identifies with the Bigger type and secretly desires to act like a Bigger but is too timid to do so.[31]

One can hardly miss the resemblance between Cross and Wright, which can be gleaned through a comparison of *The Outsider* with *Black Boy (American Hunger)*.[32] These are two black former postal workers who move from Chicago to New York to start a new life. Wright too was an intellectual with a philosophical bent of mind and a strong interest in existentialism, comfortable around other black or white intellectuals. He was raised under strict Christian discipline but was never attracted to a life of faith. He regarded himself as a man of science and favored rationality, secularism, and humanism. These characteristics (especially his intellectualism and atheism) made him somewhat alienated from ordinary black folk life, and made many blacks suspicious or frightened of him. Wright was also drawn to Marxist theory, but ultimately found that he could not abide Communists' authoritarian tendencies. Many of the claims that Cross makes in his long speech to the Communist Blimin (749–764) also appear in Wright's nonfiction writings on Western modernity, industrialization, and imperialism.[33]

Finally, Wright was himself on a quest for personal freedom, which is part of the reason he left the Communist Party and emigrated to France. "I hold human freedom as a supreme right and good for all men, my conception of freedom being the right of all men to exercise their natural and acquired powers as long as the exercise of those powers does not hinder others from doing the same."[34] Although Wright was deeply engaged by the human predicament identified by existentialists, his own conception of freedom reflects a fairly conventional, even liberal, moral outlook. Like Cross, Wright ultimately rejects nihilism, the will to power, and a life beyond good and evil. Yes, he wrote an existentialist novel. But it is one that is as much critique as it is celebration.[35]

Notes

1. Richard Wright, *The Outsider*, in *Richard Wright: Later Works* (New York: Library of America, 1991), 367–841. Parenthetical page references in the main text are to this work.

2. See Michel Fabre, "Richard Wright, French Existentialism, and *The Outsider*," in *Critical Essays on Richard Wright*, ed. Yoshinobu Hakutani (Boston: G. K. Hall & Co., 1982), 182–198.

3. For a discussion of Wright's relationship to existentialism that posits a sharper break with the tradition (particularly its French strains) than I suggest here, see Nina Kressner Cobb, "Richard Wright: Exile and Existentialism," *Phylon* 40, no. 4 (1979): 362–374. Cobb argues that Wright crafts *The Outsider* to contest the idea, associated with Sartre, that existence precedes essence and to make the case for a strong form of determinism.

4. See Richard Wright, "Blueprint for Negro Writing," in *Richard Wright Reader*, ed. Ellen Wright and Michel Fabre (New York: Da Capo, 1997), 36–49. Originally published in 1937.

5. In writing such fiction, Wright is not merely "quoting" his favorite philosophers or using philosophical ideas in a purely didactic way. He is exemplifying philosophical positions (others' and his own) through narrative, characters, situations, and symbols. To be sure, his protagonists do sometimes indulge in philosophical discourse (including long lectures and extended internal self-reflection). But Wright also embodies philosophical stances through his characters' choices and lives, and thereby shows the virtues and limits of these ideas in practice. For more on the difference between "philosophical quotation" and "philosophical exhibition," see Lewis White Beck, "Philosophy as Literature," in *Philosophical Style: An Anthology about the Writing and Reading of Philosophy*, ed. Berel Lang (Chicago: Nelson-Hall, 1980), 234–255. Also see Robert Gooding-Williams, *Zarathustra's Dionysian Modernism* (Palo Alto: Stanford University Press, 2001), 10–14.

6. For a contrasting view, see Floyd W. Hayes, III, "The Paradox of the Ethical Criminal in Richard Wright's Novel *The Outsider*: A Philosophical Investigation," *Black Renaissance* 13 (2013): 162–171. Also see Lewis R. Gordon, "Bigger-Cross Damon: Wright's Existential Challenge", in *Philosophical Meditations on Richard Wright*, ed. James B. Haile III (Lanham: Lexington Books, 2012), 3–21.

7. Lorraine Hansberry, review of *The Outsider, Freedom* 14 (April 1953). Hansberry may have been led to this reading by the fact that the theme of nothingness, as a feature of the human condition, looms large in the existentialist tradition, particularly in the early work of Sartre, whose *Being and Nothingness* is a classic in the genre. Wright explores this theme as well, but "glorification," as I will argue, is not the best way to describe his efforts.

8. Wright was often unflattering in his appraisal of the achievements of black writers before him, particularly those of the "black bourgeoisie." Here I describe his self-conception as a writer without supposing that he represented the black literary tradition accurately or that no black writer before him had similar ambitions.

9. Wright, "Blueprint for Negro Writing," 38.

10. See, for example, Ronald Ridenour, "'The Man Who Lived Underground': A Critique," *Phylon* 31 (1970): 54–57; and Michel Fabre, "Richard Wright: The Man Who Lived Underground," *Studies in the Novel* 3 (1971): 165–179.

11. Richard Wright, "The Man Who Lived Underground," in *Eight Men* (New York: HarperPerennial, 1961), 56.

12. For a reading of "The Man Who Lived Underground" that places greater weight on the fact that Daniels is a racialized subject, see Glenda R. Carpio, "Liminal Subjects, Mixed Genre: Richard Wright and the African American Story," in *Liminality and the Short Story: Boundary Crossings in American, Canadian, and British Writing*, ed. Jochen Achilles and Ina Bergmann (New York: Routledge, 2014), 213–224. Carpio argues that, though the story is no simple racial allegory, Daniels' experiences aboveground as a persecuted and marginalized racial Other are key to the philosophical import of the novella.

13. Wright, "The Man Who Lived Underground," 61.

14. Ibid., 74.

15. Ibid., 83–84.

16. Ibid., 24.

17. Ibid., 26, 25.

18. Ibid., 68.

19. Friedrich Nietzsche, *Thus Spoke Zarathustra*, trans. and ed. Adrian Del Caro, ed. Robert B. Pippin (Cambridge: Cambridge University Press, 2006), 6.

20. Claudia Tate, "Christian Existentialism in Richard Wright's *The Outsider*," *CLA Journal* 25 (1982), 370.

21. Note that while Fred Daniels, in "The Man Who Lived Underground," writes only his name and the first line of his story ("It was a long hot day"), here Cross "writes" the whole tale.

22. This brand of nihilism resembles Nietzsche's, at least on one prominent reading of that thinker's work. See Arthur C. Danto, *Nietzsche as Philosopher* (New York: Columbia University Press, 2005).

23. See Michel Fabre, *The Unfinished Quest of Richard Wright*, 2nd ed. (Urbana: University of Illinois Press, 1993), 321.

24. For a comparison that arrives at rather different conclusions than I do, see Yoshinobu Hakutani, "Richard Wright's *The Outsider* and Albert Camus's *The Stranger*," *Mississippi Quarterly* 42 (1989): 365–378. Also see Steven J. Rubin, "Richard Wright and Albert Camus: The Literature of Revolt," *International Fiction Review* 8 (1981): 12–16.

25. Albert Camus, *The Stranger*, trans. Matthew Ward (New York: Vintage International, 1998), 59.

26. Ibid., 123–124.

27. See Richard Wright, *Native Son*, in *Richard Wright: Early Works* (New York: Library of America, 1991), 724–726, 778–779.

28. Ibid., 778.

29. Ibid., 849.

30. Wright, "How 'Bigger' Was Born," in *Early Works*, 851–881.

31. Ibid., "How 'Bigger' Was Born," 874, 855.

32. Wright, *Black Boy (American Hunger)*, in *Richard Wright: Later Works* (New York: Library of America, 1991), 1–365. *Black Boy* originally published in 1945; *American Hunger* originally published in 1977.

33. See Richard Wright, *Black Power: Three Books from Exile* (New York: Harper Perennial, 2008), a volume that contains the books *Black Power* (1954), *The Color Curtain* (1956), and *White Man, Listen!* (1957).
34. Richard Wright, *White Man, Listen!* in *Black Power*, 709.
35. For invaluable critical feedback on previous versions of this essay, I thank Glenda Carpio, Julian Lucas, and Robert Gooding-Williams.

8

LAURENCE COSSU-BEAUMONT

Richard Wright, Paris Noir, and Transatlantic Networks

A Book History Perspective

This chapter sheds light on Wright's exile in France from a book history perspective. Specifically, it focuses on how Wright came to be translated, read, and commented on in postwar Paris and reevaluates Wright's achievement in Europe and his legacy while placing his work in a transnational scope. I depart from a critical approach that has focused on categories such as literary genre or nationality and seek to nuance an American centered perception of Wright. This fosters a new conversation past the boundaries of literature and across geographical and cultural borders. Considering the different networks of "cultural passeurs" or readers engaging with Wright's work in France – from agents to editors, from renowned intellectuals to unknown readers – shifts critical assessment from unfortunate isolation to fecund networks. While Paul Gilroy claimed as early as 1993 that Wright scholars had failed to confront the consensus that "as far as his art was concerned, the move to Europe was disastrous" and neglected the interactions of Wright with Europeans, a book history approach can bring fresh material to follow this lead.[1] Such material reveals the transnational impact that his work had, and the fullness of what has been called "Paris Noir."

Texts praising Paris as the city of light, as the "moveable feast," as "Harlem-sur-Seine," forge a well-known narrative of African American artists thriving in postwar Paris.[2] But little attention has been paid to the concrete ways African American texts and books reached out to foreign audiences by way of French agents and publishers, and informed new conversations in France – notably over race.[3] Richard Wright's interviews, the translations of his books, and his editorial collaborations with French and African intellectuals in Paris make for a more complex transnational network than has been conveyed by literary criticism centered on the uprootedness of his Paris fiction writing (*The Outsider*, 1953; *The Long Dream*, 1958) or the dwindling of his commitment in American issues (as purportedly evidenced by his nonfiction books, *Black Power*, 1954; *The Color Curtain*,

1956; *White Man Listen!*, 1957). This chapter's perspective stems from the scholarship in book history in the French tradition of the Annales. Roger Chartier, for instance, demonstrated the transformative power of books: how they come to be published and circulated, how audiences receive them, and how the ideas they convey can be decisive in the making of history.[4] This approach is particularly fruitful for examining African American authors whose challenges to achieve publication, reach readers, and develop strategies to receive literary attention have been demonstrated. They resonate with the struggles of African Americans to be visible and to be heard beyond the book market.[5] This book history approach intersects with the French scholarly interest in African American studies.[6] Recent publications have indeed responded to Leon Jackson's call for more scholarly research on "the nexus of African American studies and print culture."[7]

In the wealth of publications that appeared during his first months in Paris, between 1946 and 1947, Wright emerged as more than a visitor whose testimony might be sought or an admirer of the existentialist Parisian mood. In the many interviews, articles, translations, and through his personal and editorial relationship with Jean-Paul Sartre, Wright appeared as an initiator and agent of new conversations on the French literary and intellectual stage. Looking beyond the Left Bank places Richard Wright at the center of an ongoing publication network between the United States and France, and part of a larger transatlantic conversation that developed and was sustained through the Bradley agency, an American literary agency in Paris. Ultimately, the dialogue that formed in Paris spanned not just across the Atlantic but reached out to a greater network of intellectuals. Wright's support of the Négritude movement's journal, *Présence Africaine*, upon its launching in 1947 and his presence at the International Congress of Black Writers and Artists in 1956, considered in the last part of this chapter, point to the way that French-speaking Black intellectuals, alongside existentialists and African Americans, participated in a more encompassing *Paris Noir*. The threefold network charted in the chapter – French, transatlantic, transnational – extends recent critical reevaluations of Wright's work and deconstructs the myth of Wright as a "native son" at a loss in exile.

Richard Wright first visited Paris from May to December 1946 and returned to France in August 1947 for what was to become a permanent expatriation.[8] Two major publishers, Albin Michel and Gallimard, had fought for the acquisition of the rights of *Native Son* and *Black Boy* as early as 1945.[9] *Native Son* first came out in France in the fall of 1947, as did *Uncle Tom's Children* – both with Albin Michel – while Gallimard published

Black Boy in January 1948.[10] About fifty articles appeared during Wright's first eight months in Paris in 1946, while no less than 200 articles or interviews were published over the span of 1946 and 1947, before his books came out.[11]

This certainly prepared readers for Wright's masterpieces and contributed to the books' popular success.[12] The interest in, if not fascination of the French with Wright can also be explained by Wright's literary commitment. His relentless denouncing of the racial situation in the United States found affinity with the absolute necessity for *l'engagement*, a motto and prevailing practice of political engagement for French writers and intellectuals during and after World War II. *Résistance* to the enemy's oppression through literature had given a new impetus to the tradition of the public intellectual and led to the creation or continuation of journals and papers intending to fight for ideas through fiction and poetry. Books, journals and newspapers had risen as essential agents of the French political and cultural debates. The major *résistance* reviews took an interest in Wright's writings.[13] As postwar editorial and literary history show, French culture was not only intensely politicized around national concerns but also open to a conversation with an "outsider" such as Wright and with other, similar agents of resistance.

Jean-Paul Sartre undeniably emerged as the figure of *littérature engagée* and his journal *Les Temps Modernes*, started in 1945, established a reference.[14] The journal's existentialist stance condemned *l'art pour l'art* embodied by other reviews like la *Nouvelle Revue Française* whose editor had been a collaborator with the Nazis.[15] The suspicion leveled at any form of art "for art's sake" mirrored Wright's own determination to use "words as weapons."[16] In these circumstances, Wright's personal and artistic commitment to equality and freedom through literature naturally engaged French readers and critics. Yet, if *l'engagement* was a shared value, the purpose thereof was bitterly argued. The *résistance* had been composed of communist as well as right-wing patriots whose visions of France's allegiance to America in a bipolar world now diverged. The growing political and cultural Americanization of Europe and the split in the French intellectual landscape led to intense debates around Wright's critical discourse of his home country, whose culture fascinated the French but whose rising hegemony also antagonized them. The French did not forget the US contribution to France's liberation from the Nazis but they found America's refusal to address racial dis- crimination unacceptable.[17]

This fostered an original and rather disunited "community of readers."[18] Wright's literary work and discourse on race in America were appraised through the lens of France's own agenda. Wright soon became aware of this and wrote:

> Indeed political lines and ideologies are drawn so hard and sharp in France today that even "facts" are dangerous. If one so much as mentions that the majority of the world's people are hungry, you can and will be branded as Communist by the Right, so say the Communists [...] If you look at reality and speak about it in terms of how it makes you feel, you are in for trouble.[19]

Such relations of power were at the heart of the French literary, editorial and intellectual stage and have informed the way Wright's work was acclaimed or criticized – notably because of his introduction in France by Sartre. Here the book history perspective not merely contributes to establishing the cultural context in which Wright's oeuvre took on a new meaning outside the United States, it also calls for a reciprocal vision of the French American conversation thus shaped. Sartre was more than just instrumental in pushing Wright onto the French stage. The relationship between Wright and Sartre started as a personal friendship, when they first met in New York in March 1946, and continued in Paris in the form of social calls and participation in the café life in Saint Germain des Prés. But the encounter between these two powerful minds, who mutually nurtured their respective *engagement*, deserves more attention than that offered by critics that frame their relationship as fashionable Parisian influence or by those who claim that Wright's first novel written in France, *The Outsider*, was imitative of Sartre's work.[20]

In its October-November 1945 first issue, Sartre's *Les Temps Modernes* published "Fire and Cloud," one of the short stories from Wright's 1938 collection, *Uncle Tom's Children*. The September 1946 issue, devoted to the United States, featured Wright's "Early Days in Chicago," an autobiographical account of Wright's experience as an employee at the Chicago post office, as a bus boy in a restaurant, and as a hospital orderly; the account presents a scathing portrait of discrimination in the North of the United States and a tale of disillusion for the Mississippi native aspiring writer. The editors also included an extract from James Weldon Johnson's *Book of Spirituals* called "Negro Spirituals" and three excerpts from *Black Metropolis*, the 1945 comprehensive sociological study of Chicago's South Side by Horace Cayton and St. Clair Drake. This was a significant introduction for French readers to both American racial realities and African American artistic production. Early 1947, *Les Temps Modernes* serialized *Black Boy* before Gallimard published it. And while the ensuing reception epitomized the rift within the French intellectual circles and embodied the ambivalence of the French toward America, notably upon the issue of race, it also helped Sartre to (re)define his own vision of committed literature.

Sartre was sufficiently impressed by Wright's work to root some of his analysis in his essay *Qu'est-ce que la littérature?* He quoted Wright more than once and importantly argued that Wright embodied an outstanding example of what literature in its purpose of commanding action and triggering change should be.[21] This is evidence that rather than being isolated among his European peers and away from his inspirational roots, Wright was an active participant in French major publications and contributor to the French debates of the period, over "words as weapons," over race and class, over the emergence of a dominating American model, and France's own positioning in a postwar world order. While Wright's European writing was inevitably molded by this new experience, criticism has done little justice to *The Outsider* and Wright's nonfiction books. These are a continuation of his early exploration of modern alienation,[22] his commitment to *engagement* that the Black experience in America entailed,[23] and his vision of racial identity transcending American boundaries.[24]

The reciprocal exchange that occurred during Richard Wright's presence in Paris between 1946 and 1947 represents but a small fragment of a larger conversation between the French and American literary and intellectual communities and as audiences. This started much earlier with other leading figures such as those of the Lost Generation.[25] Wright inscribed himself in this tradition, exchanging hopeful letters with Gertrude Stein[26] in 1945, being welcomed and guided by her in 1946, and later passing on his experience to James Baldwin in 1948 before they fell out. But this ongoing expatriate community was built and fostered not just by the great artistic figures and minds, but also by the hands-on networks of editorial laborers. Few know the story of publishers and agents and their imprint on the American-French cultural history connection. One agency, in particular, that has yet to be fully explored, is the Bradley Agency.[27] Literary agencies such as William and Jenny Bradley's are those who made it possible for the authors to be introduced to publishers, to secure contracts and translators, and to receive funding while dwelling in France.

The archives of the Bradley Agency, located at the Harry Ransom Center at the University of Texas at Austin, contain a striking example of the ongoing French American conversation through the permanent stream of books negotiated, translated and published across the Atlantic. While it has been established by his biographers that Wright met many hurdles in obtaining a visa to come visit France, the fact that this was achieved through the connections of Jenny Bradley is never mentioned. A February 24, 1946 telegram of Richard Wright to Gertrude Stein asking that she come up with "an invitation to lecture as cultural justification" to invite him to Paris was filed in the agency's archive.[28] Bradley transferred the request to Gallimard, who kindly provided a statement that Wright was to give lectures in France and would be compensated for it.[29] The agent, invisible to biographical and literary history, was key to securing Wright's visit. The agency also devised an intricate scheme of financial redistribution of income that allowed for Wright and other American authors published in France to be duly paid.

In the 1940s, Wright was the agency's major American client in Paris for whom Bradley collected significant sums of money from French and European publishers, newspapers, journals, and even filmmakers in the case of the film version of *Native Son* whose rights were negotiated in France with Pierre Chenal. But Wright also received royalties in the United States for domestic sales through his US agent Paul Reynolds. To avoid international transfers that were complex, not to mention costly, Jenny Bradley in Paris and Paul Reynolds in New York agreed that Richard Wright would be given the "francs" that the Bradley Agency was to give the other American authors it managed for their French translations. In New York, Reynolds would retain Wright's royalties paid in the US and use these to remunerate these same American authors for their domestic sales, in dollars. This greatly facilitated the negotiations with French publishing houses that could hand over payments in French currency to Bradley without having to change currencies or wire money abroad. It happened in more than one case, notably easing the dealings with Marcel Duhamel at Gallimard.[30] Such numerous arrangements show the vitality of the publishing of American novels in postwar France and evidence of a concrete network of houses and agents sustaining African American publications.[31] This greatly benefited both Chester Himes and James Baldwin and changed their careers.[32] So while the Sartre–Wright network encourages critics to seek continuity from Wright's early career to his exile works, editorial evidence of a transatlantic stream of writers and novels suggests the permanence of a lineage. In the past decade critics have indeed started to take interest in the *confluences* rather than the *divergences* of African American artists who, despite personal fallouts, collectively built a transnational voice beyond space and time boundaries and personal disagreements.[33]

Paris afforded Wright access to a network of writers and editors beyond those comprised by American and French figures.[34] Not only did Wright meet with leading black francophone figures in Paris, such as Leopold Sedar Senghor, the poet and writer from Senegal, and Aimé Césaire, the poet from

Martinique in the French West Indies, but he also participated in the some of the founding moments of the Négritude movement, including ones of editorial nature. More specifically Wright sponsored the first issue of *Présence africaine* (1947), the magazine launched by Alioune Diop in Paris to promote both African artistic productions and creativity, and political activism. Wright participated in the first board meeting in October 1946 at the Brasserie Lipp – across the street from the existentialist haunts in Saint Germain. He contributed a piece for the first issue, the short story "Bright and Morning Star," he helped select poems, Gwendolyn Brooks's, and his own *Native Son* was reviewed in one of the magazine's columns.[35] The combination of creative vitality and political engagement found an echo in Wright's own commitment, along with the exploration of a double culture, the expression of being torn between two continents and cultures. *Présence Africaine* made a point to offer an international selection of black writers and intellectuals. This did not mean there was a perfect understanding or symbiosis between the American expatriate and the French African intellectuals nor that they shared the same agenda. But the atmosphere certainly made it possible for patterns of art and action, of creativity and combat to be confronted, discussed, mutually challenged and strengthened. The network extended to French intellectuals as well. Essays by André Gide, Emmanuel Mounier, Jean-Paul Sartre, and prominent writers and philosophers opened the first issue of *Présence Africaine* in 1947. When Senghor published the first anthology of black poetry in 1948, he asked Sartre to write the preface, "Black Orpheus."[36] Senghor's editorial project was part of a fight that was not nationally self-contained since it reached out to Africa, the West Indies, and the Indian Ocean Islands. It also signaled a transition from the individual projects and works of disseminated artists to a collective stance, a dynamics that has been suggested through this chapter.[37] These significant editorial and literary encounters molded a decade that brought independence to the French former empire, and legitimized the rise of third-world forces.

Wright embraced this vibrant and open community. He found new resonance for the African American experience. In the 1950s, he visited Kwame Nkrumah's Gold Coast (1953) and attended the Bandung Conference in Indonesia (1955) and wrote about the two experiences in *Black Power* (1954) and *The Color Curtain* (1956). That same year, the Sorbonne held the first Congress of Black Writers and Artists (1956), which showed the way identities, artistic works, and political fights now resounded in an Atlantic space.[38] Wright attended the conference along with Langston Hughes and James Baldwin, as did prominent African and Caribbean French speaking figures, the founders of the Négritude movement, and some of the future leaders of new independent nations in Africa. W. E. B. Du Bois symbolically participated through a letter read at the opening session of the Congress. This was not an exceptional and unique moment but, as I have suggested throughout this essay, the sign of an ongoing dialogue across continents and generations,[39] and within Wright's life work. Indeed Wright's 1950s travelogues helped reconnect the Mississippi field laborer, the Ghanaian farmer, and the street peddler in Djakarta years before this became a tenet of modern readings or post-colonial studies.[40] In that respect Amritjit Singh sees in Wright's career "an amazing level of unity and design, marked by his intense interest in the emerging patterns of modernity."[41] It is thus possible and high time to revisit Wright's relocation to Paris with evolving time contours and malleable spatial perimeters.[42] Wright's exiled writings should not be cut from his American ones and genres he used should not be opposed. They should be explored under the light of transnational and transdisciplinary networks, exchanges and articulations.

Until the 1990s, criticism on Wright unfolded along fracture lines and rarely sought continuity. It proceeded to cut Wright's career into space-bound and time-rigid blocks, such as "Apprenticeship," "Fulfillment," "Exile"[43] or the South, Chicago, New York, Paris.[44] It resulted in a relative inability to understand and make sense of the complexity in Wright's career course and aesthetic.[45] The discontinuity paradigm was reinforced by the many missing pieces in Wright's oeuvre. Recent explorations of the posthumously published *Rite of Passage* (1994), *A Father's Law* (2008), and the unpublished manuscripts *Black Hope* or *Island of Hallucinations* have shown the damage of a previously compartmentalized and incomplete vision of his work.[46] A more encompassing approach illuminates in a new way, not just Wright's exile works, but also his early works.[47] The promises of transnational history combined with the methodology and objects of book history could nourish disciplines like literary criticism, literary history, cultural and political history as well as further engage scholars in the issues of African American agency and of changing relations to power.

Notes

1. P. Gilroy, *The Black Atlantic Modernity and Double Consciousness* (Cambridge: Harvard University Press, 1993), 156.
2. M. Fabre, *From Harlem to Paris: Black American Writers in France 1840–1980* (Urbana and Chicago: University of Illinois Press, 1991). T. Stovall, *Paris Noir, African Americans in the City of Light* (New York: Houghton Mifflin Company, 1996).

3. Such a French-American conversation over race and the American contributions to the French debate have been celebrated in T. D. Keaton, T. D. Sharpley-Whiting, and T. Stovall, *Black France / France Noire. The History and Politics of Blackness* (Durham and London: Duke University Press, 2012).

4. R. Chartier, *The Order of Books* (Stanford: Stanford University Press, 1994 [1992]).

5. D. K. Young, *Black Writers, White Publishers: Marketplace Politics in Twentieth-Century African American Literature* (Jackson: University Press of Mississippi, 2006). L. Cossu-Beaumont and C. Parfait, "Book History and African American Studies," *Transatlantica*, 2009. G. Hutchinson and J. K. Young, *Publishing Blackness, Textual Constructions of Race since 1850* (Ann Arbor: University of Michigan Press, 2013). C. Cottenet, ed., *Race, Ethnicity and Publishing in America* (Basingstoke: Palgrave Macmillan, 2014).

6. C. Parfait, *The Publishing History of Uncle Tom's Cabin, 1852–2002* (Burlington: Ashgate, 2007). C. Cottenet, *Une histoire éditoriale:* The Conjure Woman *de Charles W. Chesnutt* (Lyon : ENS Éditions, Institut d'histoire du livre, 2012). M. Roy, "Cheap Editions, Little Books, and Handsome Duodecimos: A Book History Approach to Antebellum Slave Narratives," *MELUS* 40 (3) (2015), 69–93. M. Roy, "'Printers were almost afraid to set up types': Publishing and Circulating Antislavery Literature in Antebellum America", in M. Roy, M-J. Rossignol and C. Parfait (eds.), *Undoing Slavery: American Abolitionism in Transnational Perspective (1776–1865)*, (Paris: Éditions Rue d'Ulm, 2018), 93–112.

7. L. Jackson, "The Talking Book and the Talking Book Historian," *Book History* (Johns Hopkins University Press, Vol. 13, 2010), 295, n12.

8. M. Fabre, *The Unfinished Quest of Richard Wright* (New York: William & Morrow, 1973), 302–304 and 312–313.

9. Gallimard eventually secured the rights of *Black Boy* after they were withdrawn from Albin Michel under the translator's pressure (Marcel Duhamel) that he would not translate *Black Boy* unless it was for Gallimard. Albin Michel obtained *Uncle Tom's Children* in the bargain. I am grateful to Cécile Cottenet for bringing this to my attention and providing me with her notes from the Michel Hoffman archives located at the French Institute for Contemporary Publishing Archives (IMEC, BRH Fund, February–August 1945). Along with Jenny Bradley, considered in this chapter, Michel Hoffman was a Paris literary agent who specialized in English speaking literature.

10. *Un Enfant du Pays*, trans. H. Bokanowski and M. Duhamel (Paris: Albin Michel, 1947). *Les Enfants de l'Oncle Tom*, trans. M. Duhamel and introduction P. Robeson (Paris: Albin Michel, 1947). *Jeunesse Noire*, trans. M. Duhamel and A. Picard (Paris: Gallimard, 1948).

11. Some are listed in K. Kinnamon, J. Benson, M. Fabre, and C. Werner, eds., *A Richard Wright Bibliography: Fifty Years of Criticism and Commentary, 1933–1982* (Westport: Greenwood Publishers, 1988) and printed in K. Kinnamon and M. Fabre, eds., *Conversations with Richard Wright* (Jackson: University Press of Mississippi, 1993). The others were consulted in the form of press clippings at the Beinecke Rare Book and Manuscript Library at Yale University (Richard Wright Papers, James Weldon Johnson Memorial Collection of African American Arts and Letters [JWJ]) or in the back issues of

the French press at the Bibliothèque Nationale de France. I offer some conclusions on the reception of Richard Wright in France in "Race across the Atlantic: Jean-Paul Sartre and Richard Wright's Transatlantic Network in 1940s Paris" in H. Bak and C. Mansanti, eds., *Transatlantic Intellectual Networks* (Cambridge: Cambridge Scholars Publishing, 2018).

12. As for Wright's popular success in terms of sales, the William A. Bradley Literary Agency Records reveal that Wright was granted generous contracts and advances as well as regular royalties. While Wright received 100,000 francs for advance royalties for *Black Boy*, Gallimard offered an option for his next two (unwritten) books for 200,000 francs for each book shortly after the publication of *Black Boy*, attesting to the sales potential Wright represented on the French market (William A. Bradley Literary Agency Records, Harry Ransom Center, University of Texas at Austin, MS 04–91, Letter from Jenny Bradley to Paul Reynolds, March 10, 1948, Box 210, Folder 7 and Letter from Jenny Bradley to Richard Wright, February 24, 1948, Box 66, Folder 9; the contracts for the upcoming books were signed in May 1948).

13. One of Wright's short stories had been published during the war in a 1944 special issue of the literary review *L'Arbalète*. The review continued to appear in Vichy France as a gesture of resistance. "Big Boy s'en va" was a French translation of "Big Boy Leaves Home" by Marcel Duhamel. Another literary journal, a communist one, *Les Lettres Françaises*, came to embody the clandestine resistance. The review published Wright's "The Man Who Killed a Shadow" in 1946 (M. Fabre, *The Unfinished Quest*, 305). *Combat*, a 1942 newspaper founded by Albert Camus as a resistance paper, was the first to interview Wright on the platform of the Gare Saint Lazare on May 10, 1946. H. Rowley, *Richard Wright, The Life and Times* (New York: Henry Holt and Company, 2001), 331–332.

14. P. Baert, *The Existentialist Moment, The Rise of Sartre as a Public Intellectual* (Cambridge and Malden: Polity Press, 2015).

15. A. Beevor and A. Cooper, *Paris After the Liberation, 1944–1949* (Penguin, 2007 [1994]). See Chapter 12, "Writers and Artists in the Line of Fire."

16. R. Wright, *Black Boy* in Richard Wright, *Later Works* (New York: Library of America XE "Library of America," 1991), Vol II, 237.

17. T. Stovall, *Transnational France, The Modern History of a Universal Nation* (Boulder, CO: Westview Press, 2015), 369–376.

18. R. Chartier, *The Order of Books*, 3.

19. R. Wright, "A Personal Report from Paris," n.d., Richard Wright Papers (JWJ Collection, Beinecke Rare Book and Manuscript Library, Yale University, Box 6, Folder 130).

20. Upon publication *The Outsider* was caricatured as "the work of an adherent of Jean Paul Sartre's dark and brooding philosophy of existentialism" (Review of *The Outsider* in *The Times*, Trenton NJ, June 14, 1953, Richard Wright Papers, JWJ Collection, Beinecke Rare Book and Manuscript Library, Yale University, Box 121, Folder 1943). Wright's contemporaries such as Lorraine Hansberry and Arna Bontemps both dismissed *The Outsider* as too European; Bontemps famously referred to Wright's "roll in the hay with the existentialism of Sartre" (A. Bontemps, "Three Portraits of the Negro," *The Saturday Review*, March 28, 1953, 15–16).

21. J.-P. Sartre, *What Is Literature? and Other Essays* (Cambridge: Harvard University Press, 1988 [1948]), 78–80.

22. French scholar Michel Fabre first called for a more nuanced appraisal of Wright's supposed succumbing to existentialist illusions in "Richard Wright and the French Existentialists," *MELUS*, Vol. 5, No. 2 (Summer 1978), 39–51. More recently, S. Milgram Knapp's chapter "Recontextualizing Richard Wright's *The Outsider*: Hugo, Dostoevsky, Max Eastman, and Ayn Rand" convincingly maps out a broader existentialist ethos and aesthetic to which *The Outsider* fully contributes (in W. Dow, *et al.*, *Richard Wright in a Post-Racial Imaginary*, New York and London: Bloomsbury, 2014, 99–111).

23. In that respect one is reminded of Wright's proximity with Sartre's vision and idea of literature before he may have actually been "influenced" by them, as early as 1945. Wright's first encounter with Sartre's works was indeed spurred by Ralph Ellison's urging: "Sartre, one of the young writers, would have no difficulty in understanding your position in regards to the Left." (Letter from Ellison to Wright, July 22, 1945, JWJ Collection, Beinecke Rare Book and Manuscript Library, Yale University, Box 97, Folder 1314).

24. With the notable exception of Paul Gilroy whose delineation of the *Black Atlantic* offers a whole chapter on Wright in France. Gilroy also suggests that Simone de Beauvoir's *The Second Sex* deserves to be viewed through the lens of her exchanges on racial/gender alienation with Wright, as she herself acknowledged. P. Gilroy, *The Black Atlantic, op cit.* (on Wright, 146–186, and on Beauvoir, 186).

25. For a historical survey of Americans in Paris, see D. McCullough, *The Greater Journey: Americans in Paris* (New York: Simon and Schuster, 2011). For writers especially, see A. Gopnik, *Americans in Paris: a Literary Anthology* (New York: Library of America, 2004).

26. Richard Wright's 1945 letters to Gertrude Stein, Richard Wright Papers (JWJ Collection, Beinecke Rare Book and Manuscript Library, Yale University, Box 106, Folder 1619) and Gertrude Stein and Alice B. Toklas Papers (Yale Collection of American Literature, Beinecke Rare Book and Manuscript Library, Yale University, Box 131, Folder 246).

27. Originally funded by William A. Bradley in the 1920s, the Bradley agency was run by Jenny Bradley after her husband's death in 1939. Although the agency is responsible for the publishing of canonical authors such as Gertrude Stein, Richard Wright, William Faulkner, or Truman Capote in France and Jean-Paul Sartre, Albert Camus, or André Malraux in the United States, it has yet to be the object of a book-length study and noteworthy scholarly articles. The other pioneering literary agency, Michel Hoffman, has just been the topic of a book exploring its records. See C. Cottenet, *Literary Agents in the Transatlantic Book Trade: American Fiction, French Rights, and the Hoffman Agency* (New York: Routledge, 2017).

28. William A. Bradley Literary Agency Records, Harry Ransom Center, Box 150, Folder 7.

29. Eventually, due to the stalling of the visa emission by the State Department, other strings had to be pulled, through Claude Levi-Strauss, then cultural attaché at the French embassy in Washington who was able to secure an

invitation from the French government itself. M. Fabre, *The Unfinished Quest*, 298 and 300.

30. Marcel Duhamel was a central cultural passeur in the French American conversation. Wright's early translator, he was also the editor at Gallimard of a successful pulp collection *Série Noire* (1945–1977). In 1948, the *Série Noire* published 14 novels and in 1949, 25 novels, all of them translated from English, the majority from American authors, among them Dashiell Hammett, Raymond Chandler and later on Chester Himes.

31. Early June 1949, Wright received the royalties Geoffrey Homes had obtained for *Build My Gallow High* published in the *Série Noire* (William A. Bradley Literary Agency Records, Harry Ransom Center, Box 210, Folder 7). On June 28, 1949, Jenny Bradley informs Paul Reynolds that she has signed Richard English's *Sugarplum Staircase* with Gallimard for the *Série Noire* and writes: "I will collect the advance and pay it to Dick" (Dick being Richard Wright).

32. James Baldwin was only able to write *Giovanni's Room* in France in 1954 thanks to the financial support of his and Wright's agent Jenny Bradley who lent him money to buy coal and make ends meet (William A. Bradley Literary Agency Records, Harry Ransom Center, Box 3, Folder 4). Chester Himes gained success and financial security from his collaboration with Marcel Duhamel at Gallimard. Duhamel, translator of *If He Hollers Let Him Go* and editor of *Série Noire*, pushed Himes to write the detective novels he became known for.

33. The suggested reevaluation along the *divergence / confluence* line is borrowed from G. Holcomb – as is the emphasis. "When Wright Bid McKay Break Bread: Tracing Black Transnational Genealogy" in A. M. Craven and W. E. Dow, *Richard Wright, New Readings in the 21ˢᵗ Century* (New York: Palgrave MacMillan, 2011), 215–234.

34. Both P. Gilroy in the *Black Atlantic*, 146–186; and J. Clifford in *Routes (Routes: Travel and Translation in the Late Twentieth Century* (Cambridge: Harvard University Press, 1997), 262 have referred to Wright as a pivotal figure. See also R. D. G. Kelley "How the West Was One: The African Diaspora and the Re-Mapping of U.S. History" in T. Bender, *Rethinking American History in a Global Age* (Cambridge: Cambridge University Press, 2002), 123–147.

35. M. Fabre, *The Unfinished Quest*, 317.

36. *Black Orpheus* is Sartre's preface to L. Senghor, ed., *Anthologie de la nouvelle poésie nègre et malgache de langue française* (Paris: Presses Universitaires de France, 1948). The essay can be read in J.-P. Sartre, *What Is Literature? And Other Essays* (Cambridge: Harvard University Press, 1988 [1948]). "Black Orpheus" is 289–333.

37. F. Fanon's *Black Skin, White Masks* (1952) and *The Wretched of the Earth* (1961) takes its place in this continuum, the former for the dialectical influences it comes to terms with, the latter through the editorial strategy of having Sartre write the preface.

38. For an account of the Congress and of the debates, see B. Jules-Rosette, *Black Paris. The African Writers' Landscape* (Urbana and Chicago: University of Illinois Press, 1998). James Baldwin attended as a reporter for *Encounter*.

39. T. Stovall suggests the connection also existed between 1930s Harlem Renaissance artists visiting Paris such as Langston Hughes or Countee Cullen and the very early stages of the Négritude in 1930s Paris with young Senghor and

Césaire already elaborating their vision. T. Stovall, "No Green Pastures, the African Americanization of France," in D. Clark Hine, T. D. Keaton, and S. Small, *Black Europe and the African Diaspora* (Urbana and Chicago: University of Illinois Press, 2009), 186.

40. The encounter of the three figures is suggested by A. Singh in his Foreword to A. Craven et al., *Richard Wright in a Post-Racial Imaginary* (New York and London: Bloomsbury, 2014), x.

41. Ibid.

42. B. Hayes Edward's analysis of Black diasporic discourse in 1920s and 1930s Paris resists conclusions of influence or imitation by suggesting scholars look at "differences within unity" and articulations within the communities of African and African American intellectuals meeting in Paris. *The Practice of Diaspora. Literature, Translation, and the Rise of Black Internationalism* (Cambridge: Harvard University Press, 2003), 13–15.

43. R. Felgar, *Richard Wright* (Boston: Twayne, 1980).

44. D. Bakish, *Richard Wright* (New York: Ungar, 1973) or D. Ray et al., *Richard Wright Impressions and Perspectives* (Ann Arbor: University of Michigan Press, 1972).

45. "Wright's paramount concerns can be *isolated* into four areas: race relations in America, Marxism, contemporary international affairs, and Wright's own changing philosophical props." My emphasis. R. C. Brignano *Richard Wright: An Introduction to the Man and His Works* (Pittsburgh University of Pittsburgh, 1970), xi.

46. The two collections of essays that stemmed from the 2008 Wright Centennial Conference in Paris reflect such a critical reassessment informed by the paradigms of continuity and transnational frameworks: the need to connect the dots of a lifelong artistic and intellectual path rather than stress ruptures and conflicts (*Richard Wright, New Readings in the 21st Century*, 2011) the belief that Wright heralded a global and post-racial era of thinking and criticizing the world (*Richard Wright in a Post-Racial Imaginary*, 2014).

47. For instance *Black Hope*, an unpublished manuscript mostly drafted in 1942 and whose main voice is feminine, triggers a necessary revising of the notion that Wright failed in addressing feminine voices of the black experience. In that regard B. Foley's piece on *Black Hope* in *Richard Wright in a Post-Racial Imaginary* (2014) stands in sharp contrast with earlier criticism exemplified by Maria K. Mootry's "Bitches, Whores and Woman Haters: Archetypes and Typologies in the Art of Richard Wright" in R. Macksey and Franck E. Moorer, eds., *Richard Wright: A Collection of Critical Essays* (Englewoods Cliffs: Prentice Hall, 1984), 117–129; or Miriam DeCosta-Willis, "Avenging Angels and Mute Mothers: Black Southern Women in Wright's Fictional World" *Callaloo*, Vol 9.3 (Summer 1986), 540–549. Not much has been made of "Memories of My Grand Mother," another unpublished piece with a strong feminine voice available at the Beinecke.

9

ALICE MIKAL CRAVEN

Expatriation in Wright's Late Fiction

Black expatriate companionship and competition for recognition coexisted in Parisian African American circles in the 1950s. Following Richard Wright's move to Paris in 1947, writers such as James Baldwin, Chester Himes, and Richard Gibson, along with numerous other black artists, went to France seeking ways to exercise their individual creativity and thus find freedom from writing exclusively about the so-called Negro problem. But their dreams of freedom were frustrated by intergroup tensions created by the expectation – self- and collectively imposed – that they would write for the purposes of political protest. Such tensions were exacerbated by the fact that the United States government kept many of these artists under surveillance through the Central Intelligence Agency and the Federal Bureau of Investigation. Wright's late fiction, in particular his last published novel *The Long Dream* (1958), and its intended sequel, Wright's unpublished manuscript "Island of Hallucination," fictionalizes the dreams and frustrations of expatriate life.

The Long Dream is set in a small town in Mississippi and focuses on the relationship between Fishbelly and his father, Tyree, from whom he learns to remain silent within the white world of Jim Crow. The novel ends as Fishbelly expatriates to France while the sequel follows his expatriation. Both texts reflect the high level of paranoia in the black expatriate community, with Fishbelly's trajectory as an individual caught in a web of suspicion paralleling that of expatriated black artists at the time. The novel and manuscript also echo Wright's ultimate withdrawal from expatriate circles that he led and his desire to explore his trajectory from celebrated black American author to compromised expatriate.

John A. Williams, in his novel *The Man Who Cried I Am* (1967), models his protagonist Max Reddick on writer Chester Himes (1909–1984), an artist equally challenged by the contradictions of expatriate life. Reddick, as well as other characters, in *The Man Who Cried I Am* "measure[s] the power of US state surveillance to shape (but not to break) African American literary history."[1] While one of Williams's central characters, Harry Ames, is based on Wright in his years of exile, the novel also offers a parallel to Fishbelly's furtiveness through Harry's own secretive nature. Close readings of both Williams's depiction of Wright and of Wright's late fiction show that despite surveillance and suspicion, black expatriate artists managed to create lasting documents attesting to the value of black expatriation and its contributions to American history. Yet Wright's late fiction has been underestimated by critics, thereby complicating contemporary evaluation of Wright's legacy. Williams's fictional recreation of Wright's struggles provides a vital corrective to those critical assessments.

Both "Island of Hallucination" and Williams's *The Man Who Cried I Am* also function as "anti-files" to the voluminous public records collected by the US government against black expatriates.[2] As John A. Williams suggests through the character of Max Reddick in the *The Man Who Cried I Am*, "the secret to converting *their* change to *your* change was *letting them know that you knew*. And he now knew to what extent they would go to keep black men n***ers."[3] In commenting on this passage from Williams's novel, William J. Maxwell posits that the key to protecting the legacy of black arts was through "creating transformative anti-files that let the U.S. intelligence know that you knew of its intrigues."[4] Black artists, according to Maxwell and Williams, were actively resisting and countering what the FBI files attested to in their chronicling of black expatriate life.

Maxwell refers to the FBI's voracious surveillance as "ghost reading" designed to discover and control the secrets, and therefore the impact, of black American artists on America's image abroad. The possibility that black expatriates would challenge America's world image by exposing its racist practices was of vital concern to government surveillance agencies, as was the possibility that these writers might have Communist leanings.[5] Wright's and Williams's fiction not only describes the atmosphere of secrecy and potential betrayal that this surveillance created within black expatriate communities, but also offers alternative ways of imagining black expatriation. In the eyes of the black expatriate artists writing from within the subgenre of "black radical counterintelligence," the perpetuation of Afro-modern literary paternity was at stake.[6]

The publication of *Native Son* (1940) and *Black Boy* (1945) situated Wright as the most prominent black protest writer in the United States. Therefore, writers seeking to emulate him worked from within the protest novel tradition, the category under which Wright was best if not accurately known. Even before Wright distanced himself from America, he challenged the idea that creative fiction and political protest were mutually exclusive, but when he expatriated, he further explored artistic forms that moved away from the naturalism and protest traditions with which he was first associated. In so doing, he disoriented his followers and contenders while also creating a paradigm shift in artistic possibilities for black expatriates.

Being recognized as an eminent black writer in Wright's time was not easy. Melvin Van Peebles argues as much in his preface to Himes's novel *Yesterday Will Make You Cry* (1998): "In the States (outside of music) we were only allowed one brilliant Negro *per* profession and Richard Wright, soon to be dethroned by Jimmy Baldwin, had beaten Chester [Himes] to the wire in the protest novel department."[7] No matter how close black artists were to each other in their expatriate communities, there was always the awareness that American audiences, in expecting only "one Negro" to be recognized, were inadvertently fomenting competition. The expatriates' needs to remain relevant often led them to play the "Negro problem" card and stick to the protest tradition. Thus, companionship, government surveillance, and creative competition were closely intertwined. The infamous Gibson Affair, which involved a 1957 letter that Richard Gibson and William Gardner Smith wrote to *Life* magazine criticizing French policy in Algeria and which included Gibson's forged signature of the cartoonist Oliver W. Harrington, is a case in point. The affair disclosed the willingness of many black American expatriates to collaborate with government agencies or to undermine the comfort zone of their fellow expatriates was rooted in the spirit of competition for artistic recognition and was facilitated by their reliance upon each other for daily needs.[8]

Wright's attitudes toward his exile and his political milieu come into focus in his creation of a protagonist who struggles with his perceived need to remain silent even in the face of racial injustice. Fishbelly is modeled on the trajectory of a coming-of-age genre which is carried over from *The Long Dream* to "Island." But as Fishbelly matures, his narrative becomes more sophisticated, and he and his father eventually come to "share a dark secret" about the white world that surrounds them.[9] At first, he is deeply ashamed of his father's submission to the white world and vows not to follow in his footsteps. This is exemplified when Fishbelly's older friend Chris is killed by white men for cavorting with a white woman. Tyree, who runs a funeral service for the blacks in town, tells his son that he makes money by "gitting black dreams ready for burial." He asserts that "a black man's a dream that can't come true."[10] Tyree will not speak up against racial injustice or violence and sees silence, and even lying, as modes of survival.

Upon hearing his father's drunken tirade about the hopelessness of black lives, Fishbelly is filled with a "nameless hatred for his father."[11] But despite his shame about his father's defeatism, Fishbelly eventually embraces the practice of justified lying when he sees that his father is not invulnerable to the dictates of white supremacy. Fishbelly nonetheless reasons that though his father is not invulnerable, his *legacy* might be. Fishbelly devotes himself to protecting the one piece of evidence that can save his father's legacy after Tyree is killed. A set of canceled checks that find their way into Fishbelly's possession would prove that Chief of Police Cantley had been routinely collecting protection money from Fishbelly's father. Fishbelly zealously guards those checks so he can clear his father's name.

Rooted in a dissection of American Dream mythologies, the structure of *The Long Dream* suggests that Wright's *aesthetic* development at the end of his life was not, as critics have claimed, in a state of confusion or turmoil. Rather, Wright was focused on further constructing a transnational artistic voice (see Rinehart in this volume) through deeper explorations of literary forms and the awareness afforded by the experience of expatriation. For instance, through Fishbelly's experiences, Wright meditates on the role of silence in racial discourse. Though Fishbelly is pressured by Cantley, he holds his tongue while in the Mississippi jail and begins to dream of escaping to Europe. He reluctantly acknowledges the wisdom of his father's lessons about the "shadow" life imposed upon black men and accepts this need for silence as part of his own social condition and history. As a result, Fishbelly is most adamantly against "race talk." Early in the novel, Sam says, "You-all just 'shamed of being *black*.'" Fishbelly responds by saying, "Aw Sam, stop that kind of talk."[12] He repeatedly asks those around him to stop all their "race talk" as a way of protecting himself and others from potential racial violence.[13] But in "Island of Hallucination," Fishbelly is betrayed by race talk. For the first time in his life, he trusts and therefore openly talks about race with a white French man during his transatlantic flight. When he discovers that the man has conned him, he feels intense self-hatred. He feels that his past conditioning was the cause of his being duped and his fear of "race talk" is reinforced.[14]

Wright ends *The Long Dream* with Fishbelly's transatlantic flight departing from America to Europe, and begins "Island" with that same flight arriving in Paris. Though airport terminals began to be integrated between 1948 and 1962, transatlantic *flights* were integrated by default since flights were controlled by federal law.[15] When Fishbelly takes the plane to Paris, the physical space of the airplane cabin creates the illusion of an entry into an integrated world. At the end of *The Long Dream*, Fishbelly finds himself in an airplane cabin and he realizes that this "was the first time in his life that he had sat surrounded by white men, women and children with no degrading, visible line marking him off." But he adds that his "knees were held stiffly together, as though he expected his presence to be challenged."[16] Though he tries to avert his gaze, he eventually gives in to the temptation to look at the beautiful and luxurious head of hair of the white woman in front of him. His joy at this vision is coupled with anxiety as he witnesses "the charming trap that could trigger his deepest fears of death."[17] During the flight, he speaks with the passenger sitting next to him, an Italian American. When asked by the Italian American how it feels to be an American Negro, Fishbelly withdraws into silence. He does not contest the Italian American's image of the American Dream, but his silence reveals that Fishbelly is "not yet emotionally strong enough to admit what he had lived."[18]

Fishbelly knows he should refute what the Italian American believes to be true about America, but he remains silent in order to gain entry into the European world – his dream world. The closing pages of the novel emphasize exhilaration at the potential for a new cultural experience. But exhilaration is coupled with the anxiety of longing to know if he can belong in his newly chosen home. Metaphors of silence prevail and are interwoven with Fishbelly's dream life lying just below the surface. The shameful life he has had to live as a black American continually reemerges in his musings. As he reflects on the Italian American's questions, he notes that the "man's father had come to America and found a dream; he [Fishbelly] had been born in America and had found a nightmare."[19] Unlike the other passengers on the plane, Fishbelly "sat looking at the dream images of his life with wide-open eyes." He rejected the "curtain of dreams shielding [their] hearts from the claims of waking hours."[20]

Fishbelly's lessons in learning to be silent run parallel to the structure of dreaming. For Fishbelly, the dream of escaping to Europe was made possible through his prolonged silence while incarcerated in America. Tyree's advice to Fishbelly was to "dream only what can happen,"[21] and this is what Fishbelly believes he has managed to do. The novel's series of loosely connected memories of events in Fishbelly's life reflects its emphasis on dreaming as the memories come to have the quality of dreams. Events in *The Long Dream* become more tightly woven together when Fishbelly must act or speak in ways that have consequences on the directions his life will take. And the plot becomes more driven by Fishbelly as he internalizes his father's lesson.

The Long Dream and "Island" are structured on the interplay of dreams and frustrated desires. In "Island," Fishbelly remains aware of his longing to belong in his new environment. But he is shocked to discover that France is not actually a country free of racial prejudice, as when he is tricked by the Frenchman. Each time Fishbelly's dream of escape from racial prejudice is frustrated, his reaction is to let himself be reduced to silence. The shame and loathing he once felt for his father are increasingly directed toward himself and his actions in the world. As the narrator describes it, Fishbelly feels his "shame protecting him from the meaning of what had happened. It was as though he had struck his thumb with a hammer and was waiting for the numbness to thaw out and the searing pain to come."[22]

Wright's decisions about what to write and what to suppress in his last years are fictionalized through Fishbelly's coming-of-age experiences, while his decision to abandon the "Island" manuscript suggests that he was increasingly aware that, even though he had become a prominent writer, his racial identity could overshadow his artistic accomplishments. As he points out in his letter to James Holness dated July 7, 1959, when he declines an invitation to attend a cultural festival in London, "I shall state my case honestly. I'm an American Negro. We American Negroes who live abroad live under tremendous political pressure ... Hence I must keep clear of entanglements that would stifle me in expressing myself in terms that I feel are my own."[23] Wright decision to stop working on "Island" can thus be seen as a choice to opt for silence. Gibson's 2005 summary of the quasi-biographical conflicts presented by the manuscript, cited earlier, suggests as much. Gibson's article calls for a publication of "Island of Hallucination" as an important document showing Wright's state of mind in his final days. The article provides an overview of the relationships between the manuscript and the Gibson affair, in which Oliver "Ollie" Harrington's name was forged. The forgery placed Harrington in danger of being deported from France. Ollie Harrington, an African American expatriate cartoonist, was Richard Wright's good friend, and the fiasco caused much suspicion among members of the African American expatriate community. In this article, Gibson wants to set the record straight on what really occurred during the infamous Gibson Affair.

Gibson stresses that confusions about the Cold War fears, black expatriate fears about being accused of Communist leanings, and arguments about the question of Algeria all fueled the combative and compromised interactions between black expatriates in their social circles. The "entanglements" from which Wright wished to free himself in his last days were precisely the subject matter of the manuscript reflected in the daily interactions between the "false brothers" (African Americans willing to betray their brethren) in Parisian circles in the late 1950s. Wright's hatred of these brothers incited him to write the manuscript.[24] In abandoning the manuscript, Wright freed himself in the immediate from such entanglements. As Gibson points out, Wright's widow, Ellen followed his lead when she decided to "consign it [the manuscript] to obscurity."[25]

Despite these decisions, the manuscript has been available to the public since 1996. Its title is telling once one recognizes the importance of dream imagery to both the novel and the manuscript. It suggests that the literary value of the manuscript has been obscured by the salacious details of the context in which it was created. Following the lead of *The Long Dream*, daydreams become nightmares, and finally, in "Island of Hallucination" that most extreme of dream forms – hallucination – takes hold. Indeed, the opening section of "Island" reads like a dream become nightmare verging on the hallucinatory.

The chapter traces the inner monologues of the white American passengers surrounding Fishbelly and thus shows that the "hallucination" of the novel's title, far from alluding only to Fishbelly's experience, also pertains to the white people around him. They are appalled by him but have no legal recourse for eradicating his presence. The reactions of the white American passengers are described in detail as they gaze upon a sleeping Fishbelly. They question his foolish intentions in making his transatlantic journey, react in anger and fear to his presence, and entertain thoughts of lynching him. Fishbelly notices their hostile faces upon awaking but his dream of reaching a colorblind France leads him to dismiss their reactions. He yearns to counter the pain caused by the Americans' attitudes by embracing the overtures of the French couple he encounters on the plane. Yet Fishbelly's dream of a postracial world is shattered in his first twenty-four hours by the harsh reality of his newly adopted home.[26] Europe offers him unlimited freedom in his dreams, and isolation and disappointment in his reality.

The Paradox of Competition and Companionship in *The Man Who Cried I Am*

In *The Man Who Cried I Am*, Williams muses on the thin line between companionship and competition that presided over the African American expatriation movement during the 1950s. The novel provides valuable context by repositioning Wright's late fiction in critical circles. When Harry Ames promises and then is ultimately denied a literary prize because he is a "Negro," he echoes the account of Wright as an artist who failed to achieve his dream of being recognized as a writer on his own terms. Williams's novel is structured as a labyrinthine quasi-historical novel and takes place over a three-day period just after the death of Harry Ames. During these days, Max Reddick, the novel's protagonist, has returned to Europe to attend the funeral of his good friend Ames and to revisit his own past, as well as the past life he and Ames had shared together in Europe.[27] Much of the narration is thus a reflective review of Max's experience as an African American expatriate, and many of the episodes are evocative of actual events in the lives of other expatriates such as James Baldwin, Richard Gibson, Chester Himes, William Gardner Smith, and Wright.[28]

The paradox of competition and companionship is a constant trope. For example, at one point Reddick is offered a job as a journalist in Africa by his US newspaper, which is run by whites. He quickly realizes that by sending him across the Atlantic, the newspaper gives him a "promotion" that they couldn't give to a "Negro" in New York. He reluctantly learns that he could be promoted by white bosses if he agreed to befriend and then betray his fellow black expatriates. Many of Reddick's reflections concern the fact that in the 1950s, a black person's desire to leave the US was not understood. In fact it was feared, since white Americans were uncomfortable with the idea of black Americans representing them abroad. The inner monologue of one of the white passengers in Fishbelly's flight in "Island" spells out the fear: "Dammit, we oughtn't let niggers out of the country to run wild. No telling what kind of lies they're spreading about us."[29] This apprehension is echoed in the works of Williams and Wright.

Williams shows the irony of competition and friendly commiseration in the closing pages of his novel. In his will, Ames entrusts Reddick with important government surveillance documents. As Maxwell points out, if one considers both "Island of Hallucination" and *The Man Who Cried I Am* as anti-files, then Ames's decision to entrust secret documents to Reddick is a fictional reenactment of the way those two texts are perceived in terms of their historical significance.

The documents in Williams's novel concern a vast government conspiracy against black American expatriates and is code-named the King Alfred Plan. As Ames well knows, by sharing the documents with Reddick, he has put Reddick's life in danger. In Ames's last message to Max, Ames claims that he has entrusted Max with these documents because he was the only friend and brother Ames could trust. The companionship they share, according to Williams's depiction, parallels descriptions of the community of black American expatriates described by Oliver W. Harrington in his collection of essays *Why I Left America*.[30]

In his last message, Ames also bequeaths Reddick with the title of "father of the modern black American novel," seemingly to compensate for the fact that he has placed Reddick in harm's way. The echo of Wright in the character of Harry Ames is even more forcefully asserted here, since Wright was long recognized as the father of the modern black American novel. Williams essentially gives the Wright-based character Harry Ames the authority to decide which black author will triumph in the competitive race to be recognized. By doing so, Ames and Williams undermine the authority of white America to arbitrate on this matter.

The novels analyzed here ultimately confront white control over America's world image. Williams implies in his essay "Wright, Wrong and Black Reality" that his views on Wright and the question of black expatriate competition were very much on his mind when he wrote *The Man Who Cried I Am*. As he says, "Now that Wright is dead how we line up to celebrate his gifts! Now that he offers us no competition, how wonderful he was we say!"[31] Williams emphasizes how real the sense of competition between black expatriate artists was as a weapon against black unity and, by extension, of white America's hold on the perception of the country abroad.

Williams's ending does nonetheless recount the sudden death of Reddick and does not ultimately excuse Ames for putting Reddick's life in danger. Once authorities become aware that Reddick possessed the government documents that had previously been guarded by Ames, Reddick is killed. Williams suggests that expatriation afforded creative freedom for black artists but, through Reddick's reflections, Williams equally intimates that expatriation also entailed oppression. In the novel, secret government documents concerning a vast conspiracy against American blacks is a credible fiction. The novel also asserts that the only category admissible for black art was that of the protest tradition, even when it was penned, painted or performed on alien soil.

The conspiracy theories surrounding the mysterious death of Wright compound Williams's dire picture of the dangers of black expatriation. Wright's death has often been blamed on the government surveillance agencies which relentlessly pursued him, as Harrington points out in his collection of essays *Why I Left America*. Harrington claims that Wright routinely called either Harrington or Chester Himes before he went to the American Hospital for a check-up, and that this was the only time he did not call them in advance. He also remarks that Wright did not go to the American hospital, but rather to a private clinic on this particular visit, which resulted in his death.[32] Despite research that contradicts Harrington's conclusions, stories of his mysterious death are also reminders that the life of the expatriate artist was paradoxically freer but more perilous than imagined. Williams's novel captures the spirit of paranoia that fueled the black expatriate community in Wright's time and suggests that the situation is self-perpetuating.

Choosing One's History

In *The Fire Next Time*, Baldwin states, "The paradox – and a fearful paradox it is – is that the American Negro can have no future anywhere, on any *continent*, as long as he is unwilling to accept his past. To accept one's past – one's history – is not the same thing as drowning in it; it is learning to use it."[33] By choosing expatriation, black artists refused to drown in their histories and, instead, compelled reactions that took many forms at the time – suspicion and surveillance from Americans as well as competition from compatriots.

In Wright's late fiction and in *The Man Who Cried I Am*, expatriates struggle with their pasts in order to create new futures. As Reddick says to himself, "he did not hate. Oh, he had not forgotten; it was just that the future demanded something else."[34] To survive, one must confront and assume the burden of a past riddled with racist violence as well as accept that such violence cannot be eradicated. Wright nonetheless found solace in the fact that he could be a writer on his own terms. Revalorizing his late fiction vindicates the risks he took in that direction. In his speech at the American Church of Paris a few weeks before his death, Wright said, "You have the right to say that what I've written is good or bad but you cannot say that it was controlled by the influences extant in the black belt."[35] Wright insists that it is his *own* life of reading and his self-willed expatriation which allowed him to construct an identity free from the ideological control and conditioning of his place of origin, the deeply racist Southern United States. His late fiction needs to be reconsidered rigorously to appreciate the position he took at the end of his life. Literary critics as well as government agencies monitoring Wright's late fiction ironically bear resemblance to the ubiquitous and unyielding Chief Cantley one encounters in *The Long Dream*. Cantley dogs Fishbelly even in his jail cell, just as the CIA and FBI haunted black American expatriates through those willing to exchange information for money or favors.[36] Wright's last speech on "The American Negro Intellectual and Artist in the United States Today" established that, even as an expatriate, Wright had not stopped thinking about the literal place of black Americans. Wright's importance as the father of the modern black American novel gave him the needed visibility to forge new paths in constructing a transnational discourse about race. Yet he knew that were that discourse to consume his creative practice or derail his intellectual journey, it would short circuit any influence he might have on future generations of black American artists. American cultural history owes a debt to Wright's bravado as he faced the paradoxical world of expatriation and the final isolation and alienation it brought to him. His late fiction should be critically resituated with respect to his years of exile and his sophistication and maturity as a writer during that period must be revalorized.

Notes

1. William Maxwell, *How J. Edgar Hoover's Ghostreaders Framed African American Literature* (Princeton: Princeton University Press, 2015), 259.
2. The FBI accumulated a file on Wright that runs more than 250 pages. See James Campbell, *Exiled in Paris: Richard Wright, James Baldwin, Samuel Beckett and Others on the Left Bank* (Berkeley and Los Angeles: University of California Press, 2003), 120.
3. John A. Williams, *The Man Who Cried I Am* (New York: Tusk Ivories, 2004), location 6673 (Kindle Edition).
4. Maxwell, *J. Edgar Hoover's Ghostreaders*, 263.
5. Maxwell, *J. Edgar Hoover's Ghostreaders*, 260.
6. Maxwell, *J. Edgar Hoover's Ghostreaders*, 262.
7. Melvin van Peebles, "His Wonders to Perform." *Yesterday Will Make You Cry* (New York: W.W. Norton, 1998), 15.
8. For accounts of the Gibson affair, see also Richard Gibson's "Richard Wright's 'Island of Hallucination' and the 'Gibson Affair.'" *Modern Fiction Studies* 51.4 (2005), 896–920. The affair was an attempt to sabotage cartoonist Ollie Harrington by publishing a letter in his name that praised pro-Algerian efforts against the French governmental oppression. American expatriates were under pressure not to speak out on such a tense political situation and risked deportation to do so. Wright, a close friend of Harrington's, took the matter to heart and blamed Richard Gibson for the letter. The mundane excuse for Gibson's vengeance was that Gibson was staying in Harrington's apartment and refused to vacate upon Harrington's return to Paris. Eventually, Gibson admitted to the ruse and claimed William Gardner Smith as an accomplice, which Smith denied. It is one of the more infamous examples of just how rough infighting in the black expatriate community could be.
9. Wright, *The Long Dream* (Chatham: Chatham Booksellers, 1969), 27.
10. Ibid., 79.
11. Ibid., 79.
12. Ibid., 33.
13. Ibid., 357.
14. Ibid., 48.
15. Anke Ortleep, "The Desegregation of Airports in the American South." *The Smithsonian National Air and Space Museum* Website. May 24, 2012. https://airandspace.si.edu. In "I Choose Exile," Wright notes that his passage to Europe in 1947 was by ship: "I was not sorry when my ship sailed past the Statue of Liberty!" Putting Fishbelly on a transatlantic flight is significant since, as opposed to travel by sea, the airplane cabin was an integrated space by necessity. The change in travel settings thus serves an important narrative purpose.
16. Wright, *The Long Dream*, 378.
17. Ibid., 378.
18. Ibid., 380.
19. Ibid., 380.
20. Ibid., 382.
21. Ibid., 79.

22. Ibid., 44.
23. Richard Wright, Letter to James Holmes, July 7, 1959, Michel Fabre Papers. Manuscript. Rare Books Library. Robert W. Woodruff Library. Emory University, Atlanta, Georgia.
24. Gibson, "Richard Wright's 'Island of Hallucination' and the 'Gibson Affair'," 905.
25. Ibid., 905.
26. Wright, "Island of Hallucination." TS. Box 34, Folder 472. James Weldon Johnson Collection. Beinecke Rare Books and Manuscripts Library, Yale University, 254.
27. The Kindle edition published by Tusk Ivories (2004) includes an afterword written by John A. Williams. The afterword stresses that many believed his fictional conspiracy plot to be a true account. The King Alfred Plan, the conspiracy plot in question, was a plan to exterminate the Negro population in America (location 7059). This plot is echoed in Himes's *Plan B*.
28. Maxwell, *J. Edgar Hoover's Ghostreaders*, 260.
29. Wright, "Island," 2.
30. As Harrington points out in his essay, "The Last Days of Richard Wright," in Julia Wright, ed., *Why I Left America*, "the Tournon was Dick's favorite café in a Paris where everyone has a favorite café, and he could always be assured of an argument with his coffee (12). Harrington goes on in his essay to say that though Wright had many friends in Paris, there was always a notable hostility towards him from many of the regulars at the café. As he pointed out, there was always "a tight band of Americans who never tried to cloak their outright hatred of the great Negro writer" (12). Harrington suggests that interactions in the two main cafés for black expatriates, the Tournon and the Monaco, could range from lightweight jokes to political arguments to fistfights.
31. Williams, "Wright, Wrong, and Black Reality," *Negro Digest*, Vol. 18. December 2, 1968, 25.
32. Harrington, *Why I Left America*, 25.
33. Baldwin, *The Fire Next Time* (New York: Vintage, 1962), 81.
34. Williams, *The Man Who Cried I Am*, location 6648.
35. "The Negro Intellectual in the United States Today" (typescript and carbon copy of a speech by Richard Wright before a discussion group at the American Church in Paris, November 1960). *The Richard Wright Collection*, 1935–1967, Sc Micro R 1234–1235. c11. The Schomburg Center for Research in Black Culture, Harlem, New York.
36. Maxwell, *J. Edgar Hoover's Ghostreaders*, 259.

10

NICHOLAS T RINEHART

Richard Wright's Globalism

Introduction

In his now-classic – in some circles, infamous – study *The Black Atlantic: Modernity and Double Consciousness* (1993), Paul Gilroy mobilizes a trenchant critique of the tendencies within Americanist literary criticism and cultural studies to "overshadow" the "range and diversity of [Richard] Wright's work" by placing "fortifications" between his American writings – namely, *Uncle Tom's Children* (1938), *Native Son* (1940), and *Black Boy/ American Hunger* (1945/1970) – and the works produced following the author's self-exile from the United States in 1946. From his newfound home base in Paris, Wright published a series of existentially inflected novels often critiqued for being clumsy, stilted, and uninspired: *The Outsider* (1953), *Savage Holiday* (1954), and *The Long Dream* (1958). Perhaps the most significant and contentious works of his "post-American" era – indeed, the works on which most critical attention to his later writings has focused – were collections of travel writing and reportage: *Black Power: A Record of Reactions in a Land of Pathos* (1954), an ethnography of the Gold Coast on the eve of independence; *The Color Curtain: A Report on the Bandung Conference* (1956), on the 1955 meeting of political leaders from twenty-nine decolonizing nations across Africa and Asia in Bandung, Indonesia; and *Pagan Spain* (1957), an account of daily life under the strict Catholicism of Franco's regime.

Though aiming to demonstrate the continuities between Wright's so-called American works and the "supposedly inferior products of his European exile," namely *The Outsider*, Gilroy yet maintains that Wright's "mature position" diverged from an earlier "exclusive concern with American racial politics ... "[1] In so doing, *The Black Atlantic* typifies a dilemma that has beset Wright scholarship for several decades: the division of his life and work into nationalist and internationalist phases. Critics continue to ask whether the relationship between Wright's earlier and later output is characterized by fracture or continuity.[2] In the year of the author's death, novelist and critic J. Saunders Redding offered this evaluation:

When Richard Wright died in Paris recently his reputation stood very high with Europeans, and especially with the French, among whom he had lived for a decade. Translated into the major European languages, three of his first four books had assured him large audiences for his lectures in Italy, Holland, Germany, the Scandinavian countries and, of course, in France ...

Because of these same qualities he was much less admired in his native land, where he was too frequently charged with sensationalism, which in America, and only in America, is almost exclusively associated with the emotionally cheap, the tawdry, and the pornographic.[3]

Beyond noting the divergences in Wright's reception at home and abroad, Redding suggests that his sojourn overseas ultimately came at the expense of his literary art – thereby articulating, perhaps for the first time, an argument that has plagued Wright criticism since. Wright's own "emotions," which supplied the "power in the books for which he will be remembered, *Uncle Tom's Children*, *Native Son*, and *Black Boy*," Redding notes, "were the staple food of his childhood, youth and manhood, until he moved abroad."[4] And so if his move to Paris "in some ways completed him as a person," Redding remarks that "what was good for him as a social being was bad for his work. He had taken his Negroness with him, but he could not take with him the America that bred and fed his consciousness of Negroness."[5] This geographical and thus psychological distance drained the author's work of its power and literary lifeblood: "In going to live abroad, Dick Wright had cut the roots that once sustained him; the tight-wound emotional core had come unravelled [sic]; the creative center had dissolved; his memory of what Negro life in America was had lost its relevance to what Negro life in America is – or is becoming."[6]

Whereas Redding established a particular critical template for further "evaluations" of Wright's intellectual trajectory, others sought to prove that this very "emotional core" or "creative center" had not so much come undone or dissipated as simply evolved. Writing in 1968, Addison Gayle Jr. remarked that Wright's work – reflecting the dynamic state of African American psychic life writ large – always operated on two levels, the naturalistic or realistic and the existential. What we glimpse in the author's later post-exile work, Gayle implies, is not a wholesale abandonment or reversal of his earlier preoccupations, but more crucially a gradual shift toward "transcendence" over "pragmatism," the two forces that combine to produce the "schizophrenic quality" of Wright's work.[7] In Gayle's conception, then, *Native Son* is not simply an indictment of American society, but rather – *pace* Baldwin – "Bigger Thomas serves as the Christ figure, the martyr to the hopes of desperate men everywhere, the catalytic agent by which a society can be redeemed."[8]

By suggesting that Cross Damon, the murderous protagonist of *The Outsider*, signifies an elaboration of qualities first seen in Bigger Thomas – and further, that the nihilism of that later novel is presaged in "Bright and Morning Star," a story from Wright's debut collection *Uncle Tom's Children* – Gayle ultimately emphasizes the unity of Wright's work. "His vision, though often varied, remained true to the theme of his earlier writings," Gayle notes. Wright's post-exile work, then, does not represent a fundamental change (or loss) of vision, but more accurately a projection of his vision "on the world arena," thereby cementing the author's belief in and commitment to what he termed the "community of man."[9]

Gilroy's analysis, then, seems to synthesize the opposing positions of Redding and Gayle Jr. by suggesting that for Wright, "The image of the Negro and the idea of 'race' ... are living components of a western sensibility that extends beyond national boundaries" – in other words, that we must understand Wright's work on its own terms rather than "the same narrow definitions of racialised cultural expression that he struggled to overturn." In this rendering, Wright's post-exile work retains a peculiar racial consciousness abundant in his American work yet remains distinct from the narrower, nationalist scope thereof. My aim here is to further complicate this portrait of Wright's lifelong intellectual trajectory, positing instead that Wright's globalist imagination is not a late-stage development but rather the predominant theme that unites his *oeuvre* with a single continuous thread. This is not to uphold any rigid distinction between Wright's "Americanist" and "internationalist" periods, but more crucially to propose that his racial consciousness and globalist perspective were always already mutually constituted.

I suggest, moreover, that the globalism evident in his later work was more or less present from the outset, though admittedly in different form. The idea that "the Negro is no longer just America's metaphor but rather a central symbol in the psychological, cultural, and political systems of the West as a whole," as Gilroy writes, might not simply reflect Wright's "mature position," but his immature position, too.[10] Wright's work – including his fiction, essays, journalism, poetry, letters, and unpublished pieces spanning from the beginning of his career in the mid-1930s to his deathbed writings of 1960 – crystallizes his globalist imagination even as it shifts registers: from an anti-fascist political solidarity framed by Marxist internationalism to an affective kinship among formerly colonized peoples expressed through existentialist proto-postcolonialism, and finally toward a transcendent poetics in search of universal humanism.

Marxist Internationalism

In the summer of 1937, Wright began a stint reporting for the Communist Party's official newspaper the *Daily Worker* in Harlem. Of the pieces he wrote for the paper between July and December of that year, many were dedicated to chronicling anti-fascist activity undertaken by the CP and other allied organizations.[11] Specifically, Wright covered African American involvement in the Loyalist cause against Franco during the Spanish Civil War (1936–1939) as well as boycotts and protests against the sale of Japanese goods by local shops and retailers during the Second Sino-Japanese War (1937–1945). For Wright as well as the Harlem branch of the Communist Party that he represented as a correspondent, the nationalist struggle against Jim Crow was indelibly linked to global anti-fascist movements.

Covering an interracial women's protest outside the Italian consulate in July 1937, Wright mentions the slogans chanted by picketers, including "Stop Fascist Destruction of Women and Children in Spain and Ethiopia" right alongside "Free the Scottsboro Boys!"[12] – implying the simultaneity of these causes, their chants uttered in the same collective breath. Wright further suggests an almost metonymic relationship between anti-fascist work at home and abroad by interviewing a number of Black Americans who had volunteered to serve in the Loyalist army in Spain, one of whom remarked that, "Here [in Spain] we have been able to strike back, in a way that hurts, at those who for years have pushed us from pillar to post. I mean this – actually strike back at the counterparts of those who have been grinding us down back home."[13] The concentricity of these struggles – one against the American state, the other against Franco's regime – implies a substitutive logic: Since racial oppression in the United States is analogized to the Nationalist cause, "striking back" at one is also, in effect, striking back at both.

In another particularly telling piece from August of that year, Wright takes his reader inside "What Happens at a Communist Party Meeting in the Harlem Section":

> Leaving the blare and glare of Lenox Avenue, you walk up one flight of stairs and enter an oblong room whose walls are covered with murals depicting the historical struggles of the Negro in America. This is the Nat Turner Branch of the Harlem Division of the Communist Party. It was so named in honor of a black slave who died struggling for freedom.
>
> Before you have time to sit down, your eyes are drawn to a huge black placard.
>
> "IN MEMORY OF OUR BELOVED BROTHER, ALONZO WATSON, WHO DIED FIGHTING FOR DEMOCRACY IN SPAIN."[14]

Here, in the layout of the meeting room as in Wright's prose, the "historical struggles of the Negro in America" become metonymy for the global anti-fascist struggle, joined materially and permanently in the wounded body of the fallen "brother." Later in the article, Wright narrates the progression of the meeting: "Petitions demanding of Congress and the state of Alabama the freedom of the five remaining innocent Scottsboro Boys are passed around. Comrades are urged to have them filled out as soon as possible. The meeting is going fast now; they want to get through as soon as they can in order to listen to an educational report on the situation in China."[15] Here again we find the immediate juxtaposition of nationalist and internationalist agendas, the Scottsboro trial linked to Japanese aggression in China.

After the "educational speech" by a white student on the Sino-Japanese conflict and its connection to developments in Spain and Ethiopia, Wright remarks: "These black people who meet here in Harlem are hungry more than in one sense. They love this Communist Party which is the only organization caring enough for them to give them this world-view of things," enabling "men and women with guts and courage" to "take the world into their hands and mould it and in moulding [sic] it remake themselves."[16] In Wright's earliest professional writing, then, we glimpse how campaigns against the Scottsboro decision metonymize anti-fascist struggles in Spain, Ethiopia, Germany, and China. For Wright, this simultaneity of local matters with wartime developments on the European and Asian continents gestures toward a greater collectivity, endowing those gathered with a heightened "world-view."

Over a brief period of six months, Wright authored at least sixteen articles covering Harlem-based organizing against Franco's campaign and Japan's invasion of China, bearing titles like: "Big Harlem Rally for China Tonight," which opens "With the rallying cry that neutrality aids invasion, thousands of Harlem workers, Negro, Chinese, and white, will gather tonight at 8 PM to protest Japan's undeclared war against China"; or "Harlem Group Pushes Aid for China" in order "to build up solidarity between the people of Harlem and those of China"; or "Harlem Party to Protest Japan's Action"; or "Negro Pastor Assails Tokyo Aggression" thereby "Reflecting the aroused moral conscience of the Negro church in Harlem." Wright's early Communist Party journalism produces a periscoping effect, signifying the dynamic relation or mutual embeddedness of nationalist and internationalist causes, finding political and moral leverage in the radical juxtaposition of distant struggles.

That same year, Wright published his "Blueprint for Negro Writing" in *New Challenge*, famously lamenting the Black literary tradition while positioning himself as its unfortunate heir. "At best, Negro writing has been something external to the lives of educated Negroes themselves,"[17] he writes. Accusing previous writers of abandoning the culture of the Negro masses ("unwritten and unrecognized") for that of an itinerant Negro bourgeoisie ("parasitic and mannered"), Wright seeks to forge a new kind of expression founded upon, but never limited to, the nationalist tendencies inherent to Black culture. Wright understood the particular richness of Black life – as exemplified especially by its folklore and the Church – as the product of particular historical processes rather than the expression of any essentialist racial ontology. Black nationalism, in other words, is "a product of history alone, the stunted growth of oppression, taking shape in the absence of any other outlet for agency," writes Yogita Goyal.[18] For Wright, nationalism is thus a necessary but "reflexive" reaction to the forces of racial-capitalist modernity: in the American context, slavery and Jim Crow.[19] "The Negro people did not ask for this [way of life], and deep down, though they express themselves through their institutions and adhere to this special way of life, they do not want it now," Wright continues. "This special existence was forced upon them from without by lynch rope, bayonet and mob rule. They accepted these negative conditions with the inevitability of a tree which must live or perish in whatever soil it finds itself."[20] Black culture is "special" but endlessly contingent, forged only in the face of oppressive historical circumstance.

And it is precisely because of this seemingly "*unwanted* Black culture"[21] that Wright implores Negro writers to "accept the nationalist implications of their lives, not in order to encourage them, but in order to change and transcend them. They must accept the concept of nationalism because, in order to transcend it, they must *possess* and *understand* it."[22] In this sense, cultural nationalism is not simply the result of broader historical processes but is *itself* an historical process, "a key to self-possession but as such only a stage in the realization of a political interdependence."[23] Failing to achieve this transcendence, Wright cautions, might cause Negro writers to "alienate their possible allies in the struggle for freedom."[24] Although seemingly a blueprint for "Negro writing," Wright attunes his polemic to "world movements," remaining ever conscious of the broader implications of this work.[25] "A Negro writer must learn to view the life of the Negro living in New York's Harlem or Chicago's South Side with the consciousness that one-sixth of the earth surface belongs to the working class," he writes. "Perspective for Negro writers will come when they have looked and brooded so hard and long upon the harsh lot of their race and compared it with the hopes and struggles of minority peoples everywhere that the cold facts have begun to tell them something."[26] Building on his evident Marxist predilections, Wright articulates a daring concept of literary engagement, arguably rendering his text not only a "Blueprint for Negro Writing" but for global minoritarian discourse.

The "Blueprint" has provoked consternation – if not outright dismissal – from several critics since its publication. Harold Cruse lambasted Wright's "faulty, if penetrating, critique" in *The Crisis of the Negro Intellectual: A Historical Analysis of the Failure of Black Leadership* (1967).[27] Asserting that "Communist influence and Left literary values smother and choke black cultural expression," Cruse takes Wright to task for failing to recognize that "the cultural and artistic originality of the American nation is founded, historically, on the ingredients of a black aesthetic and artistic base."[28] Cruse continues:

> Poor Richard Wright! He sincerely tried, but he never got much beyond that starting point that Marxism represented for him. Less than eight years after his article was written, he resigned from the Communist Party and went into exile, never to return. He could not gather into himself all the ingredients of nationalism; to create values and mould [sic] concepts by which his race was to "struggle, live and die."
>
> It will never be known whether or not Wright ever grasped the extent to which vulgar Marxism had rendered him incapable of seeing unique developments of capitalism. Uncharted paths existed for the Negro creative intellectuals to explore, if only they could avoid being blinded by Communist Party propaganda.[29]

Cruse may have had good reason to express skepticism toward Wright's outsized polemical vision – insisting that "the Negro writer prepare himself for this world-shaking assignment," in Cruse's summary – but he clearly underestimated the intellectual, ideological, political, and artistic elasticity of his subject.[30] If anything, "Poor Richard Wright" would spend the next two-and-a-half decades venturing far beyond the "starting point" of his so-called "vulgar Marxism," exploring several "uncharted paths" in the further elaboration of his globalist vision.

Affective Kinship

In his essay on the conception and composition of *Native Son*, "How 'Bigger' Was Born" (1940–1942),[31] Wright begins to merge the language of Marxist internationalism and his newfound preoccupation with the shared emotional and psychic dispossession of oppressed peoples. The essay vividly elaborates the globalist rhetoric presaged in his earliest reporting and criticism, though this time without toeing the Party line. The unifying thread in Wright's own account of the novel is an emphasis on protagonist Bigger Thomas as a multiple-character: that the internal psychological, emotional, social, and political struggles of that young man in Chicago's Black Belt can be multiplied almost infinitely out into the world; that his predicament is necessarily far from unique.

Wright suggests that the critique and insight at the heart of *Native Son* can best be glimpsed from a "world-view" (to return to his earlier phrase) that repositions the novel's protagonist as a global type rather than simply a national figure of racial tension.[32] Wright envisions his protagonist beyond the Jim Crow South, even beyond the Chicago Black Belt, by recalling an image of Maxim Gorky and Vladimir Lenin walking through the streets of London and being struck by their shared experience of exclusion and outsiderness: "In both instances [that of Lenin/Gorky and Bigger Thomas] the deep sense of exclusion was identical. The feeling of looking at things with a painful and unwarrantable nakedness was an experience, I learned, that transcended national and racial boundaries."[33] As Yung-Hsing Wu writes, Wright's essay actually restages the act of literary comparison itself, oscillating constantly between the local and the global. "Wright's essay conjures a peculiar existence for Thomas – one in which he shuttles between being a specific classification and a global type," Wu notes.[34] "Without Bigger – the representative of the African American experience – as a point of comparison, the Bigger Everyman could not exist."[35]

Here, the process by which Bigger's plight "transcends national and racial boundaries" is not so much metonymic or substitutive as it is replicative, as if *Native Son*'s central character were designed as a template to be adapted or modified to new environments. But with these additive permutations come certain dangers. Perhaps most controversially, Wright also likens Bigger's political consciousness to contemporaneous developments in Nazi Germany. "And on innumerable occasions I was startled to detect [in Germany] ... reactions, moods, phrases, attitudes that reminded me strongly of Bigger, that helped to bring out more clearly the shadowy outlines of the negative that lay in the back of my mind," Wright recalls. "I read every account of the Fascist movement in Germany I could lay my hands on, and from page to page I encountered and recognized familiar emotional patterns."[36] As Frank Mehring suggests, such an affective alliance – the cross-Atlantic identification between disenfranchised subjects in vaguely similar yet culturally distinct contexts – could yield disastrous consequences. "The highly ritualized and symbolized life which dominated the political rallies of the Nazis and which fetishized national belonging had the potential to persuade a certain group of African Americans to follow a similarly aggressive plan," Mehring writes. "Wright's protagonist Bigger could easily be blinded by a leader who might claim African American superiority similar to the way Hitler assured his Nazi followers that their vanity was justified due to the alleged ethnic supremacy of the Aryan race."[37]

Here, Wright's profound skepticism toward cultural or ethnic nationalism – especially when founded on any concept of essential racial being – meets and then exceeds Marxist ideology, gesturing toward broader psychological and affective resonances. Yet embracing an avowedly Marxist framework, Wright envisions Bigger as conditioned not strictly by American race politics, but rather by global class oppression. He writes, "I made the discovery that Bigger Thomas was not black all the time; he was white, too, and there were literally millions of him, everywhere ... I sensed, too, that the Southern scheme of oppression was but an appendage of a far vaster and in many respects more ruthless and impersonal commodity-profit machine." He continues: "I approached all of these new revelations in the light of Bigger Thomas, his hopes, fears, and despairs; and I began to feel far-flung kinships, and sense, with fright and abashment, the possibilities of alliances between the American Negro and other people possessing a kindred consciousness."[38] With Wright's early journalism in mind, we might say more precisely that he began to feel *again* the analogical relationships between structural racism in the United States and racial and class oppression elsewhere.

Wright's commitment to the "possibilities of alliance" is not, by this point in his career, simply a matter of Communist Party policy (or doctrine, perhaps). Rather, it is suggestive of an active emotional engagement with questions of globality – not just in the sense of the "identical" feelings shared by Bigger Thomas's infinite replications, but also in the sense that Wright's globalist vision increasingly depends upon his own emotional labor, as he himself begins to "feel far-flung kinships" the world over. "How 'Bigger' Was Born" shows in real time how Wright shifts rhetorical registers in the elaboration of his globalist perspective: rather than finding common ground strictly in the realm of political ideology, he just as crucially emphasizes the "deep sense of exclusion" and "feeling of looking at things with a painful an unwarrantable nakedness" shared by disenfranchised peoples worldwide. What joins Bigger's "hopes, fears, and despairs" with those of the masses living under the Third Reich is not necessarily any shared political struggle, but instead a set of "reactions, moods, phrases, attitudes" and "familiar emotional patterns." Wright's essay thereby indexes most broadly the convergence of class struggle and affective dispossession in his rearticulation of the mutual constitution of racial and global, nationalist and internationalist alliances.

After Wright's formal break with the Communist Party – which he announced in the 1944 *Atlantic Monthly* article "I Tried To Be a Communist," but which had most likely occurred several years prior – and subsequent exit from the American scene, he resumed the grappling search for commonality among "people possessing a kindred consciousness" by other means. That is, rather than seeking any political or ideological binding agent, Wright located the grounds of solidarity exclusively in the realm of affect – or, as he writes in *The Color Curtain*, in his "search for the emotional landscapes of Asia."[39] Brian Russell Roberts and Keith Foulcher have recently shown how the meeting at Bandung has taken on an altogether "mythic dimension"[40] frequently at odds with "archivally verifiable history,"[41] such that romanticized accounts of the event reify its position as an inaugural moment for Third World solidarity, the nonalignment movement, and Afro-Asian and postcolonial studies writ large. It is not particularly difficult to glimpse how such historiographical romance might have been set in motion by Wright himself: "Here were class and racial and religious consciousness on a global scale. Who had thought of organizing such a meeting? And what had these nations in common? Nothing, it seemed to me, but what their past relationship to the Western world had made them feel."[42]

Rather than asserting positive linkages between dispossessed groups, Wright finds common ground in the collision of negative affect and a profound reduction of historical experience that seems to explode political affiliation altogether, writing that the meeting at Bandung "cut through the outer layers of disparate social and political and cultural facts down to the bare brute residues of human existence," that "there was something extra-political, extra-social, almost extra-human about it; it smacked of tidal waves, of natural forces."[43] If "How 'Bigger' Was Born" indexed the convergence of Marxist internationalism with a burgeoning interest in emotional and psychological malaise, here the latter predominates. *The Color Curtain* – which, as Bill Mullen notes, cemented Wright's status as either the inventor or "at the very least a founding member"[44] of postcolonial studies – instead of relying upon processes of metonymy or replication, builds its globalist vision upon a profoundly reductionist gesture, "cutting" down to life's "bare brute residues," a radical stripping-away of national, racial, and political affiliation – not periscoping, but actually telescoping the shared dispossession of the global South. In place of his earlier critique of Black cultural nationalism as an externally produced reaction to the depredations of racial-capitalist modernity, here Wright stakes his claim for global solidarity precisely in the affective kinship glinting in the twilight of colonial domination.

In this way, Wright's postcolonialism *avant la lettre* converges with what Arna Bontemps disparagingly called in a review of *The Outsider* a "roll in the

hay with the existentialism of Sartre."⁴⁵ Though Wright's particular brand
of nihilist existentialism was more indebted to Dostoevsky, Nietzsche, and
Kierkegaard than Sartre, Camus, or de Beauvoir, the writer shared with these
French intellectuals a staunch anti-colonialism rooted in "a sense of commitment and human solidarity."⁴⁶ If this putative Third World universalism
foregrounds negative identification, it also shares a reductionist impulse with
Wright's more philosophical fiction of the period, namely *The Outsider* and
The Long Dream. The late novels and reportage both demonstrate an explicit disinterest in race-based identification, instead positing the shared dispossession of both modern man and the colonial subject as the ground for
a renewed commitment to social and political connectedness. Considering
the later fiction and travel writings in tandem thus helps safeguard against
superficial readings of both – whereby Wright's alternating interest in either
radical solitude or radical solidarity seems, at best, incongruous. But as
George Cotkin notes, even *White Man, Listen!* (1957) retains a certain
"underground mentality" found in Wright's novels of the same decade –
not to mention his earlier novella "The Man Who Lived Underground"
(1944) – while his supposedly existentialist writings frequently critique
philosophical self-determination in favor of reparative sociality.⁴⁷

Indeed, several aspects of Wright's writings in exile have posed considerable difficulties for his interpreters. In Kwame Anthony Appiah's diagnosis,
the "defensive condescension" and "frank paranoia" of *Black Power*, for
example, are symptomatic of Wright's concurrent sympathies with the
oppressed masses of the Third World and with colonialist discourses of
industrialization and Western modernity.⁴⁸ This conflict between disdain-
ful contempt for and sympathetic identification with victims of Western
colonial domination in Africa and Asia is perhaps nowhere better expressed
than in "Tradition and Industrialization: The Historic Meaning of the
Plight of the Tragic Elite in Asia and Africa," collected with additional
essays in *White Man, Listen!*.⁴⁹ "Indeed, the teeming religions gripping the
minds and consciousness of Asians and Africans offend me," Wright
asserts. "I can conceive of no identification with such mystical visions of
life that freeze millions in static degradation, no matter how emotionally
satisfying such degradation seems to those who wallow in it."⁵⁰ This
impasse, produced by his "split"⁵¹ position as simultaneously a "product
of Western civilization" and "inevitably critical of the West"⁵² as a Black
man, leads Wright to articulate an ambivalent alliance with formerly colonized peoples couched in reductionist terms: "I stand, therefore, mentally
and emotionally looking in both directions, being claimed by a *negative
identification* on one side, and being excluded by a feeling of repulsion on
the other" [emphasis added].⁵³

It is in the same collection of essays, this time in his piece on "The Psychological Reactions of Oppressed People," that Wright gestures toward "the remarkable and growing body of evidence of the basic emotional kinship, empirically established[,] of all men and of all races."[54] Although the author himself expressed palpable doubt as to the viability and exigency of such perspective, conceding that "this as yet budding sense of 'the unity of man' is confined to a minority of minorities,"[55] Wright still maintains that "despite the fragility of this universal outlook, it indicates a political vista that needs must be mentioned here."[56] Here is the paradox, or at least the difficulty, of Wright's writing in exile: Though propounding explicitly scientific and militaristic programs for postcolonial self-determination (in Henry Louis Gates Jr.'s account, his belief that "colonialism was the best thing that had ever befallen the continent of Africa" for its destruction of religious primitivism and political tribalism) Wright's elitism never precludes hope for the eventual unity of man.[57] In his final writings, he would not just imagine this "universal outlook," but actually attempt to bring it into being.

Universal (Non)Humanism

If Wright sought to document the shared affective responses among those trampled by Western imperialism throughout Africa and Asia – as first hinted in his remark that Bigger Thomas's "hopes, fears, and despairs" might be dispersed and distributed across a "far vaster" global plane – his final works suggest a transcendence not just of political and racial affiliation, but even of the "bare brute residues of human existence," existential reduction superseded by poetic reduction. As his health deteriorated in the last eighteen months of his life, Wright's increasingly imminent death inspired him to compose Japanese haiku exclusively. He produced over four thousand poems, readying 817 for publication in the posthumously published collection *This Other World* (1998).[58] As Sandy Alexandre notes, Wright assumes through this body of haiku a "subjunctive mood" through which "he is empowered to divest himself of the weight of his socio-historical and racial circumstance," producing a formal, poetic Afro-Asian futurity that "exhibit-[s] an aspiration to global literature and introduce[s] possibilities for universal humanism and ecological holism."[59] Where *The Color Curtain* sought "a universal humanism" that might "bind men together in common unity,"[60] Wright's haiku perhaps imagines and brings into being, at least textually, the horizon of possibility for such relationality.[61] As Alexandre shows, through an emphasis on the harmonic integration of human and nonhuman ("I am paying rent / For the lice in my cold room / And the

moonlight too"), the elevated consciousness that comes with death's immi-
nence ("Leaving the doctor / The whole world looks different / This autumn
morning"), a disaffiliation from oneself and accompanying suppression of
subjectivity ("I am nobody: / A red sinking autumn sun / Took my name
away"), and an emptying-out of explicitly racial ideologies and themes,
Wright's consolatory haiku gesture toward a future space and time whereby
"the notion of belonging (and by extension citizenship) [becomes] more
virtuosic and certainly more worldly than the nation-state's limited and
localized definition of it," thereby "mak[ing] world citizens of its readers."[62]

Counterintuitively, we might wonder whether this moribund corpus truly
departs from the precedent set forth by Wright's earliest writing – that is,
whether this glimpse of "the whole world" signals a vision altogether different from his budding "world-view." In the second section of *Twelve Million
Black Voices: A Folk History of the Negro in the United States* (1941), for
example, Wright describes the plight of the sharecropper – the inheritor of
slavery – in the land of "Queen Cotton." An atmosphere of never-ending war
pervades this Southern scene, where "Lords of the Land" reign over the
plantation system, pitting poor white laborers against the Black underclass.
"When we feel self-disgust at our bare lot, when we contemplate our lack of
courage in the face of daily force," Wright reflects, "we are seized with
a desire to escape our shameful identification ... we seek to become protectively merged with the least-known and farthest removed race of men we
know." Here, with a "snicker of self-deprecation," Wright inserts a short
proverb:

> *White folks is evil*
> *And niggers is too*
> *So glad I'm a Chinaman*
> *I don't know what to do*[63]

Wright makes no further comment, leaving the reader to consider this
surprising gesture toward escapist, cross-racial identification in the qua-
train's third line: Why, one wonders, would a Black sharecropper invoke
the "farthest removed race of men" amidst his toil? What would it mean to
be "protectively merged" with the figure of the "Chinaman"? How does
Wright's "self-deprecating" recitation belie, or perhaps buttress, its speaker's
apparent "gladness"?

That Wright's deathbed consolations might find their curious antecedent
in the sharecropper's aphorism only further suggests how his late work
returned to – or elaborated, with increasing sophistication – a set of themes,
images, and strategies apparent even in his earliest books. Indeed, Michel
Fabre calls the prose of *12 Million Black Voices* "deliberately poetic,"[64]

while Eugene Miller posits that Wright recognized the "functional similarity between the haiku form and the lyrics of the folk blues."[65] Traditionally a poetic form dedicated to the observation and appreciation of the natural world, animate and inanimate, these haiku also recall striking moments from Wright's early fiction. In the opening story from *Uncle Tom's Children*, "Big Boy Leaves Home," the four boys swim in a nearby creek and lay out in the sun to dry off:

> They grew pensive. A black winged butterfly hovered at the water's edge. A bee droned. From somewhere came the sweet scent of honeysuckles. Dimly they could hear sparrows twittering in the woods. They rolled from side to side, letting sunshine dry their skins and warm their blood. They plucked blades of grass and chewed them.[66]

In this idyllic scene, the boys' closeness to nature, and to each other, is registered all at once by sight, scent, sound, touch, and taste. This playful innocence throws into stark relief the story's ensuing violence, as Big Boy, Bobo, Lester, and Buck must face and then flee a fatal encounter with a white woman and her husband.

While making his escape, the titular character "slowed to a walk, looking back and ahead. A light wind skipped over the grass. A beetle lit on his cheek and he brushed it off. Behind the dark pines hung a red sun. Two bats flapped against the sun. He shivered, for he was growing cold; the sweat on his body was drying."[67] This recycling of natural imagery – characteristic of what Fabre calls Wright's "truly elemental imagination" – suggests not the joy of youthful abandonment, but rather the profound breach between that former peace and this current chaos.[68] Toward the story's conclusion, Big Boy finds himself pursued by a white mob and a pack of dogs. When one of them finds his hiding place, Big Boy is forced to fight for his life:

> With strength flowing from fear, he closed his fingers, pushing his full weight on the dog's throat. The dog heaved again, and lay still ... Big Boy heard the sound of his own breathing filling the hole, and heard shouts and footsteps above him going past.
>
> For a long, long time he held the dog, held it long after the last footstep had died out, long after the rain had stopped.[69]

Big Boy's breath replaces, and thus seems to continue, the dog's final "heave." Both ultimately victims of horrid violence, their bodies remain tightly wound in a chilling image of negative identification.[70]

This thematic preoccupation with humanity's relation to the natural world – whether characterized by awe, appreciation, terror, or sympathy – recurs frequently throughout *Uncle Tom's Children*: the epic flood of "Down by the Riverside"; the chirping crickets and floating fields of "Long Black Song"; the sloping hills and bright moonlight of "Fire and Cloud"; and the rainfall that frames the first and final scenes of "Bright and Morning Star." And if we could say that Wright's late style has its antecedents anywhere in his *oeuvre*, we might also turn to the series of impressionistic catalogues appended to the author's earliest childhood recollections in *Black Boy*:

> There was the vague sense of the infinite as I looked down upon the yellow, dreaming waters of the Mississippi River from the verdant bluffs of Natchez . . .
> There was the yearning for identification loosed in me by the sight of a solitary ant carrying a burden upon a mysterious journey . . .
> There was the hint of cosmic cruelty that I felt when I saw the curved timbers of a wooden shack that had been warped in the summer sun . . .
> And there was the quiet terror that suffused my senses when vast hazes of gold washed earthward from star-heavy skies on silent nights.[71]

"Yearning for identification": This phrase perhaps best captures Wright's lifelong intellectual trajectory, itself a kind of "mysterious journey," and indeed the various modes of inquiry deployed in its pursuit. That such an image should be conjured by the "sight of a solitary ant" should not come as much of a surprise – at least not when glimpsed from the bird's-eye view of Wright's career.[72]

Conclusion

We might conclude by returning briefly to Wright's earliest criticism. At the tender age of twenty-seven, Wright began what may have been his first attempt to delineate an original aesthetic program. In an unpublished essay from circa 1935 entitled "Notes on 'Personalism,'" Wright describes the *petite bourgeoisie* as "a dream-like domain where theories sprout like mush-rooms. It is a ground strewn with statues, human statues striking unusual and outlandish poses ... It is a bog of quicksand with no bottom ... In its diffuseness it transcends petty national boundaries." Here, Wright – still three years away from publishing his debut collection – stakes his claim: "It is on the basis of this restless class of non-class that I [seek] to formulate an aesthetic theory. It is a theory of extreme individualism, or better, person-alism." "Personalism," Wright remarks in prose equally vague and grand-iose, "will foster expression of protest in terms as individual and personal as possible," he writes, concluding in a dramatic flourish: "The personalist who becomes a perfect personalist ceases to be a personalist, and becomes an artist writing for and speaking to mankind." In perfecting "personalism," then, the artist's "extreme individualism" becomes self-obsoleting in a transcendent, worldly gesture. Not simply a piece of juvenilia, the essay outlines in broad strokes several of the key tenets of the artistic and political program Wright would pursue over the next two and a half decades, claiming the outward resonances of a singular action, the dramatic interplay between the individual and all mankind, its scope "transcend[ing] petty national boundaries."

To be sure, there are clear distinctions to be upheld between Wright's youthful polemic in the "Notes on 'Personalism'" and the author's mature work – from *Native Son* to *The Color Curtain* and *This Other World*.[73] But their profound resonances compel us to conceptualize Wright's development as characterized by continuity rather than fracture. In this sense, attending to the globalist vision explicit in Wright's work throughout his earliest essays, journalism, and fiction, as well as his later expatriate writing, is not simply an anachronistic projection of current critical preoccupations. Rather, it reveals how Wright was already concerned with the possibility of global struggle, solidarity, or kinship based upon a shared humanity – as well as a profound ecological awareness of man's intimate connection to the natural world – well before the latter-day onset of globalization.

This attempt to recuperate his earliest and latest globalist imperatives ultimately works to counteract the consolidation of figures like Wright within Americanist canons such that the ways in which their political and literary imaginations transcended the nation-state and its racial signifiers might otherwise be obscured. "Wright's reach ... can be said to be much longer than that implied by the terms employed by many of his American critics. He was never merely a 'racial novelist,' a 'protest writer,' or a 'literary rebel'," Cedric Robinson notes in his famed study *Black Marxism: The Making of the Black Radical Tradition* (1983). "His work ... constituted an inquiry."[74] As such, no single ideology, intellectual tradition, political critique, or literary form could ever fully subsume the depth and range of his work or the expansiveness of his vision.

And while recent reappraisals of Wright's unheralded writings shine new and necessary light on his "post-exile" reportage and essays, this work does not always avoid the pitfall of suggesting (whether implicitly or explicitly) what could be salvaged in its likeness to his earlier output, before "he turned away from the American scene to the global one."[75] Assuming the obverse perspective, I have attempted to glance backward at Wright's career from its premature demise. Rather than positioning his later expatriate works as marking a deviation from the specifically American race consciousness of his earlier output, then, I propose that we begin to reconsider how each successive text further elaborates a globalist critique of power that was present from the outset. In that sense, tracing the increasingly sophisticated articulation of this globalist perspective means taking seriously C. L. R. James's recollection of a visit to the author's home, where Wright showed James his volumes of Kierkegaard and remarked, "I want to tell you something. Everything that he writes in those books, I knew before I had them."[76]

Notes

1. Paul Gilroy, *The Black Atlantic: Modernity and Double Consciousness* (Cambridge: Harvard University Press, 1993), 155–61.
2. This question becomes especially complex when critical efforts to emphasize one interpretation inadvertently suggest the other. In one volume, Robert Bone argues that "Wright's work is readily divided into two periods," but also that his later works demonstrate a "continuity of theme and image" through the "polar concepts" of "tradition and industrialization" that link his American and French periods, and a nihilism that "always haunted Wright's imagination." See Robert Bone, *Richard Wright* (Minneapolis: University of Minnesota Press, 1969), 13, 32, 37, 39.
3. J. Saunders Redding, "Richard Wright: An Evaluation," in Faith Berry, ed., *A Scholar's Conscience: Selected Writings of J. Saunders Redding, 1942–1977* (Lexington: University of Kentucky Press, 1992), 155.
4. Ibid., 156.
5. Ibid., 159.
6. Ibid., 160. See also J. Saunders Redding, "The Way It Was," *New York Times Book Review* October 26, 1958, reprinted in Henry Louis Gates Jr. and Kwame Anthony Appiah, eds., *Richard Wright: Critical Perspectives Past and Present* (New York: Amistad, 1993), 36. Redding had this to say about Wright's last novel: "'The Long Dream' proves that Wright has been away too long . . . Come back, Dick Wright, to life again!"
7. Addison Gayle Jr., "Richard Wright: Beyond Nihilism," in Nathaniel Norment Jr., ed., *The Addison Gayle Jr. Reader* (Urbana: University of Illinois Press, 2009), 208.
8. Ibid., 209.
9. Ibid., 211. Steven Marcus, too, made this remark about Wright's second novel: "In essence, *The Outsider* is really another *Native Son*, and Cross Damon another Bigger Thomas, no more." See Steven Marcus, "The American Negro in Search of Identity," *Commentary* November 1, 1953, reprinted in Gates and Appiah, eds., *Richard Wright: Critical Perspectives*, 36.
10. Gilroy, *The Black Atlantic*, 159.
11. On Wright's involvement with the Communist Party and its influence on his writing, see Barbara Foley, *Radical Representations: Politics and Form in U.S. Proletarian Fiction, 1929–1941* (Durham: Duke University Press, 1993); William J. Maxwell, *New Negro, Old Left: African-American Writing and Communism between the Wars* (New York: Columbia University Press, 1999); and Bill V. Mullen, *Popular Fronts: Chicago and African-American Cultural Politics, 1935–46* (Champaign: University of Illinois Press, 1999). On Wright's early poetry written for official Communist Party publications, see Keneth Kinnamon, "Richard Wright: Proletarian Poet," in

Yoshinobu Hakutani, ed., *Critical Essays on Richard Wright* (Boston: G.K. Hall & Co., 1982), 243–251; and James Edward Smethurst, *The New Red Negro: The Literary Left and African American Poetry, 1930–1946* (Oxford: Oxford University Press, 1999).

12. Earle V. Bryant, ed., *Byline, Richard Wright: Articles from the DAILY WORKER and NEW MASSES* (Columbia: University of Mississippi Press, 2014), 96.
13. Quoted in ibid., 106.
14. Ibid., 187.
15. Ibid., 189.
16. Ibid., 190.
17. Richard Wright, "Blueprint for Negro Writing," *The New Challenge* 2.2 (1937): 53.
18. Yogita Goyal, *Romance, Diaspora, and Black Atlantic Literature* (Cambridge: Cambridge University Press, 2010), 151.
19. Ibid., 151.
20. Wright, "Blueprint for Negro Writing," 57.
21. Anthony Dawahare, *Nationalism, Marxism, and African American Literature between the Wars: A New Pandora's Box* (Jackson: University Press of Mississippi, 2003), 113.
22. Wright, "Blueprint for Negro Writing," 58.
23. C. W. E. Bigsby, "Richard Wright and His Blueprint for Negro Writing," *PN Review* 7.5 (1980): 54.
24. Wright, "Blueprint for Negro Writing," 59.
25. Ibid., 61.
26. Ibid., 62.
27. Harold Cruse, *The Crisis of the Negro Intellectual: A Historical Analysis of the Failure of Black Leadership* (New York: New York Review Books, 2005), 182.
28. Ibid., 188–189.
29. Ibid., 188.
30. Ibid., 185.
31. The essay was based on a lecture delivered on several occasions in New York City and again in Chicago and Durham throughout 1940, and subsequently published in the *Saturday Review* and *Negro Digest*, then as a pamphlet of its own, and finally as a preface to a 1942 reprint of *Native Son*.
32. On Wright's revision of the *Native Son* manuscript and the novel's status as world literature, see Nicholas T Rinehart, "Native Sons; or, How 'Bigger' Was Born Again," *Journal of American Studies* 52.1 (2018), 164–192.
33. Richard Wright, *Early Works* (New York: Library of America, 1991), 863.
34. Yung-Hsing Wu, "Native Sons and Native Speakers: On the Eth(n)ics of Comparison," *PMLA* 121.5 (2006), 1465.
35. Ibid., 1467.
36. Wright, *Early Works*, 864.
37. Frank Mehring, "'Bigger in Nazi Germany': Transcultural Confrontations of Richard Wright and Hans Jurgen Massaquoi," *The Black Scholar* 39, no. 1/2 (2009), 65–66.
38. Wright, *Early Works*, 860–861.

39. Richard Wright, *Black Power: Three Books from Exile* (New York: Harper Perennial, 2008), 453.
40. Brian Russell Roberts and Keith Foulcher, eds., *Indonesian Notebook: A Sourcebook on Richard Wright and the Bandung Conference* (Durham: Duke University Press, 2016), 2.
41. Ibid., 4.
42. Wright, *Black Power*, 438.
43. Ibid., 439.
44. Bill V. Mullen, "Discovering Postcolonialism," *American Quarterly* 54.4 (2002), 701.
45. Arna Bontemps, "Three Portraits of the Negro," *The Saturday Review*, March 28, 1953, reprinted in Robert J. Butler, ed., *The Critical Response to Richard Wright* (Westport: Greenwood, 1995), 106.
46. George Cotkin, *Existential America* (Baltimore: Johns Hopkins University Press, 2003), 166. See also Michel Fabre, "Richard Wright and the French Existentialists," *MELUS* 5.2 (1978): 39–51.
47. Critics continue to debate whether *The Outsider*, especially, should be understood as an existentialist *roman à thèse* or as a full-throated critique of existentialism's limitations. See Amritjit Singh, "Richard Wright's *The Outsider*: Existential Exemplar or Critique?," *CLA Journal* 27.4 (1984): 357–370; and Jeffrey Atteberry, "Entering the Politics of the Outside: Richard Wright's Critique of Marxism and Existentialism," *MFS: Modern Fiction Studies* 51.4 (2005): 873–895. For a critique of Wright's existentialist universalism, and particularly its consequences for women in the late novels, see Stephanie Li, *Playing in the White: Black Writers, White Subjects* (Oxford: Oxford University Press, 2015), 61–93. For an analysis of Wright's depiction of Paris as a colorblind utopia in the late fiction, including his final unfinished novel *Island of Hallucination*, see Laila Amine, "The Paris Paradox: Colorblindness and Colonialism in African American Expatriate Fiction," *American Literature* 87.4 (2015), 739–768. For a reevaluation of race and *The Outsider*, see Tommie Shelby's chapter in this volume.
48. Kwame Anthony Appiah, "A Long Way from Home: Richard Wright on the Gold Coast," in Arnold Rampersad, ed., *Richard Wright: A Collection of Critical Essays* (Upper Saddle River: Prentice Hall, 1995), 199.
49. On this essay and Wright's seeming endorsement of totalitarianism, see Vaughn Rasberry, *Race and the Totalitarian Century: Geopolitics in the Black Literary Imagination* (Cambridge: Harvard University Press, 2016), 305–354.
50. Wright, *Black Power*, 706.
51. Ibid., 704.
52. Ibid., 705.
53. Ibid., 707.
54. Ibid., 679.
55. Ibid., 680.
56. Ibid. Here we might glimpse what Alexa Weik considers Wright's "cosmopolitanism in process," a striving toward the ideal of human solidarity in the face of its necessary failure. See Alexa Weik, "'The Uses and Hazards of Expatriation': Richard Wright's Cosmopolitanism in Process," *African American Review* 41.3 (2007): 459–475.

57. Henry Louis Gates Jr., "Third World of Theory: Enlightenment's Esau," *Critical Inquiry* 34.5 (2008), 195. Bone similarly writes that "No writer of the present century has celebrated the values of the Enlightenment on such a global scale." See Bone, *Richard Wright*, 37.

58. Little scholarly attention has been paid to these last works of Wright's life, with the exception of Yoshinobu Hakutani, *Richard Wright and Haiku* (Columbia: University of Missouri Press, 2014); Jianqing Zheng, ed., *The Other World of Richard Wright: Perspectives on His Haiku* (Jackson: University of Mississippi Press, 2011); Eugene E. Miller, *Voice of a Native Son: The Poetics of Richard Wright* (Jackson: University of Mississippi Press, 1990); and Michel Fabre, *The World of Richard Wright* (Jackson: University of Mississippi Press, 1985).

59. Sandy Alexandre, "Culmination in Miniature: Late Style and the Essence of Richard Wright's Haiku," in Alice Mikal Craven and William E. Dow, eds., *Richard Wright in a Post-Racial Imaginary* (New York: Bloomsbury, 2014), 246–247. For the influence of Wilhelm Reich's "orgone" theory – a cosmic life energy uniting all matter of the universe – on Wright's burgeoning universalism, see Miller, *Voice of a Native Son*, xx–xx; and Stephan Kuhl's chapter in this volume.

60. Wright, *Black Power*, 448.

61. Joshua Bennett argues to the contrary that the presence of particular "pests" in Wright's haiku suggests a "generative *disunity*," whereby "various kinds of conflict and fissure ... emerge from sharing space with unexpected visitors that have no intention of leaving." See Joshua Bennett, "Being Property Once Myself: In Pursuit of the Animal in 20th-Century African American Literature" (PhD dissertation, Princeton University, 2016), 55.

62. Alexandre, "Culmination in Miniature," 249.

63. Richard Wright, *Twelve Million Black Voices* (New York: Viking Press, 1941), 47.

64. Michel Fabre, "The Poetry of Richard Wright," in Yoshinobu Hakutani, ed., *Critical Essays on Richard Wright*, 252

65. Eugene E. Miller, *Voice of a Native Son,* 239.

66. Richard Wright, *Uncle Tom's Children* (New York: Harper Perennial, 2008), 28–29.

67. Ibid., 46.

68. Fabre, "The Poetry of Richard Wright," 257.

69. Wright, *Uncle Tom's Children*, 59.

70. Bennett similarly considers how the opening scene of *Native Son* renders Bigger Thomas "not as the savage destroyer of animal life, but as the very animal life in question, as the pest which the exterminating forces in the book seek to uncover and destroy." The rat in that novel thus signifies a model of improvisatory persistence and fugitive living amidst the environmental conditions of anti-blackness. See Joshua Bennett, "Being Property Once Myself," 35–36.

71. Wright, *Early Works*, 9–10. See also Eugene Miller, *Voice of a Native Son*, 248.

72. Robert Tener similarly notes that "the evidence of Wright's identification with nature and his use of its motifs stretches from 'Big Boy leaves Home,' with its rural events around the swimming hole, to *Black Boy* and culminates in the haiku." See Robert Tener, "The Where, the When, the What: A Study of Richard Wright's Haiku," in Hakutani, ed., *Critical Essays on Richard Wright*, 275.

73. Wright's "Notes on 'Personalism'" has received scant critical attention. For a brief summary of the essay, see Jerry Ward and Robert Butler, eds., *The Richard Wright Encyclopedia* (Westport: Greenwood, 2008), 301–2. For brief mentions of "personalism," see Miller, *Voice of a Native Son*, xv–xix; Michel Fabre, *The World of Richard Wright*, 14; and Gilroy, who identifies Wright's "aesthetics of personalism" in Frederick Douglass's *Narrative* and other writings of ex-slaves, *The Black Atlantic*, 69.
74. Cedric Robinson, *Black Marxism: The Making of the Black Radical Tradition* (Chapel Hill: University of North Carolina Press, 1983), 290.
75. Goyal, *Romance, Diaspora, and Black Atlantic Literature*, 153.
76. C. L. R. James, "Black Studies and the Contemporary Student," in Anna Grimshaw, ed., *The C.L.R. James Reader* (Oxford: Blackwell, 1992), 399.

11

STEPHAN KUHL

Richard Wright's Transnationalism and His Unwritten *Magnum Opus*

Richard Wright was born in 1908 in rural Mississippi, and he died in 1960 in Paris, where he had been living for almost fifteen years in what he once described as "voluntary exile."[1] At the moment of his death, he had seen five of the seven continents and published books set in four of them, with a plan for a novel set in a fifth unrealized. The publication of Wright's three travel books between 1954 and 1957 indicates that the thematic scope of his writings grew more international during the last decade of his life, just as his compositions in the Japanese poetic form of the haiku indicate his late work's formal transgressions of the borders of national literatures.[2] But a broad geographic reach is already inscribed into some of Wright's earliest publications from the mid-1930s.

In the 1935 poem "I Am a Red Slogan," Wright urged in a manifestly communist manner: "WORKERS OF THE WORLD, UNITE!"[3] The Marxist internationalism that Wright here makes explicit also underlies many of the more than 200 journalistic articles that he published in 1937 and 1938. Writing from the Harlem bureau of the *Daily Worker*, Wright covered conflicts in Africa, Asia, and Europe by recording their reverberations in local New York communities. So, for example, he reported on Walter Garland from Brooklyn, who had just returned from Spain, where he had fought on the side of the Loyalists in the civil war. Wright's article on Garland treats the oppression of "the Negro in America" as one specific manifestation of the situation of "all the oppressed the world over, whether in Ethiopia, Spain, or China."[4] Therefore, the text exemplifies how his coverage of the global spread of fascism took sides for Marxist internationalism and for black liberation struggles. In some of his journalistic writings Wright even established literary devices for the representation of international conflicts. For example, his reportage on the 1938 rematch between Joe Louis and Max Schmeling in Yankee Stadium figuratively emphasizes the bout's political symbolism by describing a left hook of victorious Louis that, with a truly transatlantic reach, "must have, if only slightly, jarred Hitler's

Charlie Chaplin mustache in faraway fascist Germany."[5] Thematically and stylistically, then, Wright's published writings transgressed national borders from the beginning to the end of his literary career. However, the archives provide evidence that his transnational *magnum opus* never came into existence.

In the two decades between the publication of *Native Son* in 1940 and his death, Wright planned and abandoned three different multivolume literary projects. Their extent outlines show that each one of the three would have assembled diverse novels set in various continents or nations. The inherent transnationalism of Wright's plans for his multivolume projects suggests that also his travelogues from the mid-1950s, *Black Power: A Record of Reactions in a Land of Pathos* (1954), *The Color Curtain: A Report on the Bandung Conference* (1956), and *Pagan Spain* (1957), were not merely conceived as individual texts but should be read as interdependent parts of one larger series. Accordingly, these published books represent the regions of the world that they cover, West Africa, Asia, and Spain, respectively, not as individual locales. Rather, out of these individual locales, the three books together draw one conglomerate literary map that traces the history of European colonialism. Furthermore, Wright staged his specific anti-colonial position by incorporating *Savage Holiday*, his novel on white America, into this map. In his published oeuvre, then, the literary map of transnationalism that is drawn by the three travelogues and *Savage Holiday* constitutes Wright's closest approximation to a realization of his plans for his unwritten *magnum opus*.

In 1941, Wright wrote in a letter to his editor Edward Aswell that his text for the "picture book," published that year as *Twelve Million Black Voices*, constituted "the outline of a long series of novels which I hope to write some day."[6] Wright still held this plan four years later and described, in a journal entry from January 20, 1945, which reads like a summary of *Twelve Million Black Voices*, a series of novels that should bear the term "Voyage" in its general title:[7]

> I want to take the Negro, starting with his oneness with his African tribe, and trace his capture, his being brought over in the Middle Passage, his introduction to the plantation slave system, his gradual dehumanization to the level of ramdon [sic] impulse and hunger and fear and sex. I want then to trace his embracing of religion of protestantism [sic], his gradual trek to the cities of the nation, both North and South; and his gradual urbanization UNDER JIM CROW CONDITIONS, and finally his ability to create a new world for himself in the new land in which he finds himself.[8]

While *Twelve Million Black Voices* had rendered the Black Columbiad in the first-person plural voice, "Voyage" aimed to follow one single character through over three hundred years of African and African American history and "NOT LETTING THAT CHARACTER GROW OLD AT ALL WHILE USING HIM."[9] By moving one ageless protagonist from tribal life in Africa over the Middle Passage into American slavery and urban life, this series of novels would have accentuated the transformations of subjectivity that the respective stages of this "voyage" entailed. While each individual novel of the series would have captured one of these stages, the project as a whole would have bound its individual novels into the larger unity of the protagonist's voyage in its entirety. However, the project never came to fruition.

A decade after projecting "Voyage," Wright outlined a second multivolume work in an almost forty-pages-long letter to Aswell, which he began to write on August 21, 1955, shortly after publishing *Black Power* and while working on *The Color Curtain* and *Pagan Spain*. Wright here describes a series of novels that he conceived under the title "Celebration" and that is thematically preoccupied with "the individual and his society": "That problem poses for me many paradoxes: society and man form one organic whole, yet both, by the very nature of their relationship, are in sharp conflict. [...] Society, authority, tradition, custom, government, – all of these make men human, underwrite the continuity of experience, but, at the same time, by inhibiting men's impulses, rob them of their humanity." Wright writes that this theme "is no American, Russian, or French matter; it is man's matter . . . ." In order to represent this universal theme in its variations, Wright "invented a device which I'd call an *impersonal mood*." This impersonal mood, rendered in "a kind of free verse prose, [...] champions and celebrates *any* experience having as its objects a release of the powers of the organism, and it rejects and turns aside from all that which bogs the organism down . . . ."[10] Introducing and following all the individual novelistic narratives, the mood would knit "widely disparate events, characters, stories."[11] In his outline Wright provides an exemplary passage of the free verse that is written in the first-person voice and from the perspective of the mood. This passage of free verse transitions into what Wright identifies as a "description of the growth and death of a plant."[12] In this description, the plant appears as an incarnation of or at least as in conjunction with the mood, which would also have been incarnated in or conjoined with the respective characters of the projected novels. Already Michel Fabre pointed out that Wright's elaboration of the mood was "indebted to Wilhelm Reich's orgone theory."[13] Reich, a heretic of Sigmund Freud's psychoanalysis, defined "orgone" as a "radiating energy [...] found to be present in the soil, the atmosphere, the sun radiation and in the living organism," with "living organism" here encompassing all forms of plant, animal, and human life.[14] This concept of the life energy of orgone supplied Wright with the universalism that he aimed to translate into the literary device of his mood.

In his long letter to Aswell, Wright states that he had originally intended to include *Savage Holiday* in "Celebration" and he outlines two of the novels that he plans to write for the series at length. "A Strange Daughter," set in contemporary New York, would mainly deal with the cultural conflicts arising in the relationship between a white American woman and a student from Nigeria; "When the World was Red" would depict the story of "Montezuma, the Aztec king who was conquered by Cortes [sic]."[15] In a letter from July 27, 1955, Wright had described the regional grasp of this series, here titled "Celebration of Life," to his agent Paul Reynolds: "The settings of these various novels would be Argentina, The United States, France, Spain, Africa, and Asia."[16] "Celebration," then, would have historically spanned from the early stages of European colonialism to the mid-twentieth century and geographically bridged five continents. Within this historic and geographic scope, the individual novels of the series would have described disparate characters in various forms of social organization and conflict, while the device of the mood would have established a universal link between them. However, partly due the critical reactions to his outline by Reynolds and Aswell, Wright quickly put aside "Celebration."

After abandoning "Celebration," Wright for a third time planned a multivolume series, now by conceiving his last novel published during his lifetime, *The Long Dream* (1958), as the first part of a trilogy. *The Long Dream* depicts its protagonist's coming of age in a small town in Mississippi, and it ends with him on a plane over the Atlantic, with Paris as his destination. Early in the novel, his global trajectory is foreshadowed when his nickname, Fishbelly, is described as sticking "to him all his life, following him to school, to church, tagging along, like a tin can tied to a dog's tail, across the wide oceans of the world."[17] The unpublished second volume of the series, "Island of Hallucination," takes up Fishbelly's story on the plane over the Atlantic and leaves him in Paris.[18] But it also establishes the potential for the further continuation of his journey. In Paris, Fishbelly organizes a "stag show" and muses that, if successful, "he might be able to send that show to every American military establishment in Europe."[19] A letter by Wright to Reynolds from March 13, 1959, shows that "the third Fishbelly volume," which exists only in the short outlines given in correspondences, would have realized this potential: "Fishbelly begins a tour of army camps in France and Germany, a tour which gives a bird's eye view of the Negro soldier abroad."[20] But, in addition, this third volume should have taken its protagonist "to North Africa where Fishbelly for the first time has a chance to relax and think. Here, between Europe and Africa, Fishbelly has a dawning insight into what is happening in the world, the drama of millions of people being freed."[21] After gaining this dawning insight into the processes of decolonization, he travels on "into the heart of Black Africa where Fishbelly has to come to terms with the race from which he has sprung."[22] In this outline, the novel would end with Fishbelly moving to New York; but two days later, Wright modified this plan and even projected a continuation of the Fishbelly series beyond a third book. In a letter to Reynolds from March 15, 1959, Wright writes: "If I'd try to describe the theme of this third volume, I'd say that it comprises the *beginning* of Fishbelly's gradual awakening. This process cannot be achieved in one volume, for the psychological, sexual, racial, political problems involved are much too intricate to solve in a short space of time."[23] The book would now end with reflections on the future of Fishbelly's newborn son: "Ought the child be sent to Mississippi or ought he remain in Europe?"[24] Less experimental in style than "Voyage" and "Celebration," the Fishbelly series would have followed its protagonist's evolution as he journeys back and forth over the Black Atlantic and the Mediterranean Sea. However, "Island of Hallucination" remains unpublished, and Wright never wrote a third volume for the Fishbelly series.

Wright's outlines of "Voyage," "Celebration," and the Fishbelly series indicate the enormous thematic and stylistic differences that would have existed between his three multivolume projects.[25] However, geographically, all of them aimed to span various nations or continents so that the outlines share a transnational scope. In each one of the series, every individual novel would have focused on one specific region of the globe. But the intertextual relationships between the individual novels of a project would have lifted them to the higher unity constituted by this project in its entirety. On the level of this higher unity, then, the individual nation or continent depicted in one novel would have appeared in its transnational relations with the regions of the globe depicted in the other books of the series. Thus, out of individual novels and locales, each one of Wright's unrealized multivolume projects aimed to draw one conglomerate literary map of transnationalism. While this map was not realized in the three versions of Wright's unwritten *magnum opus*, it took shape in the series of books he published in the mid-1950s.

In *Pagan Spain*, Wright hints at the common overarching theme of his travelogues when he describes Spain as "a nook of Europe [that] had completely escaped the secularizing processes that were now rampant even in Asia and Africa," the two continents treated in *The Color Curtain* and *Black Power*.[26] Similarly, at the beginning of *The Color Curtain*, Wright references his work on *Pagan Spain* and writes that he "was ready to fly to Bandung, to fly from the old world of Spain to the new world of Asia ... ."[27] If *Pagan Spain* represents the old world by treating one of the countries that had originated European colonialism, then *The Color Curtain* represents the emerging new, as it describes Wright's attendance of the 1955 Bandung Conference that convened delegates from African and Asian nations that had recently won independence from colonial rule. *Black Power* complements these two books through a detailed description of a particular locale, the Gold Coast, where out of the violent impact of the old world now emerged a new nation, Ghana. In this triangle of travelogues, Wright reflects the history of European colonialism and investigates the relation between decolonization and modernization. But since *Pagan Spain* represents Spain as a country untouched by the process of secularization, or modernization, that Wright saw taking place in Africa and Asia, this triangle alone does not depict a nation that stands for a potential destination of this process. It is the novel *Savage Holiday* that completes Wright's literary map of transnationalism through the representation of a modern Western nation: the United States. In the intertextual dialogue between his travel books and *Savage Holiday*, Wright stages his argument that Western modernity should not unequivocally serve as the ideal for the emerging nations of Africa and Asia. An analysis of the relationship between *Savage Holiday* and *Black Power*, two books that were almost simultaneously published in 1954, will localize the novel in Wright's literary map of transnationalism and trace his anticolonial position as it emerges within this map.[28]

Black Power is a travelogue, relatively consistently narrated from the perspective of the autobiographical "I," while *Savage Holiday* is a novel with a relatively consistent third-person perspective. The travelogue details Wright's three-month-long visit to the Gold Coast and his interactions with a variety of West Africans, while the novel describes the symbolic matricide committed by a white middle-class New Yorker. In the former, Wright declares that once he set foot on African soil "black life was everywhere," while the latter is his only fictional work that does not feature a major black character.[29] Beneath these superficial differences, a thematic overlap exists between the two books. Kwame Anthony Appiah claims in his essay "A Long Way from Home: Wright in the Gold Coast" that in *Black Power,* Wright employs a variety of "devices of distancing" to distinguish himself from the Africans he describes.[30] Identifying the theme of "the African body" as a central one of these devices, Appiah argues that in *Black Power* African bodies "alienate by evoking disgust."[31] Indeed, *Black Power* does extensively depict black bodies. But *Savage Holiday*, too, includes extensive depictions of bodies, albeit white ones. While *Black Power* and *Savage Holiday* share the theme of the body, they develop this theme antithetically. The two books' antithetic development of their shared theme arises from the theoretical influences of Marxism and psychoanalysis on Wright's investigation of decolonization and modernization.[32]

Wright himself states in his introduction to *Black Power* that the book employs "to a limited degree, Marxist analysis of historic events."[33] Of Karl Marx's writings on colonialism, Wright probably knew the two articles "The British Rule in India" and "The Future Results of British Rule in India," as he owned a copy of a two-volume edition titled *Karl Marx: Selected Works*, wherein they are included.[34] In these journalistic articles, Marx provides a dialectical account of English colonialism that emphasizes the exploitation, destruction, and brutality, but also the progress that it brought to India. For Marx, it was colonialism that laid the foundation for the development of India's productive powers and its appropriation of sciences. He assumed that, in particular, the introduction of machinery into the locomotion of India, as the "forerunner of modern industry," would enable the emergence of a new social order out of the destructiveness of English rule.[35] Wright shared Marx's assumption that Europe had not only brought exploitation, destruction, and brutality to its colonies but also the potential for the development of science and industry. While Wright regarded science and industry as Western heritages, he also believed that they were the necessary conditions for the independence of African and Asian nations from their European colonizers. At the same time, however, Wright remained skeptical of the modernization of former colonies according to a Western ideal and his skepticism of Westernization partly hails from the psychoanalytic dimension of his anti-colonialism. This dimension is suggested by his interest in Reich during the mid-1950s. Reich's theory did not only deviate from orthodox psychoanalysis by alleging his discovery of the orgone energy that Wright aimed to translate into the literary device of the mood in "Celebration." Reich's work also deviated from Freudian orthodoxy by seeking a synthesis of psychoanalysis and Marxism. The attempt to reach this synthesis is, for example, expressed in Reich's book *The Function of the Orgasm: Sex-Economic Problems of Biological Energy*, one of the four books by him that Wright owned.[36] In this book, Reich states: "*Sexual repression is of social-economic [...] origin.*"[37] For Reich, in Western societies, the individual's relationship to the body and its functions in general is subject to alienation, so that he writes of "the strict, obsessional training for excremental control which undermines the civilization of the white race."[38] In the antithetic development of the theme of the body in *Black Power* and *Savage Holiday*, Wright stages two different degrees of repression and inhibition as they relate to two different forms of social-economic organization.

While *Black Power* situates the theme of the body in an emergent nation that is in an early stage of the processes of industrialization and modernization, *Savage Holiday* situates the same theme in a nation that has reached a relatively late stage of these very processes.

In *Black Power*, descriptions of African bodies begin with Wright's landing at the harbor of Takoradi, and they are central to his representation of West Africa's "absolute otherness and inaccessibility."[39] Wright describes a scene that he observes through a bus window on his trip to Accra:

> I stared again at the half-nude black people and they returned my gaze calmly and confidently. What innocence of instincts! What unabashed pride! Such uninhibitedness of living seemed to me to partake of the reality of a dream, for, in the Western world where my instincts had been conditioned, nude bodies were seen only under special and determined conditions [...].[40]

When Wright later tries photographing a scene in the streets of Accra, the women he wants to capture, aware of his presence, begin to cover their breasts and he regrets that "[c]hances of a natural photograph were impossible."[41] Accordingly, on a later trip he plans to "catch the native African without warning; he would have no chance to dress up or pretend."[42] These and the book's many other descriptions of relatively uninhibited displays of the body are mirrored in its descriptions of uninhibited executions of bodily functions – and in *Black Power* Wright mentions almost all of the functions that the human body is capable of performing. He observes mothers nursing their babies, "men and women urinating publicly," the excessive spitting of "[y]oung and old, men and women, people of high and low stations in life," and even a boy who "evacuated his bowels upon the porch of his hut" while maintaining eye contact with him.[43] This defecating boy appears in Bibiani, which Wright describes as a "company town" with a gold mine upon a hill and a "native community [called Old Town] rotting away in an unhealthy depression beside a huge, muddy, scummy lagoon."[44] Since in Old Town "[p]hysical disorder was rampant; nothing repeated itself," it stands in contrast to the gold mine, a symbol of industrialization with its "faint, regular, rhythmic clang of the machinery." Wright writes,

> In the mud huts [of Old Town] life was being lived by the imperious rule of instinct; up there [at the Gold mine], instinct had been rejected, repressed, and sublimated. [...] It was clear that the industrial activity upon that hill, owned or operated by no matter what race, could not exist without the curbing and disciplining of instincts, the ordering of emotion, the control of the reflexes of the body.[45]

In Wright's description, the defecating boy, whose instincts, emotions, and bodily reflexes are undisciplined, unordered, and uncontrolled, merges with the larger panorama of Old Town's "bleakness, poverty, and dirt."[46] As Wright in this passage contrasts the boy with the orderliness of Bibiani's industrialized area, he links the degree of restraint that people exercise upon their bodily functions to the social-economic organization wherein they live. On the hill, the orderliness and regularity of the industrialized area are congruent with the orderliness of the body and the regulation of its functions; in Old Town, the physical disorder of the town is congruent with the disorder of the boy's physique, and the absence of regularity in the streets with the low degree of regulation of his bodily functions. But this boy, as a prototype of the nursing, urinating, spitting, and defecating people in *Black Power*, is not only distinct from Bibiani's industrialized area. He is also distinct from the protagonist of *Savage Holiday*.

In the longest scene of *Savage Holiday*, the protagonist, Erskine Fowler, accidentally locks himself out of his apartment, in the nude, when he wants to fetch his newspaper from the hallway of the building where he lives. Wright spends almost fifteen pages describing how his protagonist tries to regain access to his apartment while he simultaneously tries to hide his nude body from the sight of his neighbors. Erskine is alone in the hallway, unsighted, and yet:

> He became dismayingly conscious of his nudity; a sense of hot panic flooded him; he felt as though a huge x-ray eye was glaring into his very soul [...]. Erskine's moral conditioning leaped to the fore, lava-like; there flashed into his mind an image of Mrs. Blake who lived in the apartment next to his [...]; also there rose up before his shocked eyes the prim face of Miss Brownell [...] who lived just across the hall from him; and he saw, as though staring up into the stern face of a judge in a courtroom, the gray, respectable faces of Mr. and Mrs. Fenley [...] who lived in the apartment which was just to the left of the elevator.[47]

Whereas the nude people described in *Black Power* become conscious of their nudity and begin to cover their bodies only when they perceive Wright as being in sight, Erskine's panic about his nudity is initiated even in the absence of an external observer. Not a single one of the listed neighbors will see him before he manages to reenter his apartment, but they are all painfully present for him even in their absence. Erskine has internalized his social relations, as what Wright here rather crudely calls the "huge x-ray eye" that glares into his soul, and he simultaneously exercises and suffers from this eye's authority. That Erskine perceives his neighbors as if "staring up into the stern face of a judge" indicates that already the potential visibility of his body in a relatively public space is a breach of a cultural prohibition and his panic sanctions this breach. But Erskine's excessive inhibition against displaying his body is not merely the result of his individual idiosyncrasy. When in *Black Power* the boy in Bibiani merges with the bleakness, poverty, and dirt of Old Town, then in *Savage Holiday* Erskine merges with the modern Western world.

In *The Color Curtain*, Wright writes that in parts of the Western world "an astounding industrial universe [...], like a web of steel, wraps our daily lives round;"[48] and he writes similarly about Erskine in *Savage Holiday*: "From puberty onwards he had firmly clamped his emotions under the steel lid of work and had fastened and tightened that lid with the inviolate bolts of religious devotion."[49] Wright's "web of steel" and "steel lid" are reminiscent of Reich's concepts of the "character armor" and "muscular armor" that, according to him, most individuals in modernity develop "as a defense against the break-through of affects and vegetative sensations."[50] The steel lid in *Savage Holiday*, like the web of steel, signifies the inhibiting demands of a modern, industrialized society. Furthermore, Erskine's excessive inhibitions, in Reich's phrasing, "undermine the civilization of the white race." At the end of *Savage Holiday*, the conflict between Erskine's inhibitions and their underlying impulses and emotions erupts in the violence of his symbolic matricide. In this deed, the Western civilization that he personifies is heightened into the savagery that is already predicted in the novel's title. In *White Man, Listen!*, Wright wrote of "the white psychological cripples of the Western world [...] [who] can't adjust to the exacting conditions of life in New York, or London, or Paris, or Berlin," and, without doubt, naked Erskine in the hallway is his prototype of these white psychological cripples.[51] Just as Wright's representation of uninhibited African bodies in *Black Power* indicates his alienation from West Africans, so his representation of the over-inhibited white body and his heightening of "the civilization of the white race" to a pathological degree in *Savage Holiday* indicates his alienation from the Western world. Here, Wright's anti-colonial position emerges in the intertextual dialogue between the antithetic, yet at times equally hyperbolic, portrayals of bodies in *Black Power* and *Savage Holiday*.

Wright harshly condemned colonialism for its brutality and its destruction of cultures and human lives, and he ardently advocated the immediate independence of the Gold Coast from British rule. But, indebted to Marxist dialectical thought, he also believed that it was colonialism that had carried with itself its inherent contradiction and the condition for its own destruction. It was colonialism that had set the seed of science and industry in the Gold Coast, and only industrialization could lead to the economic independence that Wright saw as a premise for national independence. Industrialization, however, would not only lead to a revolution in the social structure of the Gold Coast, but also to a transformation of the subjectivity of its people. In one of the many self-reflexive passages of *Black Power,* Wright writes: "I was assuming that these people had to be pulled out of this life, out of these conditions of poverty, had to become literate and eventually industrialized. But why? [. . .] I was literate, Western, disinherited, and industrialized and I felt each day the pain and anxiety of it."[52] According to Wright's rationale, industrialization held the promise of ending the Gold Coast's subjugation under Western exploitation. But since industrialization would also institute in the people of emerging Ghana higher degrees of inhibition, it at the same time held the threat of new forms of suffering, of psychological pain and anxiety. In his literary map of transnationalism, it is Wright's position that allowed for the imagination of a utopian alternative to both, colonial exploitation and psychological suffering. As it was equally distanced from the West Africa described in *Black Power* and the white America described in *Savage Holiday*, Wright's position emerges in the transnational space between the two as a utopian one. From this transnational, utopian space, the Gold Coast and other former colonies could be envisioned as industrialized and independent nations, but also as content civilizations, free from the deformities of the white psychological cripples of the West.

Wright's position is not fully expressed in *Savage Holiday* or *Black Power* and, by extension, not fully expressed in *The Color Curtain* or *Pagan Spain*. Rather, it is situated in the intertextual and transnational crossings between these individual books as they constitute the higher unity of his literary map of transnationalism. By placing, with *Savage Holiday*, a novel within this map, Wright underlined the literary and, at times, fictional dimension of even the purportedly nonfiction travel books within it. Still, it remains hard for the reader to determine where exactly his conscious literary embellishments and fictionalizations end and where his involuntary misconceptions, for example in the form of exoticizations, begin. These misconceptions may have partly arisen from Wright's projection of his theoretical presuppositions onto the reality of the processes of decolonization and modernization that his literary map of transnationalism investigates. This map, drawn from Wright's intellectual convictions, partly composed of his fictions and conscious fictionalizations, and, surely, at times constructed according to his misconceptions, stands as an enormous literary achievement. Yet, even this achievement cannot fully compensate for the loss that world literature suffers from Wright's inability to complete any single one of the three versions of his unwritten *magnum opus*.

Notes

1. Richard Wright, "I Choose Exile," Container Number 6, Folder 110, Richard Wright Papers, Yale Collection of American Literature, Beinecke Rare Book and Manuscript Library, 1. The author would like to thank Glenda Carpio for productive feedback on earlier drafts of this essay and Magda Majewska for generously sharing her knowledge of Wilhelm Reich.
2. As Yoshinobu Hakutani and Robert L. Tener state, in 1960, Wright had selected "817 out of about four thousand haiku he had composed" (xiii) for publication under the title *This Other World: Projections in the Haiku Manner*. This selection was published in 1998 as *Haiku: This Other World*.
3. Wright, "I Am a Red Slogan," in *The World of Richard Wright*, edited by Michel Fabre (Jackson: University Press of Mississippi, 1985), 236, emphasis in original.
4. Wright, "Walter Garland Tells What Spain's Fight against Fascism Means to the Negro People," in *Byline, Richard Wright: Articles from the* Daily Worker *and* New Masses, edited by Earle V. Bryant (Columbia: University of Missouri Press, 2015), 119–121, quotation at 119.
5. Wright, "How He Did It, and Oh–Where Were Hitler's Pagan Gods?," in ibid., 163–166, quotation at 163.
6. Wright, Letter to Edward Aswell, July 20, 1941, Container Number 31, Folder 1, Michel Fabre Archives of African American Arts and Letters, Stuart A. Rose Manuscript, Archives, and Rare Book Library, Emory University, 1–2.
7. Cf. Wright, Journals / 1945, 1947, Container Number 117, Folder 1860, Richard Wright Papers, Yale Collection of American Literature, Beinecke Rare Book and Manuscript Library, 52.
8. Ibid., 51, emphasis in original.
9. Ibid., emphasis in original.
10. Wright, Letter to Edward Aswell, August 21, 1955, Container Number 85, Folder 983, Richard Wright Papers, Yale Collection of American Literature, Beinecke Rare Book and Manuscript Library, 3, emphases in original.
11. Ibid., 4.
12. Ibid., 14.
13. Michel Fabre, *The Unfinished Quest of Richard Wright*, 2nd ed. (Urbana: University of Illinois Press, 1993), 427.
14. Wilhelm Reich, *The Function of the Orgasm: Sex-Economic Problems of Biological Energy. The Discovery of the Orgone*, Vol. 1 (New York: Orgone Institute Press, 1942), 360.
15. Wright, Letter to Edward Aswell, August 21, 1955, 20.
16. Wright, Letter to Paul Reynolds, July 27, 1955, Container Number 31, Folder 2, Michel Fabre Archives of African American Arts and Letters, Stuart A. Rose Manuscript, Archives, and Rare Book Library, Emory University, 3.
17. Wright, *The Long Dream* (Boston: Northeastern University Press, 2000), 13.
18. "Five Episodes" from "Island of Hallucination" were published in *Soon, One Morning: New Writing by American Negroes, 1940–1962*, edited by Herbert Hill in 1968, 139–164. Another short passage from the novel was quoted by Julia Wright in "Foreword: A Friendship Revisited," in Oliver W. Harrington,*Why*

I Left America and Other Essays (Jackson: University Press of Mississippi, 1993), xiii.

19. Wright, "Island of Hallucination," Container Number 34, Folder 472a, Richard Wright Papers, Yale Collection of American Literature, Beinecke Rare Book and Manuscript Library, 113.

20. Wright, Letter to Paul Reynolds, March 13, 1959, Container Number 31, Folder 3, Michel Fabre Archives of African American Arts and Letters, Stuart A. Rose Manuscript, Archives, and Rare Book Library, Emory University, 1–2.

21. Ibid., 2.

22. Ibid.

23. Wright, Letter to Paul Reynolds, March 15, 1959, Container Number 31, Folder 3, Michel Fabre Archives of African American Arts and Letters, Stuart A. Rose Manuscript, Archives, and Rare Book Library, Emory University, 1–2, emphasis in original.

24. Ibid., 2. Fabre's claim about the Fishbelly project, made without giving a source in *From Harlem to Paris: Black American Writers in France, 1840–1980*, that "at the end of the third volume of the series, Wright planned to take him [i.e. Fishbelly] to Algeria and back to the United States as a civil rights militant" (190) is not supported by the quoted archival material. This material does neither identify a specific nation in North Africa nor mention the protagonist's civil rights militancy. The description that Fabre gives of the plan for a continuation of the Fishbelly series in *The Unfinished Quest of Richard Wright* also makes the claim that "Wright used Algeria [...] as the setting for Fishbelly's renaissance in volume three" (482) without giving a source. Later in that book, Fabre names the two letters by Wright to Reynolds from March 13 and March 15, 1959, as the sources for his account of the third volume and this account does not claim Fishbelly's civil rights militancy (cf. 485–486).

25. Generally, the plans for these three projects are known to Wright scholarship, as Fabre mentioned them in his biography *The Unfinished Quest of Richard Wright*. However, with the exception of the two books of the Fishbelly series, *The Long Dream* and the unpublished "Island of Hallucination," they have not yet received considerable critical attention. In particular, they have never been systematically read in relation to each other and have never been taken as the basis for a reconsideration of Wright's published material.

26. Wright, *Pagan Spain* (New York: Harper, 2008), 230.

27. Wright, *The Color Curtain: A Report on the Bandung Conference*, in Wright's *Black Power: Three Books from Exile: Black Power; The Color Curtain; and White Man, Listen!* (New York: Harper, 2008), 429–629, quotation at 443.

28. For an account of Wright's plan to write a fourth travel book, on French West Africa, which he had to abandon due to a lack of financial support, see Virginia Whatley Smith, "'French West Africa': Behind the Scenes with Richard Wright, the Travel Writer," in *Richard Wright's Travel Writings: New Reflections*, edited by Virginia Whatley Smith (Jackson: University Press of Mississippi, 2001), 179–214.

29. Wright, *Black Power: A Record of Reactions in a Land of Pathos*, in Wright's *Black Power: Three Books from Exile*, 1–427, quotation at 52.

30. Kwame Anthony Appiah, "A Long Way from Home: Wright in the Gold Coast," in *Modern Critical Views: Richard Wright*, edited by Harold Bloom (New York: Chelsea House, 1987), 173–190, quotation at 185.

31. Ibid., 186–187.
32. The intricate blend of fiction, reportage, and scientifically and theoretically guided analysis that characterizes Wright's literary map of transnationalism is partly the result of his social trajectory, throughout which he was barred from access to academic institutions, and the position in the intellectual field to which this trajectory led him. For an account of Wright's social trajectory and his position in the literary field, see Stephan Kuhl, "Intellectual Disposition and Bodily Knowledge: Richard Wright's Literary Practice," in *Power Relations in Black Lives: Reading African American Literature and Culture with Bourdieu and Elias*, edited by Christa Buschendorf (Bielefeld: transcript, 2018), 55–75.
33. Wright, *Black Power*, 12.
34. Cf. Fabre, *Richard Wright: Books and Writers* (Jackson: University Press of Mississippi, 1990), 106.
35. Karl Marx, "The Future Results of British Rule in India," in *Karl Marx: Selected Works, in Two Volumes*, Vol. 2, edited by V. Adoratsky (Moscow: Co-operative Publishing Society of Foreign Workers in the USSR, 1935), 657–664, quotation at 661.
36. Cf. Fabre, *Richard Wright*, 133–134. Reich's influence on Wright during the mid-1950s is also shown in the reference that the title of Wright's 1957 book of lectures *White Man, Listen!* makes to the former's 1948 book *Listen, Little Man!*. Wright's interest in the connection between psychoanalysis and Marxism is, furthermore, expressed in his collaborations with Fredric Wertham. For an account of the influence of Wertham's studies of matricide on Wright's *Savage Holiday*, see Stephan Kuhl, "Guilty Children: Richard Wright's *Savage Holiday* and Fredric Wertham's *Dark Legend*," in *African American Literary Studies: New Texts, New Approaches, New Challenges*, edited by Glenda R. Carpio and Werner Sollors (Spec. issue of *Amerikastudien / American Studies* 55.4, 2010), 667–684. See also, Stephan Kuhl, *Crude Psychology: Richard Wright's Literary Practice* (forthcoming).
37. Reich, *The Function of the Orgasm*, 203, emphasis in original.
38. Ibid., 201.
39. Wright, *Black Power*, 59.
40. Ibid., 58.
41. Ibid., 92.
42. Ibid., 176.
43. Cf. *Black Power*, 69, 91–92, and 183; quotations are from 137, 340, and 372, respectively.
44. Ibid., 371.
45. Ibid., 372.
46. Ibid.
47. Wright, *Savage Holiday* (Jackson: Banner, 1994), 43–44.
48. Wright, *The Color Curtain*, 607.
49. Wright, *Savage Holiday*, 80.
50. Reich, *The Function of the Orgasm*, 360.
51. Wright, *White Man, Listen!*, in *Black Power: Three Books from Exile*, 631–812, quotation at 810.
52. Wright, *Black Power*, 184.

12

ERNEST JULIUS MITCHELL

Tenderness in Early Richard Wright

Richard Wright's fame rests on his earliest books. He published the three works that made his reputation in seven years: a book of short fiction, *Uncle Tom's Children* (1938); a best-selling novel, *Native Son* (1940); and a memoir, *Black Boy* (1945).[1] In spring of 1946, he moved with his family to Paris; seven more years elapsed between *Black Boy* and his next book, *The Outsider* (1953), during which he matured as an author. Yet the consensus on Wright's artistic value calcified early, and continues to focus on his early works. Paul Gilroy once lamented the tendency of critics to exalt Wright's early writings to the exclusion of his later works; although progress has been made, the situation remains much the same today, twenty-five years later.[2]

The focus on Wright's early works has saddled him with a difficult set of stereotypes. It has long since been fashionable to dismiss him: at best, his worth resides in the sociological import of his work;[3] more likely, he is an inferior craftsman, purveying propaganda[4]; at worst, he is a misogynist, whose angry male characters promote violence against women. Together, these views created the dominant image of Wright as a kind of black Hemingway: a simplistic, violent, misogynistic, and even anti-black writer.[5]

Yet Wright has suffered from another problem – the issue of "what white publishers won't print."[6] During his lifetime, he was unable to publish his first two novels, *Tarbaby's Dawn* and *Lawd Today!* (only the second has been published to date). Even when his works appeared, they were often partially censored: no passages were cut from *Uncle Tom's Children*, but American publishers suppressed important moments in *Native Son*, as well as the entire last third of *Black Boy*.[7] These omissions shaped Wright's literary reception for decades.

The passages cut from these early works tended to focus on sex; many of these scenes are quite homoerotic. This queer dimension of Wright's early works has never been fully assessed.[8] Once seen, it recasts Wright's most famous works as attempts to dissect and diagnose the roots of misogyny, homophobia, and masculine violence.[9] Wright emerges from such rereading as a deeply feminist thinker, involved in a lifelong critique of the violence he is often accused of supporting. The portrait of sensitive masculinity that emerges from Wright's earliest writings allows us to reconsider his entire corpus under an unlikely rubric: *tenderness.*

Lawd Today! (c. 1937)

Lawd Today! devotes its second chapter to lavishly depicting a black man bathing and getting dressed. Nothing could seem stranger for a connoisseur of Wright's novels. Our entrée into Jake's morning ablutions rides the curious edge between voyeurism and kitsch. His day begins, as does *Ulysses*, with shaving.[10] Then, he deposits his adipose body into the tub for a languorous soak. For Wright's Jake (as much as for Hemingway's) bathing shows the crack in his hardboiled exterior.[11] Listen. Try to hear him singing "I Woke Up Too Soon" in the bathtub, imitating the schmaltzy, hokey croon of Archie Bleyer, Rudy Vallee, Richard Himber.[12] Hear those buttery notes aflutter over the hazy smear of big band jazz:

> *I woke up too soon*
> *The spell was broken*
> *I woke up too soon*
> *Ending a dream*

Wright had an obsession with awakenings; most of his novels begin with them.[13] He clearly learned the Proustian lesson: hypnopompic states often persist into the early moments of wakefulness. *Lawd Today!* begins with Jake awakening from a patently sexual dream and going to breakfast; afterwards, in the tub, he lapses back into a dreamlike state as sensual imagery returns:

> Deep in the tile walls he saw the dim outlines of a soft, brown body. His eyelids drooped. The water lapped at his diaphragm and his flesh swooned in oozy eddies. A sweep lump rose in his stomach and traveled upwards, filling his throat. He lifted the washrag and squeezed it slowly, making the water trickle against his skin. His lips sagged and he sighed. The woman's body hovered nearer, growing in solidity. (22)

Suddenly, he reawakens and the dream disappears, prompting him to sing "I Woke Up To Soon." The lyrics trail off suggestively: "There was such tenderness in your caress / You were almost mine ... " This tender moment echoes throughout the book; variants of "tender" mark the promise of sensual satisfaction abruptly thwarted: Jake's wife *tenderly* flips an egg just before she burns it (11); Jake lifts twelve numbers *tenderly* just before he loses the lottery (49); and Rose, a woman Jake tries to seduce, *tenderly* places her hand on his neck (197) and sleeve (208) before she steals his wallet.[14] Tenderness, both here and in Wright's later work, is always edged with melancholy, mystery, and menace.

After leaving the tub, Jake combs his hair, a ritual that reveals his ambivalent homosocial emotions. The page-long satirical depiction amuses, largely because of its has a martial edge: Jake seems "a veteran fieldmarshall inspecting the fortifications and wire entanglements of an alien army" (23); "seizing his comb like a colt .45, he tried to force an opening through enemy lines. The battle waxed furious"; after the fight, "The enemy was conquered!" but Jake has to quickly "get his hair under this peace treaty" – that is, a stocking cap (24). Later in the book, Jake flings a mental tirade at Filipinos: "*Them little cute bastards!* ... He did not like the straight, slick, black hair of the Filipinos, nor their small mouths, nor their straight noses, nor the smell of the perfume they used" (148).[15] Although he claims to hate their "straight, slick, black hair," Jake expends great effort straightening his hair until it is "a solid mass of black slickness" (24).[16] Though he claims to dislike their smell, he is the only other man in the novel who sprays himself with "perfume" (27). Moreover, he calls the male Filipinos "cute."[17] Does he hate them, or want to be them? Jake's anxiety about the Filipinos is, at bottom, anxiety about masculinity: "he remembered that one of the Filipinos was studying art at the Chicago Art Institute; he had seen him showing his water colors to white clerks on the job. *Who in hell wants to mess around with stuff like that but a sissy?*" (148).[18] Jake's fear of being a sissy shows angst about his flamboyant masculinity.

Just after combing his hair, he stands at the door of his closet, choosing the perfect suit for his day at work. He picks a green suit, with a lavender shirt, red suspenders, a yellow tie, and a purple and orange handkerchief, all after much deliberation. Upon getting dressed, he pronounces himself "Like a Maltese kitten" with evident pleasure (27). It becomes clear later that Jake is competing with Al, his co-worker at the post office, who arrives in "a yellow chinchilla coat" (76) and "a new shirt, a light green one with delicate white pencil stripes" (89). When Al first appears, Jake seems to hold him in contempt: "That nigger thinks he's a bigshot" (75).[19] Yet it quickly becomes clear that Jake is trying to live up to Al's example; if he dislikes "Al's fat face" with its "smug repose," this is only because Jake wants to "possess it, make some of the strength of that repose his own" (89). At work, Jake thinks: "Al was a soldier ... Al was a swell fellow, easy to get along with. *It'd be hot if I could get into his company ...* " (131, italics original). In the very next paragraph, Jake falls back into a dreamlike state, and "his genitals began to swell" (131). The linkage of "swell fellow" and swelling genitals clearly suggests Jake's thinly repressed queer desire, not just for Al, but for his power, charisma, and education.[20]

Al himself has a decidedly queer streak. After playing bridge with Jake and their friends Bob and Slim, he insults Bob's kinky eyebrows and bets that the hair on Bob's chest is kinky (93). Homosocial friendship veers suddenly toward the homoerotic; feeling threatened, Bob threatens to punch Al in the "puss" (lip/mouth, but an obvious double entendre); as Bob defends himself, Al pretends to flirt with him: "'Yyyyyyyyeah,' said Al, tiptoeing close and cooing into Bob's ear. You's a man, but you's a uuuuuuugyly man ... " (94).[21] The cooing of Al (and his wooing of Bob) brings out the shame and anger of their fragile masculinity, and also brings uncontrollable laughter: "Jake and Slim kicked the walls of the room with the toes of their shoes" (94). Jake's attempt to straighten his hair, his declaration of war against its "insurgent kinks" (24), seems an attempt to avoid the kind of homophobic teasing to which Al has subjected Bob.[22]

The violence Jake commits against his wife at the end of the book seems a final queer imitation of Al. Near the end of the work day, Al describes his ex-girlfriend as "a funny woman" with "damn freakish ways" and ultimately "screwy" (155). Their relationship is decidedly queer: she is ten years older and as husky as Al, whom she keeps as a kind of gigolo. Yet despite her brash demeanor, she supposedly "craved for men to beat her" (156). Jake pays close attention to Al's story; perversely, when he beats his wife at the end of the story, he does so out of narcissistic attraction: unable to be *with* Al, Jake decides to *be* Al, displacing his queer desire for his friend by means of identification with him. Like Al, he directs violence against his wife, who has been "acting queer" (123); Lil has long refused to sleep with him because she is sick from an abortion; their marital bed is full of Christian Science literature, and Jake feels her rejection of sex for religion as a mark of her queerness.[23] In other words, Jake's misogyny has a secret root: his anxiety about being seen as flamboyantly queer, which itself masks a deeper anxiety about his deeply repressed attraction to his best male friend.

In later works, Wright self-consciously disguised the queer dimensions of such violence, leading some critics to think that he was unaware of its roots. James Baldwin, who might have known better, cast a damning verdict on Wright's corpus: "The violence is gratuitous and compulsive because of the root of the violence is never examined. The root is rage."[24]. Baldwin over-simplifies here; the rage often felt by Wright's tender protagonists stems from their need to suppress so much, above all the queer aspects of their masculinity. Reading *Lawd Today!* – an early text to which Baldwin had no access – this becomes much more obvious.

Wright's novels are full of homoerotic moments, often hand-in-glove with violence. More pointedly, the violence in Wright emerges most often from homoerotic angst cut short by homophobic action. If the source of this violence "is never examined," this is no fault of Wright's; the homoerotic flashes in his works were the moments most often censored by his publishers during his lifetime (as we will soon see in our examination of *Native Son*). Only in the unexpurgated texts does it become clear that Wright linked the bursts of violence in his texts not only to interracial heterosexual desire, but also to same-race, same-sex queer desire. These "impossible" loves are policed and violently thwarted in different ways: miscegenation brings reprisal from the state; homoeroticism brings reprisal from within black communities.

Big Boy and Bigger (*Uncle Tom's Children* and *Native Son*)

What can the queer aesthetic of the posthumous *Lawd Today!* teach us about Wright's better-known early works, *Uncle Tom's Children* and *Native Son*? Jake's bathing scene and his love/hate relationship with Al provide helpful context for the first story in *Uncle Tom's Children*, "Big Boy Leaves Home."[25] Here again, as so often in Wright, we encounter a group of four black males: Buck, Bobo, Lester, and Big Boy. Although they are teenagers, much younger than the characters in *Lawd Today!*, the social dynamics are similar. Bobo is the Jake of the group, and the toady to Big Boy, who is Al's equivalent. After Big Boy jumps on the backs of the three boys, knocking them to the ground, they attempt to fight him; Big Boy escapes by wrestling Bobo painfully to the ground, nearly breaking his neck. Soon after, the boys come to a pond where they go skinny dipping (echoing Jake's bath), but not before Big Boy and Bobo have a naked wrestling match.[26] This lightly eroticized violence ends rather quickly.

We encounter a much more complicated and extended example of homoerotic tension in *Native Son*. Again, we find four friends, with twenty-year old Bigger in the role of Al. Gus plays the role of Jake: "his eyes were full of a look compounded of fear and admiration for Bigger" (465).[27] As the four plan a robbery in a pool hall, Bigger feels conflicted: he's afraid to go through with the robbery, which was Gus's idea, but he's also afraid to lose face by seeming afraid. This conundrum sets off an odd tension between Bigger and Gus, a power struggle that manifests as sexual tension. While Gus stands "toying with a cue stick," Bigger stops the game by sweeping his arm across the table, "then looked straight at Gus as the gleaming balls kissed" (467). Waiting for Gus to speak, Bigger feels his "stomach tighten; he was hot all over. He felt as if he wanted to sneeze and could not ... He grew hotter, tighter" (468). Suddenly, "Bigger felt a curious sensation – half-sensual, half-thoughtful ... He edged toward Gus, not looking at Gus, but feeling the presence of Gus all over his body, through him, in and out of him, and hating himself and Gus because he felt it" (468). Tension rides a razor thin line between sex and violence: refusing to speak ("I don't have to use my tongue unless I *want* to!"), "Gus leaned on his cue stick and gazed at Bigger and Bigger's stomach tightened as though he were expecting a blow and were getting ready for it" (469). Finally, Bigger threatens Gus: "I'll take one of those balls and sink it in your Goddamn mouth" (469).[28] At last, Gus agrees to the robbery, angering Bigger, who dreams of stabbing, slapping, kicking, or tripping "Gus for making him feel this way" (470).

Although the ambivalence in the preceding passage seems patent, it makes more sense not only in light Jake's relation to Al in the posthumous *Lawd Today!* but also in connection with the scene that follows, one of the few that was cut from the original *Native Son*. After his near-fight with Gus, Bigger "longed for a stimulus powerful enough to focus his attention and drain off his energies" (471). Gus and his friend G. H. leave, and Bigger walks with Jack to a movie theater to watch *Trader Horn* (1931), a film set in Africa and starring Edwina Booth as Nina Trent.[29] Bigger begins to masturbate in the darkness, "polishing [his] nightstick" as Jack watches him, laughs, and does the same. Bigger and Jack – the pun deserves no comment – are not yet watching Edwina Booth, for the film has not begun. Their moment of queer intimacy occurs in the absence of women; only after finishing do they see a newsreel on Mary Dalton, the daughter of Bigger's new employer.[30] Bigger's homoerotic impulses find conflicting outlets: *jouissance* with Jack, violence toward Gus.

Later in the afternoon, Bigger replays a more intensely sexualized version of the pummeling Big Boy gives Bobo. Back at the pool hall, waiting for Gus to return, Bigger's "entire body hungered for keen sensation, something exciting and violent to relieve the tautness" (478). When Gus arrives, Bigger kicks him, chokes him, punches him, trips him, then threatens him with a knife. Bigger, "his body tingling with elation," forces Gus to lick his knife (138); their friends and the pool hall owner look on, laughing. Viewed in the context of the posthumous Wright – the homoerotics of *Lawd Today!* and the omitted masturbation scene of *Native Son* – the repressed queer dimension of Bigger's anxieties seems clear.[31]

The centrality of the pool hall scene should not be overlooked: both Wright and Ellison later agreed that the pool scene was the first of *Native Son* to be written.[32] How might we trace its implications the relationship of desire and violence in *Native Son*? A prevailing view, first laid out by James Baldwin soon after Wright's untimely death, holds that in most of Wright's work, as in black writing generally, "there is a great space where sex ought to be; and what usually fills the space is violence" (251).[33] There are at least two problems with this claim. First, it only holds for heterosexual desire. That is, even if we agree that the desire for heterosexual encounter in Wright is often frustrated and leads to violence, we should also note that the desire for same-sex violence is also often frustrated and leads to homoeroticism. Briefly, a formula:

Heterosexual desire expresses itself violently;
Homosocial violence expresses itself sexually.

This helps to explain why the violent threats between men (of the same race) seldom lead to actual violence, but dissipate in homoerotic tension, while heterosexual tension (almost regardless of race) tends to move as if inexorably toward violence.[34] But even with this modification, Baldwin's adage seems wrong for a second, subtler reason: he treats sex and violence as opposed and fully separable. But Baldwin's own work shows all too clearly the intricate lacework of sex and violence: they form a delicate tissue, both sensual and cruel. Sex is often threaded with violence, violence laden with sex; the desire to comfort, and the urge to crush, lie disturbingly close together.

Bigger's interactions with Mary and her communist boyfriend Jan should be viewed through the erotics of the pool hall scene. Much has been made of Bigger's supposedly strong reaction to Mary, given the taboo on interracial heterosexual sex. Yet when Mary appears, Bigger barely reacts, simply touching his cap and thinking that "she was kind of pretty" (503). Whatever "fear she inspired in him" (506) comes more from her inscrutable actions than anything specific to her whiteness. By contrast, Jan's appearance provokes an existential dread in Bigger that is hard to explain; as Jan extends his hand for a shake,

Bigger's entire body tightened with suspense and dread ... Bigger extended a limp palm, his mouth open in astonishment. He felt Jan's fingers tighten about his own. He tried to pull his hand away, ever so gently, but Jan held on, firmly, smiling ... he did not wish to meet Jan's gaze ... He was very conscious of his black skin and there was in him a prodding conviction that Jan and men like him had made it so that he would be conscious of that black skin ... He felt that he had no physical existence at all right then; he was something he hated, the badge of shame which he knew was attached to a black skin ... He felt naked, transparent ...   (507–508)

Bigger's reaction seems disproportionate; although justifiably anxious about touching a white man for the first time, a more than racial anxiety seems afoot. Bigger's hand is "limp"; his conviction is "prodding"; suddenly, he feels "naked." The homoerotic overtones are prominent. No comparable sexual frisson occurs when he touches Mary: the feel of her thigh against his receives but a sentence.

Bigger's desire has a bisexual edge. As he drives them home, he watches Jan and Mary in the backseat "spooning," another scene cut from the original edition (509). Bigger looks not only at Mary, but also at Jan. Suddenly "*filled* with a sense of them*,*" he quickly "sat up *straight,* fighting off the stiffening feelings in his loins" (518, emphases mine). Straightness must quickly be reasserted to avoid being filled with queer desire. After Jan leaves, Mary passes out and Bigger drunkenly carries her to her room, moved more by her scent than by physical contact. His sexual desire for Mary only rekindles as he recalls her link to Jan: kissing her, "the thought and conviction that Jan had had her a lot flashed through his mind" (524). The cutting of these passages erases not only Jan's spooning with Mary, but also Bigger's triangulated desire for both of them.

Although I would like to avoid replaying the violent deaths of Mary and Bessie, it seems appropriate to pause here and reflect on the role of violence in the text.[35] As in most of Wright's fiction, depictions of actual violence take up little space in the book, yet their intensity and vividness seem to overpower the narrative. Wright's perfection of techniques for intensifying violence was almost too successful: his compelling accounts of violence often leave readers unable to recall other aspects of his texts. Violence curbs our literary appreciation, hides the effects of style, camouflages the literary art involved in its own construction.

Yet depicting violence in this way demands exquisite technique. These depictions of violence affect Wright's readers intensely because they seem to emerge at random from idyllic scenes of tenderness. Violence comes without transition; its sudden onset obliterates all that came before it. What stands out in memory are instants of violence; one seldom remembers quiet beginnings, tender moments, or beautiful descriptions in Wright: the whiplash of topic and mood induces forgetfulness.[36] Such abrupt transitions are a hallmark of Wright's early style. The violence, in other words, is a carefully prepared effect, which relies on the forgettable backdrop of neutral or pleasant emotions.

Following this pattern, Bigger's moments alone in his jail cell are often forgotten in the mounting excitement of his interrogation and subsequent trial. Most readers focus on Boris Max's tour-de-force monologue near the end of Book Three; in doing so, they miss what Baldwin saw so clearly in "Everybody's Protest Novel" (1949): that "Bigger's tragedy is not that he is cold or black or hungry, nor even that he is American, black; but that he has accepted a theology that denies him life" (18).[37] Readers generally see Bigger's problem as tied to his race, or class, or masculinity; but Baldwin saw, as few others did, the theological dimension: that Bigger's "desire to crush all faith in him was in itself built upon a sense of faith" (701); that he rejects Christianity yet views this rejection as "his first murder" (710); his knowledge that he is unable to believe (725); that "he wanted to believe, but was afraid" (783). Bigger has some certainties: he does not believe in an afterlife (725) or the soul (762); about God's existence, he remains agnostic (778). He experiences moments of a messiah complex, believing that he can atone for others by taking upon himself "the crime of being black" (721).

As Wright explained elsewhere, Bigger reveals the true "moral horror" of black American life in his last conversation with Boris Max.[38] In these final moments, Bigger finally comes to believe in himself; but with his infamous conclusion ("what I killed for, I *am*!"), he also denies his own capacity for moral choice, displacing morality in favor of ontology (849). If Bigger simply exists to kill, and if he had killed long before killing Bessie, as he firmly believes, then he is metaphysically unfree, beyond the reach of the moral as a category. Baldwin rejects this firmly: on the one hand, he grows up just like Bigger: poor, black and hungry in an American metropolis. Like Bigger, he rejects the consolation of the church. But unlike Bigger, he refuses to capitulate to a theology that dehumanizes him. Baldwin slips, only slightly, when he says that the protest novel fails to endorse Bigger's theology. But the narrator doesn't seem to endorse it, and Wright himself certainly does not.

The critical habit has been to comment on the contrast between the work and the life; how different the brutal, violent characters of Wright's fiction seem from the soft-spoken, mild-mannered, laughing author.[39] What most surprises is how much the characters *resemble* Wright in their tenderness; they seem to differ in their violence, but the violence is often accidental, or out of fear, largely instinctual. No, the major way in which Wright differs from his characters is in his specific spirituality. All of his works stage the failures of theologies (or atheisms) that are not his own. An agnostic, his agnosticism still diverges profoundly from that of his agnostic characters. The nature of this theological difference can best be examined through an exploration of his memoir *Black Boy/American Hunger*.

Black Boy and *American Hunger*

Of the two parts of Wright's memoir, only *Black Boy* (1945), which follows him from childhood through his escape from the South for Chicago at age nineteen, was published during his lifetime. Unlike many of his early protagonists (like Jake, Big Boy, and Bigger), young Wright is shy, small, and pretty. That is, he does not particularly relish speaking to others;[40] he is underfed and thus underweight;[41] and he is viewed as somewhat non-normative for his gender, being light skinned and well educated.[42] None of this quite adds up to Wright being sexually queer.[43] Although Wright repeatedly insists on his oddity, the primary markers of his difference from his peers are his poverty, his religion (Seventh Day Adventist), and forever being the new kid at school. The tension between physical qualities (shyness, smallness, prettiness) and those foisted on him by his family (poverty, religion, itinerancy) shapes his existence.

Wright's childhood self, as the protagonist of *Black Boy*, is depicted as *tender*.[44] The term first appears in a description of his palm after it is stung by a bee (49), but is subsequently deployed to describe Wright's personality: by age twelve, he had become "strangely tender and cruel, violent and peaceful" (96); later, after being abruptly fired, he "lived carrying a huge wound, tender, festering" (186);[45] and in the conclusion of the original edition, he summarizes his childhood thus: "The shocks of southern living had rendered my personality tender and swollen, tense and volatile" (879).[46] This depiction of Wright as constitutionally "tender" serves two purposes. First, it shows him as someone marked by violence, and thus inclined to respond to the world in kind ("tender *and cruel, violent* and peaceful"). Second, it marks him as a sensitive yet skeptical observer, detached yet hypersensitive.

This tenderness arises as a direct result of his fear of white Southerners. Long before he experiences any threats to his person, he develops an almost paralyzing fear that whites will attempt to kill him or his loved ones. Counteracting this fear are his fantasies of violent revenge, both tragic and laughable since he is barely ten years old. These fantasies become "a culture, a creed, a religion" for him (72); these terms are not randomly chosen. A particular challenge for Wright as he ages is replacing this religious creed of fantastical violent reprisals with a set of beliefs that responds in a positive way to his environment. He struggles to replace this theology of violence with a belief in nonviolence.

Wright's failed religious conversion at the center of *Black Boy*, which is also the site of his successful rebirth as a writer, deserves our attention in this regard. In his eyes, the strict Seventh Day Adventist theology of his grandmother embodies the fantasies of violence that he seeks to escape. His most religious relatives are inclined to beat him sadistically. The church services themselves are superficially a site of tenderness: he speaks of "loving the hymns for their sensual caress" (107) and finds himself lusting after the elder's wife (though "the contrast between budding carnal desires and the aching loneliness of the hymns never evoked an sense of guilt in me," 108). Yet these services belong to the economy of violence; his reference to the "masochistic prayers" suggests that under the cover of the hymns, the congregation was led to take pleasure in doing spiritual violence to themselves (108). His inability to believe disappoints his grandmother deeply, though the older Wright notes "I knew more than she thought I did about the meaning of religion, the hunger of the human heart for that which is not and can never be" (114).[47] This hunger leads to a conversion of sorts to a spirituality of writing.

By turning to writing, Wright discovers an alternative theology. After promising his Grandmother to spend his afternoons in prayer, Wright still finds himself unable to believe. But unlike Bigger, who finds no substitute for religion, he discovers a love for writing when he finds himself unable to pray.[48] One day, instead of praying, he writes a story. Writing quickly becomes a substitute for prayer, both opposed to yet aligned with religious practice.[49] Wright is all too similar to his protagonists who fail because they make bad theological choices; he shares their anxieties, yet diverts them into writing, which he views as a mode of criminality,[50] but also spirituality.

The decision to write becomes a *theological* choice for Wright. He finally sees writing as a kind of positive tenderness, an attempt to becomes conscious of his interiority. This can be contrasted with his earlier negative tenderness, which was externally focused on the world of Southern racism. And it is in this respect that we should understand his infamous use of "tenderness" in *Black Boy*:

> (After I had outlived the shocks of childhood, after the habit of reflection had been born in me, I used to mull over the strange absence of real kindness in Negroes, how unstable was our tenderness, how lacking in genuine passion we were, how void of great hope, how timid our joy, how bare our traditions, how hollow our memories, how lacking we were in those intangible sentiments that bind man to man, and how shallow even was our despair ... Whenever I thought of the essential bleakness of black life in America, I knew that Negroes had never been allowed to catch the full spirit of Western civilization, that they lived somehow in it but not of it. And when I brooded upon the cultural barrenness of black life, I wondered if clean, positive tenderness, love, honor, loyalty, and the capacity to remember were native with man ... (37).

There are two crucial things to note here. First, this is not Wright's final position on the matter. The verb tense is carefully chosen: the thirty-five year old Wright locates this statement *after* childhood, but *before* the present day: "I used to" suggests that he no longer sees things this way. Second, there is still an important distinction to be made between the "unstable" or reactive tenderness he feels in his youth, and the "clean, positive tenderness" to which he aspires. Wright never claims to be in full possession of the virtues that conclude his list, but his writer's faith is a practice moving him closer.

The latter third of the autobiography, *American Hunger*, was not published in full until 1977. During Wright's life, it was issued piecemeal: the first three chapters as "The Man Who Went to Chicago" (1945) in *Cross Section* magazine;[51] chapters four through six in Richard Crossman's edited volume, *The God That Failed*.[52] Both were published with many omissions, beyond the scope of this essay to fully catalogue.[53] But many of the cuts fall into two basic categories.

A first set downplays Wright's paradoxical investment in both Protestantism and Communism. Although he had broken from their dogmas and doctrines, Wright saw himself as faithful to the spirit of both; he praises "the spirit of the Protestant ethic" as the lifeblood of free thought and, then points out that the Communist Party had ironically sworn itself to defending that heritage in ways that tended to stamp it out (120), only to quickly pivot and praise the party's moral code, which had no need for "the injunctions of the supernatural" (121), as "the future of mankind ... for good or bad" (122). Wright's uses the competing extremes of Church and Party to critique one another.

The second sort of omission comes as a further critique of this opposition: in many deleted passages, Wright asserts the independence of the solitary writer over against both Christianity and Communism. "Writing," he insists, "had to be done in loneliness and Communism had declared war on human loneliness" (123). Elsewhere, Wright casts the opposition in equally bold terms: "The artist and the politician stand at opposite poles" (92). In asserting his role as an artist, Wright commits to standing alone in racial terms as well: "my country had shown me no examples of how to live a human life . . . . the whites were as miserable as their black victims" (135). This passage, not published until 1977, helps to clarify Wright's infamous critique of Negro life in *Black Boy*: the "absence of real kindness" and the instability of "tenderness" are a larger American problem not at all specific to black folks.[54]

Conclusion

What do we gain from unpacking the strain of tenderness in Wright's early, most famous works? Above all, such a reading allows us to stop rehearsing old debates on the misogyny, homophobia, and racial self-hatred of his early writings. Seen in the light of his relentless attention to tenderness, these early works necessarily appear as critiques of violent masculinity, delicate diagnoses of how it fails. To see the tenderness so often missed in Wright requires us to read him well: attending to these details reveals his writerly sensitivity. He emerges as a deft technician of subtle lexical details: his tenderness lives at the level of form and content.

More importantly, revising our view of the early works makes room for considering his later ones. Since the majority of Wright's output was produced in Parisian exile, we can reasonably view his most famous works, including *Native Son* and *Black Boy*, as juvenilia.[55] His later fiction develops the exploration of masculinity, attempting to dissect it with ever-finer tools. Noting Wright's tenderness also prepares us to look anew at his sympathetic depictions of women, from *Pagan Spain*, which Gilroy has called his most woman-centered published text,[56] to *Black Hope*, his still-unpublished novel on women domestic workers.[57]

Above all, a focus on Wright's tenderness helps us to rethink the entire genealogy of black American letters. For years, Wright has occupied an outsized place in the tradition as the icon of masculinist protest. Such a view has led us to misread his cautious, exploratory tone; we have often taken him as a spokesman instead of a quietly independent thinker, urging us to think for ourselves. If Wright is not tough, but tender, we need not oppose him to Hurston and black women writers; we can also see new continuities between his work and that of earlier black male writers like Langston Hughes or Claude McKay. We equip ourselves to read black American writing with nuanced sensitivity, to write about it with precision, always *tenderly*.

Notes

1. Wright also published two texts in collaboration with others during this period: a theatrical script of *Native Son* with Paul Green, and the photobook *Twelve Million Black Voices* (1941) in collaboration with Edwin Rosskam.
2. Paul Gilroy, *The Black Atlantic: Modernity and Double Consciousness* (Cambridge: Harvard University Press, 1993), 150, et passim.
3. Werner Sollors, *African American Writing: A Literary Approach* (Philadelphia: Temple University Press, 2016), 137–143. While diagnosing the trend of sociological readings of Wright, Sollors also offers one of the strongest defenses of Wright's literary capacity in *Ethnic Modernism* (Cambridge: Harvard University Press, 2008), discussed below.
4. Editors of his writings often approach the task with a barely implicit question: *could Richard write?* See Yoshinobu Hakutani, ed., *Critical Essays on Richard Wright* (Boston: G. K. Hall, 1982); Harold Bloom, ed., *Richard Wright: Modern Critical Views* (New York: Chelsea House, 1987); Henry Louis Gates Jr., and K. A. Appiah, *Richard Wright: Critical Perspectives Past and Present* (New York: Amistad, 1993), xi–xii. Bloom's critiques have been especially astringent.

5. This view of Hemingway has been challenged somewhat by the posthumous publication of *The Garden of Eden* (New York: Charles Scribner, 1986), a novel with a queer and proto-feminist slant. For an incisive critique of racism and misogyny in Hemingway's texts, see Toni Morrison, *Playing in the Dark: Whiteness and the Literary Imagination* (New York: Vintage, 1992). For a more recent and recuperative take on Wright's literary relationship to Hemingway, see Charles Scruggs, "Looking for a Place to Land: Hemingway's Ghostly Presence in the Fiction of Richard Wright, James Baldwin, and Ralph Ellison," in Gary Edward Holcomb and Charles Scruggs, eds., *Hemingway and the Black Renaissance* (Columbus: Ohio State University Press, 2012).

6. The title of an essay by Zora Neale Hurston, herself the victim of unsympathetic editors for the latter part of her career, this phrase describes a common problem for black writers in general. See Cheryl A. Wall, ed., *Folklore, Memoirs, and Other Writings* (New York: Library of America), 950–955.

7. The scenes cut by his publishers did not appear in print for decades; most were only restored in the publication of a two-volume edition of his works by the Library of America; its editor, scholar-biographer Arnold Rampersad, restored the texts of five major works to their unexpurgated versions.

8. There are, as of yet, precious few queer readings of Wright. When authors discuss this at all, they frequently focus on Aggie West, the gay character in Wright's last published novel, *The Long Dream*: see Paul Gilroy, *The Black Atlantic: Modernity and Double Consciousness* (Cambridge: Harvard University Press, 1993), 183–184; Marlon B. Ross, "Beyond the Closet as Raceless Paradigm," in *Black Queer Studies: A Critical Anthology*, edited by E. Patrick Johnson and Mae G. Henderson (Durham: Duke University Press, 2005), 161–189, especially 181–182; and Robert Reid-Pharr, "The Funny Father's Luck" in *Once You Go Black: Choice, Desire, and the Black American Intellectual* (New York: New York University Press, 2007), 37–67, especially 57–65. For an essay on the most recent of Wright's posthumously published novels, see John C. Charles, "A Queer Finale: Sympathy and Privacy in Wright's *A Father's Law*," in Alice Mikal Craven and William E. Dow, eds., *Richard Wright: New Readings in the 21st Century* (New York: Palgrave MacMillan, 2011), 147–166.

9. Paul Gilroy suggested a proto-feminist Wright in *The Black Atlantic*, but relied on Wright's later writings to do so.

10. Wright's emphasis on Jake's fat in the shaving episode calls to mind Joyce's "plump Buck Mulligan" (though Jake is far less *stately*, and shaves far less *warily, neatly, evenly* ...). The allusion seems hardly accidental, since the novel uses the twenty-four hour conceit of *Ulysses*. Although Wright does not use the term "plump" in this passage, he notes that Jake is fat, and uses Joyce's juicy adjective three times in the text: "A plump, brownskinned girl passed" (43); "[the snakecharmer's] lips were plump and loose" (95); and "a plump, mulatto girl [at Walgreens]" (102). All quotations from *Lawd Today!* come from Richard Wright, *Early Works*, edited by Arnold Rampersad (New York: Library of America, 1991), 1–220.

11. Werner Sollors, *Ethnic Modernism* (Cambridge: Harvard University Press, 2008), 124.

12. All three singers recorded the song in the mid-1930s.

13. Those that do not still tend to foreground dreams.

14. Jake's friend Bob, who has a painful venereal disease, crosses his legs "with a slow, tender motion" (110), and the radio explains that Lincoln "lingered among tender friends" until he died from his gunshot wound (190).

15. After this passage, Jake observes that Filipinos seems to prefer marriage to white women; a similar passage occurs shortly thereafter. These reflections on marriage distract from the blatant homoeroticism of the passage.

16. The overlay of martial imagery and Filipino hair points to geopolitics: the American occupation of the Philippines had recently been challenged by the passage of the Philippine Independence Act of 1934.

17. "Cute" appears one other time, when Blanche tries to seduce the men: "We got the cutest beds ... " (198).

18. His hatred of so-called "sissies" appears again at the jazz club: "He did not want to smoke any Marihuana cigarettes ... *That's a sissy's way to get high*" (196). One of the well-established tropes for 1920s jazz clubs was the marginal presence of queer characters. The depiction of the jazz club in Part III draws on tropes established by James Weldon Johnson's *Autobiography of an Ex-Coloured Man* (1912), and developed further by Ernest Hemingway's *The Sun Also Rises* (1926), Carl Van Vechten's *Nigger Heaven* (1926), and McKay's *Home to Harlem* (1928), as well as Hurston's evocation of a jook joint in *Mules and Men* (1934).

19. This line foreshadows his comment on the young white mail clerks: "them white boys always in a hurry to get somewhere. And soon's they get out of school they's going to be bigshots" (117).

20. A few pages later, in the bathroom, "Al edged close, buttoning his pants and holding a crumpled newspaper under his arm" (134). The phallic newspaper links the two: Jake and Al are the only two people in the novel who read the papers, and reading itself is seen by Jake as an act that threatens to make one crazy, or "queer" – Jake remembers "a schoolmate of his who had become queer from trying to memorize the Bible" (69).

21. Only one other character coos in the novel: in the jazz club, after someone shouts "Lawd, today!" (205), Blanche coos at Jake while seducing him.

22. Multiple strands of homoscopic, homosocial, and homoerotic behavior converge in the word "kink" – a term uniting curly hair, madness, sexual perversity, social deviance, blackness, and criminality ("kink, n.1," OED online).

23. Wright marks the sexualization of their bed with his use of the word "edge" – when Jake lies down, he strikes his head against the "sharp edge" of a Christian Science booklet. Later, under the eye of white women, "he felt the edges of his wet BVDs cutting into his loins" (143); [BVDs were a form of long underwear popular before the 1950s, named after the initials of its makers, Bradley, Voorhees & Day; "B.V.D., n.," OED online]. In the final scene, he finds Lil kneeling "on the edge of a circle of light" (216); she defends herself with "a jagged edge of windowpane" (219).

24. James Baldwin, "Alas, Poor Richard," originally in *Nobody Knows My Name* (1961); cited here from James Baldwin, *Collected Essays*, edited by Toni Morrison (New York: Library of America, 1998), 251.

25. Wright wrote the story in 1936, at a time when he was also revising *Lawd Today!* All quotations from "Big Boy Leaves Home" come from *Uncle Tom's Children* in Richard Wright, *Early Works*, 221–442.

26. "Bobo crouched, spread his legs, and braced himself against Big Boy's body. Locked in each other's arms, they tussled on the edge of the hole, neither able to throw the other" (246).

27. All quotations from *Native Son* come from Richard Wright, *Early Works*, 443–850.

28. Billiard balls carry a homoerotic charge in *Lawd Today!*, where Jake's "nappy forelocks . . . had to be bullied into a billiard ball smoothness" (23), using a hair pomade that was "fatal to insurgent kinks" (24).

29. The original film trailer refers to her as "the beautiful White Goddess of paganism."

30. Buckley, the prosecutor, wrongly imagines that the boys masturbated to the image of Mary Dalton, imagining her rape and murder (831). Jonathan Elmer notes the absence of the newsreel, but doesn't acknowledge the homoerotic stimulus involved in Jack watching Bigger; see his "Spectacle and Event in *Native Son*," in Harold Bloom, ed., *Richard Wright's Native Son, New Edition* (New York: Bloom's Literary Criticism, 2009), 138.

31. Abdul R. JanMohamed offers a reading of the scene with the knife as a "mock rape/castration" which also serves as an act of mirrored violence: "because of the insistently specular nature of the relations between Bigger and Gus, what Bigger does to Gus, he does to himself. The implication thus is that Bigger rapes and castrates himself . . . " (89, 90). However, JanMohamed does not refer to this narcissistic violence as homoerotic, nor does he connect it to the larger thematics of homoeroticism woven through the early parts of the novel. Abdul R. JanMohamed, "Specularity as a Mode of Knowledge and Agency in Richard Wright's Work," in *Philosophical Meditations on Richard Wright*, edited by James B. Haile III (New York: Lexington Books, 2012), 83–96.

32. Ellison, "That Same Pleasure, That Same Pain," in *The Collected Essays of Ralph Ellison*, edited by John F. Callahan (New York: Modern Library, 2003), 63–80; Wright, "How Bigger Was Born," in Wright, *Early Works*, 851–881. Like Jake's bath in *Lawd*, the pool hall scene occupies the second position in the story, after the infamous opening in which Bigger kills a rat at home.

33. "Alas Poor Richard" (1961). See also Marilyn Waniek's, "The Space Where Sex Should Be" (1975).

34. Threats of interracial violence between men almost always lead to violence in Wright; but such threats often veil anxieties about interracial heterosexual sex: in such cases, the men use violence to prevent miscegenation.

35. On similar ethical reserve, see Saidiya Hartman, *Scenes of Subjection* (1997) and Christina Sharpe, *In the Wake* (2016).

36. In his use of transitions, Wright closely resembles Hurston's discussion of the "rhythm of segments." See her essay "Characteristics of Negro Expression" (1934) in Zora Neale Hurston, *Folklore, Memoirs, and Other Writings*, edited by Cheryl A. Wall (New York: Library of America, 1995), 835.

37. James Baldwin, *Collected Essays*, edited by Toni Morrison (New York: Library of America, 1998).

38. "The lawyer, Max, was placed in Bigger's cell at the end of the novel to register the *moral* – or what *I* felt was the *moral* – horror of Negro life in the United States" ("How Bigger Was Born," 880). Earlier in this essay, Wright also writes:

"The degree of *morality* in my writing depended on the degree of felt life and truth I could put down upon the printed page" (877, my emphasis).

39. A more sophisticated version of this argument is Ellison's claim, in letter to Albert Murray in 1952, that Wright "could never bring himself to conceive a character as complicated as himself." Albert Murray and John F. Callahan, eds., *Trading Twelves: The Selected Letters of Ralph Ellison and Albert Murray* (New York: Vintage, 2000), 29.

40. For analogues to Wright's introversion, we might look to Audre Lorde's claim "I did not speak until I was four" in *Zami: A New Spelling of My Name* (Berkeley: Crossing Press, 1982), 31; a similar, more recent example is the resolute silence of the young Chiron in the first third of Barry Jenkins' film *Moonlight* (2016). For a broader meditation on the overlooked place of introversion and quiet in representations of black subjects, see Kevin Quashie, *The Sovereignty of Quiet: Beyond Resistance in Black Culture* (New Brunswick: Rutgers University Press, 2012).

41. Soon after turning fifteen, Wright seeks employment at a sawmill; at his interview, Wright recounts, the foreman "put his hands under my arms and lifted me from the floor, as though I were a bundle of feathers," before concluding "You're too light for our work" (*Black Boy*, 163). All quotations from *Black Boy (American Hunger)* come from Wright, *Later Works*, edited by Arnold Rampersad (New York: Library of America, 1991), 1–366.

42. "Many of the naïve black families bought their insurance from us because they felt that they were connecting themselves with something that would make their children 'write 'n speak lak dat pretty boy from Jackson" (Wright, *Black Boy*, 131).

43. Victor Anderson goes so far as to call him "a quare kid" (66, 71); but he also adds, a bit late: "This is not to mark Wright with a queer identity, which is a hotly contested description when assigned to straight or same-sex – same-gender loving black writers or people. Quare does not stand in for an identity at all. [...] My *quare* reading of the everyday of Richard Wright does not signify a fixed, stable identity" (78); Victor Anderson, "Fear, Trembling, and Transcendence in the Everyday of Richard Wright: A *Quare* Reading," in *Philosophical Meditations on Richard Wright*, edited by James B. Haile III (New York: Lexington Books, 2012), 65–81.

44. Wright only calls himself "tender" in *Black Boy*, while he is still a teenager before he leaves the South; the term does not occur in *American Hunger*.

45. Elsewhere in the memoir, Wright often speaks of his mind or body reacting like an ulcer to his surroundings.

46. This ending was moved to an appendix when *Black Boy* and *American Hunger* were released together in 1991.

47. Compare the failed conversion in Langston Hughes's autobiography *The Big Sea* (1940), which Wright had reviewed negatively.

48. See Hemingway's *The Sun Also Rises* (1926), where the protagonist Jake pauses in a Catholic church and tries to pray, only to realize that he is doing a poor job: "I was thinking of myself as praying, I was a little ashamed, and regretted that I was such a rotten Catholic, but realized there was nothing I could do about it, at least for a while, and maybe never, but that anyway it was a grand religion, and I

only wished I felt religious and maybe I would the next time … " (New York: Scribner, 2006), 103.

49. Compare "How Bigger Was Born," where Wright claims to write "in an attitude almost akin to prayer" (876).

50. After including the word "Hell" in the title of his first published story, "I felt that I had committed a crime" (*Black Boy*, 161).

51. Copyrighted in 1945 by L.B. Fischer Publishing Corporation with the title "Early Days in Chicago." See Richard Wright, *Eight Men* (Cleveland: The World Publishing Company, 1961), 4.

52. Prior to *The God That Failed* (New York: Harper, 1949), parts of these chapters had appeared in *Atlantic Monthly* (August/September 1945) as "I Tried to Be a Communist" and "American Hunger" in *Mademoiselle* (September 1945). See Richard Wright, *Later Works*, 869.

53. For a useful introduction, see Janice Thaddeus, "The Metamorphosis of Richard Wright's *Black Boy*" in *Richard Wright's* Black Boy (American Hunger): *A Casebook* (New York: Oxford University Press, 2003).

54. This may, perhaps, seem a bit cold. But compare Lukács's note on the misperception of Stefan George as a "cold" writer: "He is cold because the notes he strikes are so delicate that not everyone can hear them; because his tragedies are such that the average reader of today does not yet feel them as tragic"; György Lukács, *Soul and Form*, edited by John T. Sanders and Katie Terezakis, translated by Anna Bostock (New York: Columbia University Press, 2010), 100. Nathan A. Scott was rare in correctly perceiving Wright's warm sensitivity, his existential heat: "his books take us into the hot psychic climate of *crisis* and *anguish* and *dread* in which we have lived" (emphases original); see Nathan A. Scott, "Search for Beliefs: Fiction of Richard Wright" in *University of Kansas City Review* 23.1 (October 1956), 19.

55. In the fifties, Wright published nearly a book a year, from *The Outsider* (1953) until *The Long Dream* (1958), as well as writing several other works, some of which were published posthumously, some of which have yet to appear.

56. " … most directly concerned with questions of women's social subordination … " Gilroy, *Black Atlantic* (182–183).

57. See Barbara Foley, "'A Dramatic Picture … of Woman from Feudalism to Fascism': Richard Wright's *Black Hope*," in *Richard Wright in a Post-Racial Imaginary*, eds., William Dow and Alice Mikal Craven (New York: Bloomsbury, 2014), 113–126.

FURTHER READING

Primary Works, Fiction

Wright, Richard. *A Father's Law*. New York: Harper Perennial, 2008.
Bright and Morning Star. New York: International Publishers, 1941.
Eight Men. Cleveland and New York: World Publishing Company, 1961.
Haiku: This Other World. New York: Arcade Publishers, 1998.
Lawd Today! New York: Avon Books, 1963.
Native Son (The Biography of a Young American): A Play in Ten Scenes. With Paul Green. New York: Harper, 1941.
Native Son. New York: Harper & Brothers, 1940.
Rite of Passage. New York: HarperCollins, 1994.
Savage Holiday. New York: Avon Books, 1954.
The Long Dream. New York: Doubleday, 1958.
The Outsider. New York: Harper & Brothers, 1953.
Uncle Tom's Children: Five Long Stories. New York: Harper, 1940.
Uncle Tom's Children: Four Novellas. New York: Harper & Brothers, 1938.

Primary Works, Nonfiction

Wright, Richard. *American Hunger*. New York: Harper & Row, 1977. A continuation of Black Boy; Wright's account of his years in Chicago; published posthumously.
Black Boy: A Record of Childhood and Youth. New York: Harper & Brothers, 1945.
Black Power: A Record of Reactions in a Land of Pathos. New York: Harper & Brothers, 1954.
Byline, Richard Wright: Articles from the Daily Worker and New Masses. Columbia: University of Missouri Press, 2015.
Pagan Spain. New York: Harper & Row, 1957.
The Color Curtain. Cleveland: World Publishing Company, 1954.
Twelve Million Black Voices: A Folk History of the Negro in the United States. Photo direction by Edwin Rosskam. New York: Viking Press, 1941.
White Man, Listen! New York: Doubleday, 1957.

Important Short Pieces, Articles, Reviews, Letters, Etc.
Not Included in Books

Wright, Richard. "A Sharecropper's Story" (Review of *I Was a Sharecropper*, by Harry B. Kroll). *New Republic*, XCIII (December 1, 1937), 109.

"A Tale of Folk Courage" (Review of *Black Thunder* by Arna Bontemps). *Partisan Review and Anvil*, 3 (April 1936).

"A World View of the American Negro." *Twice a Year*, no. 14–15 (Fall 1946–Winter 1947), 346–348.

"Adventure and Love in Loyalist Spain" (Review of *The Wall of Men*, by William Rollins). *New Masses*, XXVI (March 8, 1938), 25–26.

"Alger Revisited, or My Stars! Did We Read That Stuff?" (Review of Horatio Alger's Collected Novels). *P.M. Magazine* (September 16, 1945), m8.

"American G.I.'s Fears Worry Gertrude Stein" (Review of *Brewise and Willie* by Gertrude Stein in the form of a letter to Roger Pippett). *P.M. Magazine* (July 26, 1946), m15–m16.

"American Negroes in France." *Crisis*, LVIII (June–July 1951), 381–383.

"Between Laughter and Tears" (Review of *These Low Grounds* by Walters E. Turpin and *Their Eyes Were Watching God* by Zora Neale Hurston). *New Masses*, 25 (October 5, 1937), 22–25.

"Blueprint for Negro Writing." *New Challenge*, II (Fall, 1937), 53–65.

"Gertrude Stein's Story is Drenched in Hitler's Horrors" (Review of *Wars I Have Seen* by Gertrude Stein). *P.M. Magazine* (March 11, 1945), m15.

"How 'Bigger' Was Born." *Saturday Review*, 22 (June 1, 1940), 4–5, 17–20.

"How He Did It, and Oh!–Where Were Hitler's Pagan Gods?" *Daily Worker* (June 24, 1938), 1, 8.

"How Jim Crow Feels." *True Magazine* (November 1946), 25–27, 154–156. On Wright's trip to Mexico and the South in the summer of 1940.

"I Bite the Hand That Feed Me." *Atlantic Monthly*, CLV (June 1940), 826–828.

"I Support the Soviet Union." *Soviet Russia* (September 1941), 29.

"I Tried to Be a Communist." *Atlantic Monthly*, CLXXXIV (August 1944), 61–70; (September 1944), 48–56. Included in Richard Crossman, ed., *The God That Failed*. New York: Harper, 1949.

"Inner Landscape" (Review of *The Big Sea* by Langston Hughes). *New Republic*, 103 (October 24, 1940), 600.

"Introduction," in George Lamming, *In the Castle of My Skin*. New York: McGraw-Hill, 1953, ix–xii.

"Introduction," in George Padmore, *Pan-Africanism or Communism?* London: Dobson, 1956, 11–14.

"Introduction," in Horace R. Cayton and St. Clair Drake, *Black Metropolis*. New York: Harcourt Brace, 1945, xvii–xxxiv.

"Introduction," in J. Saunders Redding, *No Day of Triumph*, p. I. New York: Harper, 1942.

"Introduction," in Nelson Algren, *Never Come Morning*, pp. ix–x. New York: Harper, 1942.

"Introductory Note to 'The Respectful Prostitute,'" in *Art and Action, A Book of Literature, the Arts, and Civil Liberties (10th Anniversary Issue, Twice a Year, 1938–1948)*. New York, 1948, 14–16.

"Joe Louis Uncovers Dynamite." *New Masses*, 17 (October 8, 1935).

"Lynching Bee" (Review of *Trouble in July* by Erskine Caldwell). *New Republic*, 102 (March 11, 1940), 351.

"Neurosis of Conquest" (Review of *Prospero and Caliban* by Octave Mannoni). *The Nation*, 183 (October 20, 1956), 330–331.

"Not My People's War," *New Masses*, 39 (June 17, 1941), 8–9, 12.

"Preface," in Chester Himes, *La Croisade de Lee Gordon*, Paris: Correa, 1952, 7–8.

"Psychiatry Comes to Harlem." *Free World*, XII (September 1946), 49–51. Reprinted in *Twice a Year* (1946–1947) under the title "Psychiatry Goes to Harlem."

"Richard Wright and Antonio Frasconi: An Exchange of Letters." *Twice a Year*, no. 12–13 (1945), 256–261.

"Richard Wright Describes the Birth of Black Boy." *New York Post*, November 30, 1944, B6.

"Spanish Snapshot: Granada, Seville." *Two Cities (Paris)*, No. 2 (July 1959), 25–34.

"The Shame of Chicago." *Ebony*, 7 (December 1951), 24–32. On Wright's return to Chicago in 1949.

"The Voiceless Ones" (Review of *The Disinherited* by Michel Del Castillo). *Saturday Review*, 443 (April 16, 1960), 53–54.

"There Is Always Another Café." *The Kiosk (Paris)* no. 10, 1953, 12–14.

"Two Million Black Voices." *New Masses*, 18 (February 25, 1936).

"Two Novels of the Crushing of Men, One White, One Black" (Review of *Focus* by Arthur Miller and *If He Hollers Let Him Go* by Chester Himes). *P.M. Magazine* (November 25, 1945), m7–m8.

"Urban Misery in an American City: Juvenile Delinquency in Harlem." *Twice a Year*, no. 14–15 (Fall 1946–Winter 1947), 339–345.

"What You Don't Know Won't Hurt You." *Harper's Magazine*, CLXXXVI (December 1942), 58–61.

Poetry

Wright, Richard. "A Red Love Note." *Left Front*, no. 3 (January–February 1934), 3.

"Ah Feels It in Mah Bones." *International Literature*, 4 (April 1935), 80.

"Between the World and Me." *Partisan Review*, 2 (July–August 1935), 18–19.

"Child of the Dead and Forgotten Gods." *The Anvil*, no. 5 (March–April 1934), 30.

"Everywhere Burning Waters Rise." *Left Front*, no. 4 (May–June 1934), 9.

"Haiku Poems." A number of haikus have appeared in Ollie Harrington, "The Last Days of Richard Wright." *Ebony* 16 (February 1961), 93–94. Reprinted in (1) Arna Bontemps and Langston Hughes, *The Poetry of the Negro*. New York: Doubleday, 1964; (2) Constance Webb, *Richard Wright: A Biography*. New York: Putnam, 1968, pp. 393–394; (3) Richard Wright, "Haikus." *Studies in Black Literature*, I (Summer 1970), 1; (4) "10 Haiku." *New Letters*, 38 (Winter 1971), 100–101.

"Hearst Headline Blues." *New Masses*, 21 (May 12, 1936), 14.

"I Am a Red Slogan." *International Literature*, 4 (April 1935), 35.
"I Have Seen Black Hands." *New Masses*, 11 (June 26, 1934), 16.
"King Joe" ("Joe Louis Blues"). Lyrics for OKEH record no. 6475. Reprinted in *New York Amsterdam Star News*, October 18, 1941, p. c16.
"Obsession." *Midland Left*, no. 2 (February 1935), 14.
"Old Habit and New Love." *New Masses*, 21 (December 15, 1936), 29.
"Red Clay Blues." *New Masses*, 32 (August 1, 1939), 14. Written in collaboration with Langston Hughes.
"Red Leaves of Red Books." *New Masses*, 15 (April 30, 1935), 6.
"Rest for the Weary." *Left Front*, no. 3 (January–February 1934), 3.
"Rise and Live." *Midland Left*, no. 2 (February 1935), 13–14.
"Spread Your Sunrise." *New Masses*, 19 (July 2, 1935), 26.
"Strength." *The Anvil*, no. 5 (March–April 1934), 20.
"We of the Streets." *New Masses*, 23 (April 13, 1937), 14.

Fiction

Wright, Richard. "Almos' a Man." *Harper's Bazaar*, 74 (Jan. 1940), 40–41. Included with slight revisions, in Wright, *Eight Men,* as "The Man Who Was Almost a Man."
"Big Black Good Man." *Esquire*, 50 (Nov. 1957), 76–80. Included in *Eight Men.*
"Big Boy Leaves Home," in *The New Caravan*, eds. Alfred Kreymborg, Lewis Mumford, and Paul Rosenfeld (New York: W. W. Norton, 1936), 124–158. Included in *Uncle Tom's Children.*
"Bright and Morning Star." *New Masses*, 27 (May 10, 1938), 97–99, 116–124. Included in *Uncle Tom's Children* (1940 edition).
"Fire and Cloud." *Story Magazine*, 12 (March 1938), 9–41. Included in *Uncle Tom's Children.*
"Five Episodes," in *Soon, One Morning*, ed. Herbert Hill (New York: Knopf, 1963), Excerpts from "Island of Hallucinations," an unpublished novel completed in 1959.
"Silt." *New Masses*, 24 (August 24, 1937), 19–20. Included in *Eight Men* as "The Man Who Saw the Flood."
"Superstition." *Abbot's Monthly Magazine*, 2 (April 1931), 45–47, 64–66, 72–73.
"The Man Who Killed a Shadow." *Zero* (Paris) I (Spring 1949), 45–53. Included in *Eight Men.*
"The Man Who Lived Underground." *Cross Section*, ed. Edwin Seaver. New York, 1945), 58–102. Included in *Eight Men.*
"The Voodoo of Hell's Half Acre." *Southern Register* (Jackson, MS), 1924. (Precise date unknown – no copy available).

Plays

Daddy Goodness, an adaption of and collaboration with Louis Sapin. A Negro Ensemble Company Production. 1959.

Native Son, the Biography of a Young American. A Play in Ten Scenes. By Paul Green and Richard Wright. New York: Harper & Brothers, 1941.
The Long Dream, a collaboration with Ketti Frings. An October Productions, Inc., produced by Cheryl Crawford and Joel W. Schenker. 1960.

Biographies

Fabre, Michel. *The Unfinished Quest of Richard Wright.* New York: Morrow, 1973.
Gayle, Addison. *Richard Wright: Ordeal of a Native Son.* New York: Doubleday, 1980.
Rowley, Hazel. *Richard Wright: The Life and Times.* New York: Henry Holt, 2001.
Walker, Margaret. *Daemonic Genius: A Portrait of the Man, A Critical Look at His Work.* New York: Warner Books, 1988.
Webb, Constance. *Richard Wright: A Biography.* New York: Putnam, 1968.
Williams, John A. *The Most of Native Sons: A Biography of Richard Wright.* New York: Doubleday, 1970.

Interviews

Wright, Richard. *Conversations with Richard Wright.* Edited by Keneth Kinnamon and Michel Fabre. Jackson: University Press of Mississippi, 1993.

Selected Video Recordings

Graham, Maryemma, Hazel Rowley, Sonia Sanchez, John Edgar Wideman, and Julia Wright. "Richard Wright at 100. Richard Wright's Centennial Celebration: A Panel Discussion." Langston Hughes Auditorium in the Schomburg Center, New York City, Lecture. 2008. https://www.c-span.org/video/?204687–1/richard-wright-100.
Native Son. Directed by Pierre Chenal, performances by Richard Wright, Gloria Madison, Nicholas Joy, Ruth Robert, and Jean Wallace. Argentina Sono Film S. A.C.I., 1951.
Richard Wright – Black Boy. Directed and produced by Madison Davis Lacy. San Francisco, CA: California Newsreel, 1994.
Richard Wright: Native Son, Author and Activist. Directed by CreateSpace. Venice, CA: TMW Media Group, Inc., 2005.

Selected Critical Studies

Single Author Books

Bone, Robert. *Richard Wright.* Minneapolis: University of Minnesota Press, 1969.
Brewton, Butler E. *Richard Wright's Thematic Treatment of Women in Black Boy, Uncle Tom's Children, Native Son.* Bethesda: Academia Press, 2010.

Butler, Robert. *Native Son: The Emergence of a New Black Hero*. Boston: Twayne Publishers, 1991.

Hakutani, Yoshinobu. *Richard Wright and Haiku*. Columbia: University of Missouri Press, 2014.

JanMohamed, Abdul R. *The Death-Bound-Subject: Richard Wright's Archaeology of Death*. Durham: Duke University Press, 2005.

Joyce, Joyce Ann. *Richard Wright's Art of Tragedy*. Iowa City: University of Iowa Press, 1986.

Kinnamon, Keneth. *The Emergence of Richard Wright: A Study in Literature and Society*. Urbana: University of Illinois Press, 1972.

McCall, Dan. *The Example of Richard Wright*. Carbondale: Southern Illinois University Press, 1969.

Tuhkanen, Mikko. *The American Optic: Psychoanalysis, Critical Race Theory, and Richard Wright*. Albany: State University of New York Press, 2009.

Parts and Chapters in Books

Baker, Houston. *Long Black Song: Essays in Black American Literature*. Charlottesville: University Press of Virginia, 1972.

Bell, Bernard. *The Afro-American Novel and Its Tradition*. Amherst: University of Massachusetts Press, 1987.

Bergin, Cathy. *'Bitter with the Past but Sweet with the Dream': Communism in the African American Imaginary, Representations of the Communist Party, 1940–1952*. Chicago: Haymarket Books, 2016.

Bone, Robert. *The Negro Novel in America*. New Haven: Yale University Press, 1958.

Campbell, James. *Exiled in Paris: Richard Wright, James Baldwin, Samuel Beckett, and Others on the Left Bank*. New York: Scribner, 1995.

Cappetti, Carla. *Writing Chicago: Modernism, Ethnography, and the Novel*. New York: Columbia University Press, 1993.

Cooke, Michael. *Afro-American Literature in the Twentieth Century: The Achievement of Intimacy*. New Haven: Yale University Press, 1984.

Davis, Arthur P. *From the Dark Tower: Afro-American Writers, 1900 to 1960*. Washington, DC: Howard University Press, 1974.

Dolinar, Brian. *The Black Cultural Front: Black Writers and Artists of the Depression Generation*. Jackson: University Press of Mississippi, 2012.

Fabre, Michel. *The French Critical Reception of African-American Literature: From the Beginnings to 1970: An Annotated Bibliography*. Westport: Greenwood Press, 1995.

Fabre, Michel. *From Harlem to Paris: Black American Writers in France, 1840–1980*. Urbana: University of Illinois Press, 1991.

Gaines, Kevin. *African Americans in Ghana: Black Expatriates and the Civil Rights Era*. Chapel Hill: University of North Carolina Press, 2006.

Garcia, Jay. *Psychology Comes to Harlem: Rethinking the Race Question in Twentieth Century America*. Baltimore: John Hopkins University Press, 2012.

Gayle, Addison. *The Way of the New World: The Black Novel in America*. New York: Doubleday, 1975.

Gloster, Hugh M. *Negro Voices in American Fiction*. Chapel Hill: University of North Carolina Press, 1948.

Griffin, Farah Jasmine. *'Who Set You Flowin'?: The African-American Migration Narrative*. New York: Oxford University Press, 1995.

Hutchinson, George. *Facing the Abyss: American Literature and Culture in the 1940s*. New York: Columbia University Press, 2018.

Jackson, Lawrence. *The Indignant Generation: A Narrative History of African American Writers and Critics, 1934–1960*. Princeton: Princeton University Press, 2010.

King, Richard. *Race, Culture and the Intellectuals, 1940–1970*. Baltimore: John Hopkins University Press, 2004.

Maxwell, William. *F.B. Eyes: How J. Edgar Hoover's Ghostreaders Framed African American Literature*. Princeton: Princeton University Press, 2015.

Mills, Nathaniel. *Ragged Revolutionaries: The Lumpenproletariat and African American Marxism in Depression-era Literature*. Boston: University of Massachusetts Press, 2017.

Morgan, Stacy. *Rethinking Social Realism: African American Art and Literature, 1930–1953*. Athens: University of Georgia Press, 2004.

Rasberry, Vaughn. *Race and the Totalitarian Century: Geopolitics in the Black Literature Imagination*. Cambridge: Harvard University Press, 2016.

Scott, Daryl Michael. *Contempt and Pity: Social Policy and the Image of the Damaged Black Psyche, 1880–1996*. Durham: University of North Carolina Press, 1997.

Smith, Valerie. *Self-Discovery and Authority in Afro-American Narrative*. Cambridge: Harvard University Press, 1987.

Stovall, Tyler. *Paris Noir: African Americans in the City of Light*. New York: Houghton Mifflin, 1996.

Taylor, David A. *Soul of a People: The WPA Writers' Project Uncovers Depression America*. Hoboken: John Wiley & Son, 2009.

Articles

Allred, Jeff. "From Eye to We: Richard Wright's *12 Black Million Voices*, Documentary and Pedagogy." *American Literature* 78.3 (September 2006): 549–583.

Blair, Sara. "The Photographs as History: Richard Wright, *Black Power*, and Narratives of the Nation." *English Language Notes* 44.2 (2006): 65–72.

Brannon, Costello. "Richard Wright's *Lawd Today!* and the Political Uses of Modernism." *African American Review* 37.1 (Spring 2003): 39–52.

Brivic, Sheldon. "Conflict of Values: Richard Wright's *Native Son*." *Novel* VII (Spring 1974): 231–245.

Butler, Robert James. "The Function of Violence in Richard Wright's *Native Son*." *Black American Literature Forum* 20 (Spring–Summer 1986): 9–25.

"Signifying and Self-Portraiture in Richard Wright's *A Father's Law*." *CLA Journal* 52.1 (September 2008): 55–73.

Dixon, Nancy. "Did Richard Wright Get It Wrong? A Spanish Look at *Pagan Spain*." *Mississippi Quarterly* 61.4 (Fall 2008): 581–591.

Dubek, Laura. "Till Death Do Us Part: White Male Rage in Richard Wright's *Savage Holiday*." *Mississippi Quarterly* 61.4 (Fall 2008): 593–614.

Dunbar, Eve. "The Multiple Frames for a Dynamic Diaspora in Richard Wright's *Black Power*." *Papers on Language and Literature: A Journal for Scholars and Critics of Language and Literature*, 50.3–4 (2014 Summer-Fall): pp. 269–280.

Ferris, William. "Richard Wright and the Blues." *Mississippi Quarterly* 61.4 (Fall 2008): 539–552.

Garcia, Jay. "Richard Wright and the Americanism of *Lawd Today!*" *Journal of American Studies* 49.3 (2015): 505–522.

Grinnell, George C. "Exchanging Ghosts: Haunting, History, and Communism in *Native Son*." *English Studies in Canada* 30.3 (September 2004): 145–174.

Hakutani, Yoshinobu. "Richard Wright's Experiment in Naturalism and Satire: *Lawd Today*." *Studies in American Fiction* 14.2 (Autumn 1986): 165–178.

Hayes, Floyd W. "The Cultural Politics of Paul Robeson and Richard Wright: Theorizing the African Diaspora." *Valley Voices: A Literary Review* 8.2 (2008): 81–98.

Hernton, Calvin. "The Sexual Mountain and Black Women Writers." *Black American Literature Forum* 18 (Winter 1984): 138–145.

Iadonisi, Richard. "'I am nobody': the Haiku of Richard Wright." *MELUS* 30.3 (2005): 179–200.

Jackson, Blyden. "Richard Wright: Black Boy from America's Black Belt and Urban Ghettos." *CLA Journal* 12 (June 1969): 387–423.

Jackson, Candice Love. "Tougaloo College, Richard Wright, and Me: Teaching Wright to the Millennial Student." *Papers on Language & Literature* 44.4 (Fall 2008): 374–381.

Jackson, Lawrence. "The Birth of the Critic: The Literary Friendship of Ralph Ellison and Richard Wright." *American Literature* 72.2 (June 2000): 321–355

"Richard Wright and Black Radical Discourse: The Advocacy of Violence." *Critical Review of Social and Political Philosophy*. Vol. 7 (2004): 200–226.

Joyce, Joyce Ann. "Style and Meaning in Richard Wright's *Native Son*." *Black American Literature Forum* 10 (Summer 1982): 112–115.

Keady, Sylvia H. "Richard Wright's Women Characters and Inequality." *Black American Literature Forum* 10 (Winter 1976): 124–128.

Kent, George E. "Richard Wright: Blackness and the Adventure of Western Culture." *CLA Journal* 12 (June 1969): 322–343.

Kiuchi, Toru. "Teaching Richard Wright's Haiku in Japan." *The Black Scholar* 39.1–2 (April 2009): 59–62.

Kuhl, Stephan. "Guilty Children: Richard Wright's *Savage Holiday* and Fredric Wertham's *Dark Legend*." *Amerikastudien/American Studies* 55.4 (2010): 667–684.

Lordi, Emily. "Vivid Lyricism: Richard Wright and Bessie Smith's Blues." *Black Resonance: Iconic Women Singers and African American Literature*. New Brunswick, NJ: Rutgers University Press, 2013: 27–65.

Lowe, John W. "The Transnational Vision of Richard Wright's Pagan Spain." *Southern Quarterly* 46.3 (Spring 2009): 69–99.

Nagel, James. "Images of 'Vision' in *Native Son*." *University Review* 35 (December 1969): 109–115.

Pudaloff, Ross. "Celebrity as Identity: Richard Wright, *Native Son*, and Mass Culture." *Studies in American Fiction* 11 (Spring 1983): 3–18.

Redden, Dorothy. "Richard Wright and *Native Son*: Not Guilty." *Black American Literature Forum* 10 (Winter 1976): 111–116.

Schettler, Meta L. "'The Rifle Bullet': African-American History in Richard Wright's Unpublished Haiku." *Valley Voices* 8.2 (2008): 66–80

Shelby, Tommie. "The Ethics of Uncle Tom's Children." *Critical Inquiry* 38.3 (Spring 2012): 513–532.

Siegel, Paul. "The Conclusion of Richard Wright's *Native Son*." *PMLA* 89 (May 1974): 517–532.

Tremaine, Lewis. "The Dissociated Sensibility of Bigger Thomas in Wright's *Native Son*." *Studies in American Fiction* 14 (Spring 1986): 63–76.

Tuhkanen, Mikko. "Queer Guerrillas: On Richard Wright's and Frantz Fanon's Dissembling Revolutionaries." *Mississippi Quarterly* 61.4 (Fall 2008): 615–642.

Weik, Alexa. "The Uses and Hazards of Expatriation': Richard Wright's Cosmopolitanism in Process." *African American Review* 41.3 (October 2007): 459–475.

Werthan, Frederic. "An Unconscious Determinant in *Native Son*." *Journal of Clinical Psychopathology and Psychotherapy* 6 (Winter 1944): 111–115.

Whitted, Quiana J. "'Using My Grandmother's Life as a Model': Richard Wright and the Gendered Politics of Religious Representation." *The Southern Literary Journal* 36.2 (Spring 2004): 13–30.

Zheng, Jianqing. "The South in Richard Wright's Haiku." *Notes on Contemporary Literature* 37.2 (March 2007): 6–9.

Collections of Essays

Appiah, Kwame Anthony and Henry Louis Gates, eds., *Richard Wright: Critical Perspectives Past and Present*. New York: Amistad, 1993.

Baker, Houston, ed., *Twentieth Century Interpretations of "Native Son."* Englewood Cliffs: Prentice-Hall, 1972.

Bloom, Harold, ed., *Richard Wright*. New York: Chelsea House Publishers, 1987.

Butler, Robert, ed., *The Critical Response to Richard Wright*. Westport: Greenwood Press, 1995.

Craven, Alice M. and William Dow, eds., *New Readings in the 21st Century*. New York: Palgrave Macmillan, 2011.

Craven, Alice M., William Dow and Yoko Namura, eds., *Richard Wright in a Post-Racial Imaginary*. New York: Bloomsbury Academic, 2014.

Fabre, Michel, ed., *The World of Richard Wright*. Jackson: University of Mississippi Press, 1985.

Foulcher, Keith and Brian Russell Roberts, eds., *Indonesian Notebook: A Sourcebook on Richard Wright and the Bandung Conference*. Durham: Duke University Press, 2016.

Kinnamon, Keneth, ed., *New Essays on Native Son*. Cambridge: Cambridge University Press, 1990.

Reilly, John, ed., *Richard Wright: The Critical Reception*. New York: Franklin, 1978.

Smith, Virginia Wheatley, ed., *Richard Wright's Travel Writings: New Reflections*. Jackson: University Press of Mississippi, 2001.

ed., *Richard Wright: Writing America at Home and from Abroad*. Jackson: University Press of Mississippi, 2016.

Zheng, Jianqing, ed., *The Other World of Richard Wright: Perspectives on His Haiku*. Jackson: University Press of Mississippi, 2011.

General Reference Books

Fabre, Michel, ed., *Richard Wright: Books & Writers*. Jackson: University Press of Mississippi, 1990.

Kiuchi, Tōru and Yoshinobu Hakutani, eds., *Richard Wright: A Documented Chronology, 1908–1960*. Jefferson: McFarland & Company, 2013.

Ward, Jerry and Robert Butler, eds., *The Richard Wright Encyclopedia*. Westport: Greenwood Press, 2008.

INDEX

Index

Index

Index

Johnson, Charles S., 100n1
journalism, xv
juvenilia, 211

Kelley, Robin, 63
Kent State University, xviii
Kevin (*Moonlight* character), 107
Kierkegaard, Soren, 51, 180
killing. *See also* murder
  existentialist meditation on, 130
King Alfred Plan, 159
Koestler, Arthur, xvii

Ladner, Joyce A., 89
Lane, Lionel (*Outsider* character), 110,
  129, 130
language, 40
laughter, 105
  in *The Outsider*, 113
Lawson, Elizabeth, 93
League of American Writers, 61
Leak, Jeffery, 104
Left Front, xv, 61
l'engagement, 141,
Lenin, Vladimir, 60, 69, 171
Lerneer, Sammy, 75
Les Temps Modernes, 141, 142,
Lester (*Big Boy* character), Jim's shooting
  of, 108
Levi, Carlo, xvii
Levine, Caroline, 60
Levine, Lawrence, *Black Culture and Black
  Consciousness*, 104
Lewis, Sinclair, 28, 33
library
  of Cross, 131
  Wright discovery of, 27
Library of America, xx, 25
life
  interconnection of forms, 23
  possibilities, 32
Lil (*Lawd Today!* character), 202
literary communities, conversation between
  French and American, 143
literary creation, aesthetic challenge in,
  30
literature, and sociology, 88–89
living, meaning of, 27
Locke, Alain, 9
Louis, Joe, 185
lynch song, 74
lynching, 104, 107, 158
  music on, 77

machinery, introduction in India, 191
Mademoiselle, 34
magic, 126
magnolias, 75
The Man Who Killed a Shadow, 148
Marks, Gerald, 75
Marx, Karl, 126
  *Karl Marx
    Selected Works*, 191
  writings on colonialism, 191
Marxism
  connections, xv
  critics, 58
  discontentment with, 25
  explanation of history, 24
  impact on Wright, 9
  internationalism, 167–170, 185
  synthesis with psychoanalysis, 191
  theory of history, 59
    Wright and, 67
  Wright study of, 62
Marxist theory, 8
Mary (*Native Son* character)
  Bigger and, 205
  death of, 206
masculinity, 211
  adolescent, 107
  black
    expectations about, 108
    humorless approach to, 103
  humorless approach to, 103
  Jake's anxiety about, 201
masturbation, 204
Max, Boris, 23, 206, 207
Maxwell, William, 59, 63, 153
McCarthy, Harold, *American Literature*
  essay, 6
McCarthy, Mary, 11, 42, 52
Meadman, Dhimah, xvi
meaning, 121
  Bigger's search for, 24
Mehring, Frank, 171
melancholia, 126
Melville, Herman, 88–89
Memphis, public library, 27
Mencken, H.L., xiv, 7, 28, 33
  A Book of Prefaces, 28
Menti (*Outsider* character), 113
Meursault
  Cross compared to, 132
  execution, 133
Meyerson, Gregory, 67
Michel, Albin, 140

233

Index

Cambridge Companions to ...

AUTHORS

Edward Albee edited by Stephen J. Bottoms

Margaret Atwood edited by Coral Ann Howells

W. H. Auden edited by Stan Smith

Jane Austen edited by Edward Copeland and Juliet McMaster (second edition)

Balzac edited by Owen Heathcote and Andrew Watts

Beckett edited by John Pilling

Bede edited by Scott DeGregorio

Aphra Behn edited by Derek Hughes and Janet Todd

Walter Benjamin edited by David S. Ferris

William Blake edited by Morris Eaves

Boccaccio edited by Guyda Armstrong, Rhiannon Daniels, and Stephen J. Milner

Jorge Luis Borges edited by Edwin Williamson

Brecht edited by Peter Thomson and Glendyr Sacks (second edition)

The Brontës edited by Heather Glen

Bunyan edited by Anne Dunan-Page

Frances Burney edited by Peter Sabor

Byron edited by Drummond Bone

Albert Camus edited by Edward J. Hughes

Willa Cather edited by Marilee Lindemann

Cervantes edited by Anthony J. Cascardi

Chaucer edited by Piero Boitani and Jill Mann (second edition)

Chekhov edited by Vera Gottlieb and Paul Allain

Kate Chopin edited by Janet Beer

Caryl Churchill edited by Elaine Aston and Elin Diamond

Cicero edited by Catherine Steel

Coleridge edited by Lucy Newlyn

Wilkie Collins edited by Jenny Bourne Taylor

Joseph Conrad edited by J. H. Stape

H. D. edited by Nephie J. Christodoulides and Polina Mackay

Dante edited by Rachel Jacoff (second edition)

Daniel Defoe edited by John Richetti

Don DeLillo edited by John N. Duvall

Charles Dickens edited by John O. Jordan

Emily Dickinson edited by Wendy Martin

John Donne edited by Achsah Guibbory

Dostoevskii edited by W. J. Leatherbarrow

Theodore Dreiser edited by Leonard Cassuto and Claire Virginia Eby

John Dryden edited by Steven N. Zwicker

W. E. B. Du Bois edited by Shamoon Zamir

George Eliot edited by George Levine

T. S. Eliot edited by A. David Moody

Ralph Ellison edited by Ross Posnock

Ralph Waldo Emerson edited by Joel Porte and Saundra Morris

William Faulkner edited by Philip M. Weinstein

Henry Fielding edited by Claude Rawson

F. Scott Fitzgerald edited by Ruth Prigozy

Flaubert edited by Timothy Unwin

E. M. Forster edited by David Bradshaw

Benjamin Franklin edited by Carla Mulford

Brian Friel edited by Anthony Roche

Robert Frost edited by Robert Faggen

Gabriel García Márquez edited by Philip Swanson

Elizabeth Gaskell edited by Jill L. Matus

Edward Gibbon edited by Karen O'Brien and Brian Young

Goethe edited by Lesley Sharpe

Günter Grass edited by Stuart Taberner

Thomas Hardy edited by Dale Kramer

David Hare edited by Richard Boon

Nathaniel Hawthorne edited by Richard Millington

Seamus Heaney edited by Bernard O'Donoghue

Ernest Hemingway edited by Scott Donaldson

Homer edited by Robert Fowler

Horace edited by Stephen Harrison

Ted Hughes edited by Terry Gifford

Ibsen edited by James McFarlane

Henry James edited by Jonathan Freedman

Samuel Johnson edited by Greg Clingham

Ben Jonson edited by Richard Harp and Stanley Stewart

James Joyce edited by Derek Attridge (second edition)

Kafka edited by Julian Preece

Keats edited by Susan J. Wolfson

Rudyard Kipling edited by Howard J. Booth

Lacan edited by Jean-Michel Rabaté

D. H. Lawrence edited by Anne Fernihough

Primo Levi edited by Robert Gordon

Lucretius edited by Stuart Gillespie and Philip Hardie

Machiavelli edited by John M. Najemy

David Mamet edited by Christopher Bigsby

Thomas Mann edited by Ritchie Robertson

Christopher Marlowe edited by Patrick Cheney

Andrew Marvell edited by Derek Hirst and Steven N. Zwicker

Herman Melville edited by Robert S. Levine

Arthur Miller edited by Christopher Bigsby (second edition)

Milton edited by Dennis Danielson (second edition)

Molière edited by David Bradby and Andrew Calder

Toni Morrison edited by Justine Tally

Alice Munro edited by David Staines

Nabokov edited by Julian W. Connolly

Eugene O'Neill edited by Michael Manheim

George Orwell edited by John Rodden

Ovid edited by Philip Hardie

Petrarch edited by Albert Russell Ascoli and Unn Falkeid

Harold Pinter edited by Peter Raby (second edition)

Sylvia Plath edited by Jo Gill

Edgar Allan Poe edited by Kevin J. Hayes

Alexander Pope edited by Pat Rogers

Ezra Pound edited by Ira B. Nadel

Proust edited by Richard Bales

Pushkin edited by Andrew Kahn

Rabelais edited by John O'Brien

Rilke edited by Karen Leeder and Robert Vilain

Philip Roth edited by Timothy Parrish

Salman Rushdie edited by Abdulrazak Gurnah

John Ruskin edited by Francis O'Gorman

Shakespeare edited by Margareta de Grazia and Stanley Wells (second edition)

Shakespearean Comedy edited by Alexander Leggatt

Shakespeare and Contemporary Dramatists edited by Ton Hoenselaars

Shakespeare and Popular Culture edited by Robert Shaughnessy

Shakespeare and Religion edited by Hannibal Hamlin

Shakespearean Tragedy edited by Claire McEachern (second edition)

Shakespeare on Film edited by Russell Jackson (second edition)

Shakespeare on Stage edited by Stanley Wells and Sarah Stanton

Shakespeare's First Folio edited by Emma Smith

Shakespeare's History Plays edited by Michael Hattaway

Shakespeare's Last Plays edited by Catherine M. S. Alexander

Shakespeare's Poetry edited by Patrick Cheney

George Bernard Shaw edited by Christopher Innes

Shelley edited by Timothy Morton

Mary Shelley edited by Esther Schor

Sam Shepard edited by Matthew C. Roudané

Spenser edited by Andrew Hadfield

Laurence Sterne edited by Thomas Keymer

Wallace Stevens edited by John N. Serio

Tom Stoppard edited by Katherine E. Kelly

Harriet Beecher Stowe edited by Cindy Weinstein

August Strindberg edited by Michael Robinson

Jonathan Swift edited by Christopher Fox

J. M. Synge edited by P. J. Mathews

Tacitus edited by A. J. Woodman

Henry David Thoreau edited by Joel Myerson

Tolstoy edited by Donna Tussing Orwin

Anthony Trollope edited by Carolyn Dever and Lisa Niles

Mark Twain edited by Forrest G. Robinson

John Updike edited by Stacey Olster

Mario Vargas Llosa edited by Efrain Kristal and John King

Virgil edited by Fiachra Mac Góráin and Charles Martindale (second edition)

Voltaire edited by Nicholas Cronk

David Foster Wallace edited by Ralph Clare

TOPICS